Armed Conflict and the New Law:

Aspects of the 1977 Geneva Protocols and the 1981 Weapons Convention

Edited by

Michael A. Meyer

CONTRIBUTIONS

Geoffrey Best
M.H.F. Clarke
L. Doswald-Beck
G.I.A.D. Draper
Hans-Peter Gasser
T. Glynn
C.J. Greenwood
Françoise Hampson
F. Kalshoven
H. McCoubrey
Michael A. Meyer
Adam Roberts
A.P.V. Rogers
R. Scott

BRITISH INSTITUTE OF INTERNATIONL AND COMPARATIVE LAW
LONDON 1989

Published in 1989 by the
British Institute of International and Comparative Law
17 Russell Square, London WC1B 5DR

Printed by The Chameleon Press Ltd.
5–25 Burr Road, Wandsworth, London SW18 4SG

British Library cataloguing in publication data
Armed conflict and the new law: aspects of the
1977 Geneva Protocols and the
1981 UN Weapons Convention
1. War. International Legal aspects
I. Meyer, Michael Anthony, 1952-341.6

ISBN 0-903067-30-7

TABLE OF CONTENTS

349

PREFACE

Professor Geoffrey Best

Between 1968 and 1980 a series of conferences, convened variously by the United Nations, the Swiss Federal Government, the International Red Cross in general and its Geneva-based International Committee in particular, culminated in the production of two multilateral treaties whose shared purpose was to bring up-to-date and extend the scope of, the international laws of armed conflict.

Humankind has through many centuries evolved these laws and their accompanying customs for the combined purposes of damage limitation and moral self-respect. Whatever the value of the law of war - and the contributors to this book share to the full the conviction of the legal, diplomatic, military and humanitarian fraternities to which they belong that it is indispensably valuable - there is nothing unhealthy in approaching it with a certain scepticism. As one who has gone a good deal into its history and striven to understand why its story is a mixed and somewhat tragic one, I would not wish any prospective reader to suppose that we do not know it to be so.

Some of the factors which regulate the degree of its observance are as old as the hills, others areas new as the radar screen and the cruise missile. The passionate and chancy business of war has never been and can never be helpful to the practice of that coolness and self-control which respect for any sort of law ideally requires. Adversaries rarely have such mutual regard and sense of shared interest that they will strive to keep their conflict limited. Wars for religious, racial and ideological causes, wars between whole nations and peoples, and civil wars and anarchies within weak States - the kinds of war, in fact, which characterise our own times - make enormous difficulties for the law of war's classic prohibitions and restraints. What works for one age will not necessarily work for another. Insofar as the law's failures can be ascribed to defaults or decrepitude, reaffirmations and developments like those of 1977 and 1981 must be hopefully welcomed. But how likely is the record of the future to be better than the record of the past? The rational well-wisher may still hesitate before (I cite Albert E. Clattenburg, an American official prominent in the making of the main humanitarian treaties of the previous generation) putting over much trust in 'international legislation as a means of eliminating evil from the minds of men'; he may find continuing reason to remark that the ready availability of appropriate international law is no guarantee that attention will be paid to it; and he will be thankful that organisations concerned to protect and relieve the victims of armed conflict are well accustomed to work through other channels beside those with bright legal markers along them; 'humanitarian diplomacy', for example, and perhaps not-so-diplomatic private or collective humanitarian enterprise.

And yet the law itself, the treaties, customs and fixed principles scrutinised in these pages, is of crucial and singular importance to millions more than the relatively tiny band of lawyers who serve at its altar. Without it there would be no clear directions, no common language, for those who seriously value its principles and who seek to maintain some respect for it amidst and notwithstanding all the mist and mud and muddle outside the shrine. In a less imperfectly organised world - a world, say, in which the obligations of international law would be serious-mindedly acknowledged, violations of it for the most part prevented and the unpreventable residue of violators effectively brought to justice - the law thus enforced in the ladder of national courts leading up to an International Criminal Court would be the whole body of the law as the experts themselves know it. In the world as it is and as we have to make our way in it, that law becomes a good deal bruised in its obstacle race to whatever modified recognition may be within its would-be practitioners' reach. Virtually all States pay it the lip-service of formal acknowledgment (of the 171 States on the global list at the end of 1988, 165 were parties to the Geneva Conventions), but acknowledgment is one thing meaningful acceptance is another, and evasion is, given the present poor state of world law and order, easy and commonplace. The 1982 war between the UK and Argentina over the Falkland/ Malvinas Islands was an honourable exception. It offered an uncommon contemporary example of an unmixedly international armed conflict, conducted by the belligerents with considerable respect for legal and (so far as they were anything else) humanitarian proprieties, and making for the International Committee of the Red Cross nearly all the room it needed for the exercise of its proper functions. But most of the armed conflicts that rack our world are by no means so simply classifiable and are conducted either with little earnest respect for the law of war or in circumstances which make such respect difficult to sustain. What the world sees of the law in such cases tends to be little more than a view in a distorting mirror; the best that the belligerent parties can manage for the time being, the nearest to that craggy complete original that can be got by way of simplification, approximation, analogy and extrapolation. What alone keeps it nevertheless from the shipwreck which sometimes seems to threaten is the hold of its anchors in that legal rock and the evidently wide-spread belief that no matter how much they may drag, it would be a fearful moral disaster for humankind and for civilisation if their chains should irreparably break.

The application of the new law to armed conflict then is a matter of intense interest to many besides the warriors and lawyers who are, admittedly, the most intimately and expertly concerned. Beneath the sometimes tangled trunks and branches of the forest trees through which they have to thread their way lie the broad contours of the hills and valleys among which we live and hope to go on living. Our general wish (I write simply as one of the civilian host of interested non-experts) to share their concern is all the more reasonable and weighty because their course through that forest is in fact largely determined by the decisions we make, or fail to make, as participants in politics and as molecules of public opinion. What sort of a war we would wish ourselves or anyone else to become involved in is, after all, no less momentous a question than whether we wish to become involved in a war at all and both questions evidently lie equally within the proper scopes of rational politics and responsible citizenship. That is why the International Committee of the Red Cross has since 1977, the birth-year of the more important of the treaties studied in these pages, taken the lead in a world-wide programme to disseminate knowledge of those treaties and all the other laws, customs and principles which go with them. That no doubt is the explanation of the continuing crop of writings about the legal and ethical aspects of war, on all levels, from technical treatise to school textbook and popular paper-back. And that is why this particularly learned and thoughtful addition to that crop will find a larger readership than could have seemed possible a generation ago.

INTRODUCTION

This collection of essays arises from a Discussion Group held under the auspices of the British Institute of International and Comparative Law during the period 1985-88. It covers some of the most important advances and outstanding problems in the Laws of Armed Conflict as developed by the two 1977 protocols additional to the four Geneva Conventions of 1949 and by the 1981 Weapons Convention and its protocols.

A significant number of States nearly half the international community, are now parties to the 1977 protocols and a growing number are parties to the 1981 Weapons Convention (see the Table at the end of this volume). The United Kingdom along with other leading States east and west has signed the two 1977 protocols and the 1981 Weapons Convention but at the date of writing, it has yet to ratify these agreements. It is hoped that the publication of this collection will help to stimulate interest in these treaties, which as Professor Best points out in his preface, merit everyone's concern as members of individual States and as members of the world community.

It is also hoped that the publication of these papers, written by a combination of academics, armed forces lawyers and Red Cross officials, will be of value to anyone interested in the regulation of warfare, the protection of human beings and humanitarianism during armed conflicts. In particular, the book may prove useful to professional soldiers, lawyers, scholars and students of international law or of international relations, and persons associated with the Red Cross and Red Crescent Movement or with other humanitarian organisations.

The volume is in four parts coinciding with the scope of each paper. Each author writes in a strictly personal capacity, and does not represent the views of his or her respective institution or Government.

Part I contains four papers covering general aspects of the law. Colonel Professor Draper, who participated in the drafting of the 1977 Protocols, discusses the development of the humanitarian strand in the Laws of Armed Conflict. In keeping with the overall approach of the collection not only positive features are noted.

Mr. McCoubrey takes a rather novel, philosophical approach to the subject, whilst Miss Hampson shows the important confluence and relevance of Human Rights and Humanitarian Law (the Laws of Armed Conflict) in the vital area of internal conflicts. Dr. Gasser of the International Committee of the Red Cross (ICRC) brings together his legal knowledge and his experience of discussing the Protocols with Governments to explain some of the legal considerations behind formal acceptance of these treaties.

Part II is concerned with several of the main categories of persons covered by the 1977 Protocols. Three British Army lawyers - Brigadier Clarke, Lt.Colonel Glynn and Lt.Col. Rogers, discuss the development of the law governing combatant and prisoner of war status, an area which has adapted to the realities of guerrilla warfare, with varying views on its viability. Although these officers write in a personal capacity, it is useful to have professional soldiers' opinion of these issues. Mrs. Doswald-Beck, now of the ICRC Legal Division, elucidates one of the main advances in the Protocols: the increased protection given to the civilian population. She demonstrates that on balance, by virtue of many of these provisions alone (some of which represent customary law), the two treaties merit ratification or accession.

Part III addresses the topic of humanitarian assistance, of which there is little written. Professor Roberts describes the new international regime of civil defence, and shows why it merits serious attention. I myself who currently hold the position of legal adviser to the British Red Cross discuss the articles in the Protocols on the provision of relief. These rules represent further progress in the law and illustrate the realism necessary in the Laws of Armed Conflict.

The final part of the book covers aspects of the subject of the use of weapons. Mr. Greenwood writes on one of the more controversial matters in the first Protocol of 1977: reprisals and reciprocity. This topic is fundamental to the entire question of implementation of the Laws of Armed Conflict. Professor Dr. Kalshoven discusses the making of the 1981 Weapons Convention, in which he was a participant. Finally, Major General R. Scott gives an Army physician's view of the traditional law of war concept of unnecessary suffering. General Scott's contribution illustrates that many points of view require consideration when legal norms relevant to armed conflict are formulated.

A number of significant components of the Modern Laws of Armed Conflict remain to be examined. These include national and international measures of implementation; advances in the law governing the use of transport; questions of the use of nuclear weapons and of chemical weapons; mine warfare, and the increasingly important area of naval warfare, to name but a few. The Discussion Group at the British Institute is continuing to meet, and it is hoped that in due course, a second volume of papers will be published.

The following acknowledgments are made, with thanks. The International Committee of the Red Cross, through the kind offices of Dr. Hans-Peter Gasser, Legal Adviser to the Directorate, gave permission to publish the information in the Table on the present state of ratifications and accessions to the Geneva Conventions and their Additional Protocols. Similarly the United Nations has allowed us to print the information on the state of ratifications, etc. to the 1981 Weapons Convention. This information was taken from the publication "Multilateral Treaties Deposited with the Secretary-General - Status as at 31st December 1987" (ST/LEG/SER/E/6) and from the Treaty Section, Office of Legal Affairs, United Nations.

Thanks are due to Lady Fox, Director of the British Institute of International and Comparative Law, for supporting both the Discussion Group on the Laws of Armed Conflict and the publication of this volume. Ms. Anne Goldstein of the British Institute is responsible for the typing of the papers and Ms. Helen Helston compiled the index.

November 1988 — Michael A. Meyer

NOTE ON CONTRIBUTORS

Professor Geoffrey Best
Formerly Professor of Modern History at the Universities of Edinburgh and Sussex, author of Humanity in Warfare (1980)

Brigadiar M.H.F. Clarke
Army Legal Corps, Commander, Army Legal Group UK

Mrs. L. Doswald-Beck
Member of the Legal Division International Committee of the Red Cross, Geneva; formerly Lecturer in Law at the University of London (University College)

Colonel Professor G.I.A.D. Draper, OBE
Emeritus Professor of Law at the University of Sussex; Fellow of the North Atlantic Treaty Organisation; formerly Colonel, Directorate of Army Legal Services; Member of the United Kingdom delegation to the Diplomatic Conference on the Reaffirmation and Development of International Humanitarian Law Applicable in Armed Conflicts 1974-77

Dr. Hans-Peter Gasser
Legal Adviser to the Directorate, International Committee of the Red Cross, Geneva

Lt. Colonel T. Glynn
Army Legal Corps presently serving with the British Army of the Rhine

Mr. C.J. Greenwood
Fellow of Magdalene College Cambridge, and Lecturer in Law in the University of Cambridge

Miss Francoise Hampson
Lecturer in Law at the University of Essex

Professor Dr. F. Kalshoven

Holder of the Red Cross Chair in International Humanitarian Law at the University of Leiden, The Netherlands; Member of the Dutch delegations to the Diplomatic Conference on the Reaffirmation and Development of International Humanitarian Law Applicable in Armed Conflicts 1974-77, and to the meetings of governmental experts in 1974 and 1976 which led to the adoption of the 1981 Weapons Convention and protocols, at which he also served as Rapporteur

Mr. H. McCoubrey

Lecturer in Law at the University of Nottingham

Mr. Michael A. Meyer

Head Legal and Committee Services, British Red Cross

Professor Adam Roberts

Montague Burton Professor of International Relations in the University of Oxford and Fellow of Balliol College. Joint editor of *Documents on the Laws of War*, rev. ed. Oxford, 1989.

Lt. Colonel A.P.V. Rogers, OBE

Army Legal Corps, Staff officer responsible for International Law matters at the Ministry of Defence

Major General R. Scott, QHS

Commandant and post-graduate Dean, Royal Army Medical College; Member of the United Kingdom delegation to the meetings of governmental experts in 1974 and 1976 which led to the adoption of the 1981 Weapons Convention and Protocols.

PART I

GENERAL ASPECTS

HUMANITARIANISM IN THE MODERN LAW OF ARMED CONFLICTS

G.I.A.D. Draper

1. The Theoretical perspective

Warfare being one of the oldest collective activities of mankind, it is no surprise that it has attracted a considerable body of law governing its conduct. The history of that law is long and involved. It is, in fact, almost the oldest part of the law of nations, known in our day as International Law. Yet, it has been stated that "the very idea of a legal regulation of a condition of mere force has appeared to many incongruous to the point of absurdity".[(1)*] One of the most distinguished jurists of our time, the late Sir Hersch Lauterpacht, who devoted much time and attention to the law of war, was prepared to concede that: "if international law is in some ways, at the vanishing point of law the law of war is perhaps even more conspicuously at the vanishing point of international law".[(2)] It was he who in the aftermath of World War II, urged with considerable intellectual power and moral fervour that "we shall entirely fail to understand the true character of the law of war unless we realise that its purpose is almost entirely humanitarian in the literal sense of the word, namely, to prevent or mitigate suffering and in some cases, life, from the savagery of battle and passion. This, and not the regulation of hostilities is its essential purpose. Rules of Warfare are not primarily rules governing the technicalities and artifices of a game. They have evolved or have been expressly enacted for the protection of actual or potential victims of war"[(3)]

These words, written in 1952, were true of the law as it existed when he wrote them. They have been more than justified by the substantial developments in that which have been established since that time.

* For footnotes see p. 20.

The expression "International Humanitarian Law" has not been without its critics. Some have stressed the inherent contradiction between the nature of acts of warfare and humanitarian conduct designed to reduce loss of life and suffering in warfare. Other critics have pointed out that the fundamental purpose of war is not to display humanity. Others contend that the fact that the law of war is in large part prohibitory presupposes that the salient purpose of war is the overpowering of the enemy by force with the minimum of time, casualties and logistics outlay. The classical juridical definition of war is "a contention between two or more States through their armed forces for the purposes of overpowering each other and imposing such conditions of peace as the victor pleases".[4] The law of war seeks to regulate such contentions, by imposing obligations both upon States and upon the individuals who comprise them. Thus, war is an activity recognised and regulated by law.

Today we talk of "The International Humanitarian Law of Armed Conflict" to indicate that the principle of humanity dominates the modern Law of War, Humanitarianism in warfare is no longer an ideal exclusive to the Red Cross movement. It is accepted by States and repeatedly confirmed by the United Nations.

Since 1950 International Humanitarian Law has found a powerful ally in the expanding regimes of Human Rights, whether international or regional. Both are based in their fundamental nature upon the dignity and value of the individual being. So close is the intimacy, in theory, between the two regimes that the UN General Assembly resolutions relating to the development of International Humanitarian Law have appeared under the title of "Human Rights in time of armed conflict'. The exact juxtaposition of the two bodies of law may in juridical terms, present some difficulties, but it is apparent that the one has supported the other. Human Rights regimes are applicable primarily in peace-time. War and other emergencies are, under the Human Rights regimes, occasions when human rights are subject to derogation. The International Humanitarian Law of armed conflict has a minimal relevance to peace-time. Human Rights consist essentially of <u>rights</u> conferred upon individuals in relation to the Government. The International Humanitarian Law of Armed Conflict consists primarily of a series of duties imposed upon States and individuals, enforceable by penal processes and punishment. These duties are designed to restrain that conduct in warfare which imposes unnecessary suffering on combatants, all warfare directed against those civilians not engaged in the armed conflict, and all inhumane conduct against those who are defenceless in the hands of the enemy by the tide of war whether members of armed forces or civilians. The range of these humanitarian prohibitions is wide.

The dichotomy between acts of warfare and humanitarian conduct is stark and dramatic. Yet the two phenomena have co-existed within the regime of the law of war in some degree since the late 18th century, and more overtly from the close of the 19th century. The history of the appearance and gradual ascendance of the humanitarian ideal in the law of war has not yet been narrated. It is part of the history of civilisation. The consonance of reason and humanitarianism is part of the history of natural law ideas and the perennial interplay between reason and goodness on the one hand, and passion and brutality on the other.

2. The Historical perspective

The International Humanitarian Law of armed conflicts is:-

(1) a part of International Law;

(2) a part of the International Law governing armed conflicts, whether international or internal, and

(3) humanitarian in nature, i.e. designed to prevent or mitigate loss of life and suffering and to reduce the destructive effects of hostilities upon civilian life, health, habitat and well being.

Humanity is one of the principles which have determined the growth of the law of war. Its role has been thus described:

> "The whole growth of the laws and usages of war is determined by three principles. There is, first, the principle that a belligerent is justified in applying any amount and any kind of force which is necessary for the realisation of the purpose of war - namely, the overpowering of the opponent. There is, secondly, the principle of humanity at work, which postulates that all such kinds and degrees of violence as are not necessary for the overpowering of the

> opponent should not be permitted to a belligerent. Thirdly, there is in operation the principle of chivalry, which arose in the Middle Ages and introduced a certain amount of fairness in offence and defence and a certain mutual respect. In contradistinction to the savage cruelty of former times, belligerents gradually adopted the view that the realisation of the purpose of war was in no way hampered by consideration shown to the wounded, prisoners and to private individuals who do not take part in the fighting"(5)

What we have witnessed over the centuries is the gradual elimination of the ideals of chilvalry, a code limited to those of the knightly and professional men-at-arms class and the emergence of a major role accorded to the principle of humanity. Early religious prohibitions of the use of certain types of weapon e.g. the cross and longbow, were based on the idea that they were "deadly and odious to God".(6) The prohibition was not disassociated from the desire of knights not to be laid low by a cowardly and dishonourable archer who killed noble knights from a safe range. The mounted knight showed little humanity for the archers in close combat.

Nevertheless the early 'Law of Arms' established a number of restraints designed to spare women, merchants, religious clerks and children, but often with little effect. There were legal restraints drawn from canon law, military usage, chivalry and from Roman law. Grotius in his work *De Jure Belli ac Pacis* (1625) argued for restraints from the Law of God (Divine Law) the Law of Nature (Natural Law) and from ancient military usage. Unfortunately, he is far from clear as to the distinction between the war practices of his day and the law of war as he conceived it to be. As he wrote during the Thirty Years War (1608-1648), the result was worse than confusion. Certain it is that Grotius, a devout Christian, hated war and all its brutalities with a deep loathing. Indeed it was his response to war which launched him upon his great work. He argued with intellectual brilliance that the totality of inter-State relations, including war, should be subject to the Rule of the Law of Nations. Further, he never ceased to stress that this conception of man-made law both international and municipal was based on the Law of Nature i.e. reason and goodness. All law including the Law of Nations, which included the Law of Arms, was made for the benefit of man. His plea for the principle of humanity is explicit.

At the close of his work, he set out his *temperamenta belli* or "moderations" in the existing savage and cruel practices of warfare. His plea for their acceptance was not without some effect. He was the powerful advocate for restraint in war. His influence and reputation was outstanding even in his lifetime. He helped to achieve some accommodation between the nature of war and a law of war based upon a measure of humanity. Before the time of Grotius, the predominance of the religious idea of the 'just war' did much to obstruct the acceptance of legal restraints binding both belligerents equally. The party waging the 'just war' i.e. with God behind it was not so bound. Grotius, by secularising the idea of the 'just war', removed in part that formidable obstacle. He urged that, irrespective of the 'justness' or otherwise of the war, the law of war bound the 'just' and the 'unjust' belligerent equally.

In a famous introductory passage which marks a substantial development of the civilised approach to war and warfare, Grotius wrote:

> "Throughout the Christian World I observed a lack of restraint in relation to war such as even barbarous races would be ashamed of. I observed that men rush to arms for slight causes, or no cause at all, and that when arms have once been taken up, there is no longer any respect for law, divine or human; it is as if, in accordance with a general decree, frenzy had openly been let loose for the committing of all crimes."

In the 18th century these ideas of Grotius, as expressed in his *temperamenta belli* had some impact upon the customary law of war, even if the war practices still left much to be desired.

The 18th century, with its limited historical sense and its enthusiasms for a Natural Law equated with reason, witnessed a major change in relation to practices of warfare. Part of this creditable development is properly attributable to Rousseau. His revolutionary work *Le Contrat Social* (1752) was burnt by the public executioner in Geneva, the city of his birth. He advanced the idea that "war is not a relation between man and man, but a relation between State and State in which individuals are enemies only accidentally not as men or even as citizens, but as soldiers, not as members of any particular community but as its defenders". From this novel idea of doubtful legal validity, Rousseau advanced the theory that:

> "The object of war being the destruction of the enemy State, one has the right to kill its defenders only when they have weapons in

their hands; but immediately they put them down and surrender, thus ceasing to be enemies or agents of the enemy, they once more become ordinary men, and one no longer has any right to their life. Sometimes one can extinguish a State without killing a single member of it; moreover, war confers no right other than that which is necessary for its purpose. These principles are not those of Grotius, are not founded upon the authority of poets, but they flow from the nature of things and are founded upon reason."(8)

Rousseau prepared the way for the humanitarian ideal in warfare in his philosophy of rationalism and sensibility.

In the second half of the 19th century a number of factors combined to accelerate the humanitarian approach to war. This movement is visible in the conclusion by States of various international Conventions. These Conventions sought to codify in written form and develop the existing customary law of war. Thus the law of war was the first part of International Law to be subjected to codification. That is one of the reasons why the law of war has, in our day, become out of date. There is a price to kay for precocity in legal development.

The 'Declaration' of St. Petersburg of 1868, established under Czar Alexander II, formulated two salient aspects of the humanitarian ideal in the preamble thereto:

(i) "... having by common agreement fixed the technical limits at which the necessities of war ought to yield to the requirements of humanity ...."

(ii) "Considering that the progress of civilisation should have the effect of alleviating as much as possible the calamities of war; ... that this object [to weaken the military forces of the enemy] would be exceeded by the employment of arms which uselessly aggravate the sufferings of disabled men, or render their death inevitable; that the employment of such arms [explosive projectiles under 400 grammes weight] would therefore be contrary to the laws of humanity ....."(9)

This prohibition was directed at the new explosive bullets (not shells) which exploded in contact with a hard or soft surface, e.g. the human body. The rationale of the 1868 Declaration was carried forward into the Hague Declaration of 1899 prohibiting projectiles whose sole purpose was the diffusion of asphyxiating or deleterious gases. The prohibition "is based upon the laws of humanity".

The close of the 19th century marked the high tide of the doctrine of State sovereignty and of legal positivism. It was a time of considerable activity in the establishment of International Law. The European States adopted 13 Conventions in 1907, of which 12 dealt with war. The majority of them dealt with the law of war at sea. These instruments reflected the moral climate of the day: secular, human and 'civilised'. Among the factors which led to the establishment of these 13 Conventions were:

(i) the huge increase in the size of land armies, by resort to conscription, which had been a feature of the Napoleonic wars;

(ii) a modest sophistication in the emergent technology of weaponry, particularly in the use and destructive power of artillery;

(iii) the failure of the massive infantry formations to succeed against this artillery. Thus, at the battle of Gettysburg, 1862, "when some 15,000, the flower of Virginia" infantry perished under point-blank artillery fire from the Federalist forces; and

(iv) the failure of military medical skills and resources to handle the enormous casualties and terrible wounds.

At the battle of Solferino in 1859 38,000 men were killed or wounded within the space of 15 hours. The wounded remained untended the doctors having retreated with the army upon which they depended, being at that time liable to capture as prisoners of war. The heat was intense and the water shortage was acute. Here, on the battlefield among the wounded, was born the modern universal humanitarian ideal of the Red Cross. Henri Dunant, a Swiss national and failed banker from Geneva, was present as a civilian at Solferino by chance. He improvised medical relief from local civilians, procured water from homes and church fonts, and women's clothing was torn up for bandages. Many thousands of the wounded perished from thirst and lack of care. After the battle, Dunant wrote an account of his experience in a pamphlet, "A Memory of Solferino", which appeared in 1861. This had a considerable impact in Europe. It led to the foundation of the International Committee of the Red Cross (ICRC) in Geneva and of the National Red Cross Societies, devoted to the relief of suffering in time of war. A further result was the first Geneva Convention for the relief of the wounded and sick of armies in the field, established in 1864. By 1867, 12 Great Powers had ratified it.

An important initiative in 1863 was the redaction ordered by President Lincoln for the benefit of the Federal armies in the American Civil War. The text produced was issued as General Order No. 100. It was prepared by an American law professor, Francis Lieber, with a committee of Federal generals and formed the basis for the abortive Brussels Declaration on the Law of War on Land of 1874 which failed to secure adoption at the Brussels Conference convened by Czar Alexander II. This draft was adopted, substantially unaltered, at the Hague Peace Conference of 1899 and became in due course the Hague Convention No. IV of 1907 concerning the Law and Customs of War on Land.

This Convention was established at the second of the Hague Peace Conferences convened by Czar Nicholas II, in the year 1907. The Hague Convention No. IV was probably the most important instrument of the time and purported to reduce into written rules the existing customary law of war on land. The architect and dominant jurist at both Conferences was Professor de Martens, who held the Chair of International Law at the University of St. Petersburg and was appointed legal adviser to the Imperial Foreign Ministry for the purpose of these Conferences. He is responsible for the famous 'de Martens Preamble' to the Hague Convention No. IV which contains the principles of the Convention and which now forms part of our modern Convention law. It recites:

> "... these provisions, the wording of which has been inspired by the desire to diminish the evils of war, as far as military requirements permit, are intended to serve as a general rule of conduct ...
> Until a more complete code of the laws of war has been issued, the ... Parties declare that in cases not included in the Regulations, the inhabitants and the belligerents remain under the protection and governance of the principles of the law of nations, as they result from the usages established among civilized peoples, from the laws of humanity and the dictates of the public conscience."[10]

The Regulations appended to this Convention deal with combatant status, prisoners of war, hostile operations, pacific relations between belligerents and the occupation of enemy territory. They were in force and operative during World Wars I and II. Their gross violation was the basis of part of the Indictment presented to the International Military Tribunal at

Nuremburg in 1945. From these Regulations Appended to this Convention much of the post war International Humanitarian Law of Armed Conflicts has been derived, by developing the general principles therein codified so as to apply to means and methods of modern warfare. In particular Article 22 of the Hague Regulations of 1907 is one such principle:

> "The right of belligerents to adopt means of injuring the enemy is not unlimited."

Article 23(e) provides another:

> "... it is especially prohibited ... to employ arms, projectiles or material calculated to cause unnecessary suffering."

These principles have now been made applicable to uses of specific modern weaponry and means and methods of combat.

In the Nuremburg I.M.T. Judgment of 1946, the Hague Convention No. IV was considered to be a statement of the customary law of war in force at the time of World War II and therefore bound all States engaged in that war. Thus three outstanding individuals, Dunant, de Martens and Lieber, each in his different way, has a claim to be considered as the architect of the codification of the law of war on land. This law is illuminated by the principle of humanity which was foremost in the mind of each of them.

Since 1864, the International Committee of the Red Cross in Geneva has been the standard-bearer for humanitarian principles in the conduct of warfare. It has promoted a series of International Conventions for the benefit of war victims. Their first foothold was the securing of protection and respect for the sick and wounded in armed forces in the field and the neutrality of military doctors, medical equipment and transport achieved in the Geneva Convention of 1864. This was followed by further Geneva Conventions of 1906, 1929, 1949 and by additional Protocol I of 1977. The protection and care of sick and wounded members of armed forces on land was extended to maritime warfare in 1899, 1907 and 1949. These Conventions replace each other for those States which subscribe to the later ones. They are detailed, complex and technical.

The treatment of prisoners of war, as to which there is a long history of customary law from ancient times, was codified in Hague Convention No. IV of 1907. This was followed by the

Geneva (POW) Convention of 1929 after World War I, and the Geneva (POW) Convention of 1949 after World War II. Finally additional Protocol I of 1977 completed the story to date. The whole now constitutes a considerable and detailed body of written law.

Between 1907 and the First World War in 1914, no further law-making was undertaken. The First World War was remarkable for the scale of the casualties and the appalling conditions of trench warfare in which hostilities were mainly conducted.

Thereafter, disarmament stood high in the aspirations of States in the early days of the League of Nations, but these ambitions failed. The rise of totalitarianism in the USSR, Germany, Italy and Japan which marked the 1930s, was not encouraging. There were the abortive Hague Rules of Aerial Warfare of 1925. Although not adopted, these have not been without value in contributing to the development of customary rules of air warfare and additional Protocol I of 1977. They included rules confining aerial attacks to military targets of which a definition was attempted.

The Geneva Gas Protocol of 1925 was established under the auspices of the League of Nations. This instrument is somewhat misnamed. The Protocol confirmed the existing prohibition of the use of poisoned gas and extended that prohibition to bacteriological methods of warfare. The London (Submarine) Protocol of 1936 required certain humanitarian rescues of those who were victims of submarine attacks on merchant ships. Both these instruments were in force during World War II, the latter forming part of the modern law of sea warfare.

A more substantial achievement was the establishment of two Geneva Conventions of 1929. One Convention was adopted for the protection of prisoners of war and the other for the protection and proper treatment of the sick and wounded in the armed forces in the field, following upon earlier Geneva Conventions on that topic. These two instruments were widely accepted by States and provided a detailed body of humanitarian rules for protection and humane treatment for these two classes of war victims.

This was the limit of the law of war making between the two World Wars.

3. The Development of International Humanitarian Law in the post-1945 Era

The experiences of World War II left a scar upon the minds of those who survived it, and upon Governments. Although the casualties in the armed forces of the belligerents were large particularly on the Eastern European front the scale of loss of life and suffering among the civilian populations attained gargantuan proportions. This arose from indiscriminate aerial and land bombardments, and, also on a large scale, from the deliberate extermination of ethnic groups accompanied by the barbarous treatment of detained civilians by the agencies of the Third Reich. This interlude of inhumanity was of a nature and scale that strain the resources of language to describe. The last days of the Far Eastern War saw the dropping of two nuclear bombs upon two Japanese cities, Hiroshima and Nagasaki. The scale of the destruction, the number of deaths which ensued, and the nature of the injuries of those who survived, are now part of the history of the inhumanity of man to man.

The treatment of POWs in the Eastern European and Far Eastern theatres of war was the very denial of humanity. The conditions imposed on civilians in occupied territory, from the Bay of Biscay to the Caucasus, especially in Poland and the USSR, attained a degree of inhumanity rarely matched by belligerents in times past.

When the account of human suffering came to be taken at the end of the War by an 'audit' of war criminality, the law of war was found to be defective in many respects, not least in the monitoring of its observance and the securing of its enforcement.

To the jurist, perhaps the most noticeable defects in the existing law of war apparent in 1945 were the inadequate rules for the protection of civilians from the direct or incidental effects of hostilities.

Moreover, the system of the neutral Protecting Power willing to undertake to protect nationals of one belligerent in the hands of the enemy had, by 1945, broken down even where it had existed in earlier years. The ICRC had done its best as an impartial humanitarian agency to secure humane treatment for prisoners of war and sick and wounded in the forces, but its presence depended on the consent of the belligerents. It had no right to enter POW or concentration camps. In some cases, e.g. in the USSR, the ICRC was not allowed to carry out its humanitarian functions at all.

The response of the ICRC to these events was to secure the adoption of the four Geneva Conventions of 1949. They are now the main part of the International Humanitarian Law of Armed Conflicts. These Conventions are now binding upon 165 States.[11] They embrace in all some 417 detailed humanitarian articles. They relate, respectively, to:-

(i) the Sick and Wounded in the Armed Forces,

(ii) the Sick, Wounded and Shipwecked of such Forces at Sea,

(iii) POWs,

(iv) civilians whether in occupied territory or in the territory of the enemy.

Except in limited and vestigial areas, they do not purport to apply to battle conduct, i.e. weaponry targetry and modes of fighting. They are admirable in their humanitarian and detailed, but elaborate content; their purpose is the protection and securing of humane treatment for war victims of the categories described, i.e. all those who fall defenceless, by the tide of war, into the hands of the enemy. *Lacunae* arising from the last war have been substantially removed. One article common to each Convention, includes a microcosm of the main humanitarian prohibition of each Convention, to be applied in "internal' armed conflicts, i.e. those "occurring in the territory of a State Party and which are not of an international character". In the light of the number of such conflicts, often conducted with great cruelty, since 1949, it can be seen that this one provision of law has been put to the maximum strain.

These Conventions had sought to increase the efficacy of the Protecting Power System for supervising their observance. This system rests on the consent of at least three States - two or more belligerents, and one or more neutral protecting State. Sovereignty can preclude each such consent. The ICRC may be invited in default, but no belligerent need accept the presence of the ICRC. The supervising system rests on the good will of the belligerents and the volunteering of the neutral States. It is thus a system of marked fragility.

For the first time in history, these four Conventions of 1949 have introduced a system of obligatory penal repression of defined "grave breaches"(war crimes) of those instruments, by whomsoever committed. There is, however, no obligation upon a State to hand over the accused or the evidence against him to a demandant State. Although many gross atrocities have been committed in armed conflicts since 1949, not one single person has yet been brought to trial for a "grave breach" of any of these Conventions.

In the years 1950 to 1970, the number of internal and 'mixed' armed conflicts greatly exceeded the number of international armed conflicts. (The total number of such conflicts since 1945 is approximately 200.) In the case of the former, the law (common Article 3 of the Geneva Conventions of 1949) is modest in content but difficult to monitor or enforce, whilst the suffering is acute and is aggravated by conflicting ideologies.

The experience of those 20 years has indicated that members of armed forces, wounded, sick, shipwrecked and captured, enjoyed in law a high level of protection in international armed conflicts. Civilians, however, were not in like position. Above all, the law of battle conduct remained substantially the customary law codified in 1907. In the face of modern weaponry, it was clear that the protection of the civilian population from the effects of hostilities was in law seriously defective. Accordingly in 1971 the ICRC called to Geneva a number of Government experts who worked for three years to assist the ICRC to prepare, for submission to the United Nations, two Draft Protocols additional to the four Geneva Conventions of 1949, and to reaffirm and modernise the law of hostilities of 1907. In 1974, the United Nations requested the Swiss Federal Government to convene a Diplomatic Conference of States in Geneva to consider the Drafts prepared by the ICRC and the Government experts as Working papers. This Conference was attended by some 120 States. For the first time, 'liberation movements' attended, of which three - the PLG, SWAPO and the ANC - 'signed' the agreed texts of the two Protocols when these were finally established in June 1977.

Protocol I, confined to international armed conflicts, is an important and substantial contribution to our modern Humanitarian Law of Armed Conflicts. It extends previously accepted general principles of the law of war to meet modern conditions of combat. The main achievement of Protocol I has been to secure a more extensive and precise protection, in law, for civilians, from the effects of modern weaponry. This was achieved by a narrow definition of military objects (Article 52) and by confining lawful attacks exclusively to such objectives, whether from the land air or sea. 'Attacks' are widely defined. These rules are reinforced by a general prohibition on attacks directed against civilians as such or against civilian objects, and on indiscriminate attacks causing excessive loss of life and injury of civilians or destruction of civilian objects, i.e. 'excessive' in relation to the "concrete and direct military advantage anticipated". The general principle of exemption of civilians from 'attack' is formulated in Article 48:-

> "In order to ensure respect for and protection of the civilian population and civilian objects, the Parties to the conflict shall at all times distinguish between the civilian population and combatants and between civilian objects and military objectives and accordingly shall direct their operations only against military objectives."

For this purpose civilian objects are all objects which are not 'military objectives'. The latter are:-

> "those objects which by their nature, location, purpose or use make an effective contribution to military action and whose total or partial destruction, capture or neutralisation, in the circumstances ruling at the time, offers a definite military advantage."

All attacks against the civilian population or individual civilians or civilian objects, are expressly prohibited as are such attacks "by way of reprisal".

A reprisal is an act, otherwise illegal, taken as a last resort to compel the enemy to desist from previous illegalities. Such reprisals are limited by proportionality and must cease with the cessation of the enemy's illegalities. Since 1929, reprisals have been forbidden against POWs sick and wounded and shipwrecked in armed forces. The prohibition of reprisal attacks against civilians and civilians objects is considered by some to mark considerable progress in achieving a higher level of humanity in warfare. On the other hand, the threat of such reprisals has often, in the past, been effective in securing the enemy's regard for the law. In terms of humanity, resort to reprisals frequently means that the 'innocent' suffer.

Starvation of civilians, a method of war of great antiquity, is now prohibited, as is the destruction of the objects indispensable to the survival of the civilian population, who may not be the object of reprisals. It is also forbidden to expose the natural environment to "widespread, long-term and severe damage", and there may be no reprisals of that nature. Dams, dykes and nuclear electrical generating stations are to have protection from attack or reprisal attacks. Any attacks likely to cause incidental loss of civilian life or injury, or damage of civilian objects excessive to concrete military advantage are prohibited. If this is not practicable the attack must be cancelled or suspended.

The Protocol confers wide protection upon, and requires care and treatment for all the wounded, sick and shipwrecked (service or civilian) of the parties to the conflict. All must be treated humanely and receive such medical treatment as can be given, swiftly and without distinction other than medical urgency. This is probably the most effective humanitarian achievement of the Protocol. It is the one most likely to be observed. The question of nuclear weaponry prohibition was marked by a consensus of silence. The text of the Protocol, as adopted, provided in Article 35 a repetition of the humanitarian principles established in 1899: that the means of injuring the enemy are not unlimited and that weapons causing superfluous injury or unnecessary suffering are prohibited. To the extent that some of the prohibitions might be considered to extend, by their literal terms, to certain uses of nuclear weaponry, the United Kingdom and the United States made express statements of understanding at the time of signature. The UK declaration is in these terms:

> "(e) that the new rules introduced by the Protocol are not intended to have any effects on and do not regulate or prohibit the use of nuclear weapons."

The United States made a similar, but less cautious, statement. Neither of them, nor the USSR, nor France has as yet ratified the Protocol. The prohibition of reprisal attacks has not added to the enthusiasm of the United Kingdom for doing so.

One jarring note in the humanitarian endeavour was Article 47 governing the position of mercenaries, as defined therein. Such persons are not entitled to combatant or POW status but may be entitled to the benefit of the fundamental guarantees for all persons in the hands of the enemy who are not entitled to more favourable treatment under the Geneva Conventions or the Protocol. They are not to be treated inhumanely and are to be entitled to fair trials, as specified therein. Their fighting will, as such, expose them to trial. The Protocol deals extensively with the protection of women and children, and civilian relief. It also confers protection on journalists engaged on "dangerous missions", an inclusion received without noticeable enthusiasm.

The most defective parts of the Protocol, apart from its technical complexity, relate to the measures to supervise its observance and for the penal repression of listed "grave breaches". The USSR showed no marked enthusiasm for the former because it represented an inroad upon its sovereignty, but it displayed considerable enthusiasm for the latter in that it extended the exercise of its sovereignty. "Grave breaches" include attacks upon civilians and civilian objects, indiscriminate attacks, and *apartheid* practices, presumably in relation to persons entitled to protection under the Geneva Conventions and the Protocol. States are required to bring the offenders, whoever they are, to trial. A novel requirement is that legal advisers be available to advise commanders in the field as to the application of the Geneva Conventions and the Protocol.[12]

Protocol II dealing exclusively with internal armed conflicts of a high level of intensity, nearly failed to secure adoption. It finally emerged in a much debilitated text. The original intention was that it should echo as many of the provisions of Protocol I as possible. New States displayed minimal enthusiasm for conferring extended rights upon rebels. Protocol II cannot be considered a substantial advance of humanitarian principles in the law of internal armed conflicts an area in which it is particularly needed.

4. An Appraisal

The conclusions to be drawn from this limited account of the development of the Humanitarian Law of Armed Conflicts demand caution. In the 150 years of its development, the progress of the humanitarian law of war has been remarkable. With out doubt the humanitarian principles have gained at the expense of military requirements. This has certain beneficent aspects in that all efforts to reduce human suffering and loss of life in warfare are for the good of mankind. 'Poor suffering humanity' is more than a sentimental cry. At the same time, the extent to which the new law, particularly that developed in Protocol I of 1977, may have disregarded the essential nature of warfare, may expose the law to the traditional criticism of a certain mischievous propensity to artificiality. The prohibiting of attacks that may seriously injure civilians, civilian objects and the natural environment, and of reprisal attacks of a like nature, may well, in the light of the capacity of modern conventional and nuclear weaponry bring the law into disregard and thereby weaken its moral and legal force. The non-use of certain classes of conventional weapons may not be easily achieved by drastic targetry and attack restrictions. Disarmament is probably not going to be achieved by such oblique methods. The reaffirmation of the prohibition of disproportionate killing and injury of civilians, and of all direct attacks against civilians, is assuredly to be welcomed. Jurists have rendered a service by developing the broad principles of humanity contained in the Hague Regulations of 1907 and deducing from them specific rules to apply to the methods of modern warfare.

The consensus of silence about the use of nuclear weapons is neither diplomatic hypocrisy nor moral cowardice. In political terms, it may be urged that the humanitarian gains achieved in other areas of the law of war, as outlined above, would not have been possible if the use of nuclear weapons had been before the Conference which established Protocol I. Humanitarian Law is as strong and as weak as the Governments of the States of the world wish to make it. Had the nuclear issue been before the Conference, it is doubtful whether it would have achieved more than an exchange of rhetoric, damaging to consensus upon other issues.

Further legal inroads upon the use of certain classes of conventional weaponry were, in part, attained later by the UN Convention on Conventional Weaponry of 1981 in force 2nd December 1985.(13) Therein, the use of weapons such as mines, booby traps, incendiary weapons, and those which injure by fragments which in the human body escape X-ray detection are to be subject to legal prohibitions. This Convention develops the general principle of law, and of humanity, which prohibits weapons which may be excessively injurious or which have indiscriminate effects.

The extended list of "grave breaches" of the Geneva Conventions, outlined in Article 85 of Protocol I, and their penal repression, can operate only after the law has been violated. In humanitarian terms the harm is already done by the time that war crimes prosecutions are mounted. The protecting power and "substitute' system of monitoring observance, particularly of combat law, remains fragile to the touch of State sovereignty. The ICRC does its best. Fact-finding Commissions, provided for in Article 90 of Protocol I are based entirely on agreement and joint acceptance. Instruction of members of all armed forces in the Humanitarian Law of Armed Conflicts is now mandatory and has been so since 1950. It is only partially honoured by States. There is considerable humanitarian value in this requirement. Moreover, education may frustrate the criminal orders of Governments and of military commanders.

At the end of the day, the perpetual quest for a balance between military requirements and humanitarian dictates remains. The balance is not easy to attain. At the moment it is quite possible that humanitarianism may have outstripped its practical limits.

Grotius' great principle that the laws of war bind all parties to hostilities, irrespective of the legality or illegality of the resort to war by any belligerent, has stood firm to this day. Necessity and humanity demand no less even in the era of the UN Charter. All persons of goodwill must labour to improve their knowledge of the Humanitarian Law of Armed Conflicts in order to make it more effective by improved mechanisms of pressure, both legal and meta-legal. In our imperfect world, the only environment we know, humanitarianism is now enshrined in the law of war. It must stand as a barrier against the brutalities and suffering in war for as long as mankind is unable to conduct his affairs without armed struggles. We cannot afford to dispense with, or to ignore, the contemporary Humanitarian Laws of Armed Conflicts.

FOOTNOTES

* This article is published with the kind permission of the David Davies Memorial Institute of International Studies. It was originally delivered as the 'Adam Weiler Memorial Lecture' at the University of Sussex on 22 November 1984 and first appeared in (1985) 8 *Int. Relations* 380.

1. H. Lauterpacht: *International Law, Collected Papers* (1975) Vol. 2, Cambridge University Press, p. 37.

2. H. Lauterpacht: "The Revision of the Law of War", *The British Year Book of International Law*, vol. 29 (1952) pp. 381-382.

3. *Ibid.* p. 382.

4. Oppenheim: *International Law*; vol. 2, "War, Disputes and Neutrality", 7th edition, (1952), Longmans, p. 202.

5. *Ibid.* pp. 226-227.

6. Second Lateran Council, 1139, Canon XXIX.

7. Grotius; *Prolegomena*, 29.

8. Rousseau: *Contrat Social*; Book 1, Ch.iv.

9. Imperial Russia was the main inspirer of the humanitarian ideal in the written Law of War established in the second half of the 19th century.

10. This famous "Martens clause" is reproduced, in somewhat modernized form, in Geneva Protocol I of 1977, Article 1(2).

11. As at 31 December 1987. For text, see 75 U.N.T.S. 31, 85, 135 and 287.

12. Article 82 of Protocol I requires legal advisers to be available "when necessary" to advise military commanders at the appropriate level on the application of the Geneva Conventions of 1949 and of the Protocol. The phrase "when necessary" was insisted upon by the USSR at the Diplomatic Conference which established the Protocol.

13. For text adopted 10th October 1980 see 19 *I.L.M.* 1523; *Cmnd.* 8370.

JURISPRUDENTIAL ASPECTS OF THE MODERN LAW OF ARMED CONFLICTS

H. McCoubrey

According to the American Realist thinker Karl N. Llewellyn one of the basic functions of any legal system is the avoidance or at any rate safe "channelling" of disputes which might otherwise be damagingly disruptive of the community in which they occur.[(1)*] This would seem to be at least as much applicable to Public International Law as to any system of municipal law. In this light it must appear something of a jurisprudential oddity that such a category as the laws of armed conflict should exist. There is certainly no real parallel to be found in developed systems of municipal law. There are defences of "self-defence" to charges of murder, manslaughter, assault and so on but in all cases the basic rule is of the form "thou shalt not", there are no rules for the "proper" conduct of such activities. The practical answer to this paradox lies of course in the truism that the power of the institutions of public International Law *vis-a-vis* the entities subject to it is much less than that held over the subjects of developed municipal legal systems and consequently a wider latitude of action, including armed conflict, must of necessity be contemplated. Nonetheless the undeniable jurisprudential oddity of this category of law has important consequences for its substantive content and application.

1. The Relationship between Legal provisions pertaining to Armed Conflict

There are broadly three areas of Public International Law relating to armed conflict which fall into two categories, the *jus ad bellum* and the *in bello*. The former relates to the use of force by states. Some commentators such as Geza Herczeg

* For footnotes see p. 49.

prefer the term *jus contra bellum*[2] as a truer reflection of the present state of Public International Law as embodied in the United Nations Charter. Unfortunately the broadening exceptions to the ban upon resort to force, *inter alia* through the concept of "wars of national liberation", renders this, in Benthamite terms, increasingly a censorial rather than an expositorial proposition. The *jus in bellum* which is properly the law of armed conflict, is divided usefully, although not strictly accurately, into "Hague Law" and "Geneva Law". The former makes provision for the permitted means and methods of warfare, the later provides for the protection of designated categories of people during armed conflict. These two are different in kind although overlapping to some extent and the nature of their relationship will call for comment in due course. First however the relationship of both to the international law of the use of force requires examination.

In principle there should be no relationship between the *jus ad bellum* and the *jus in bello* as they have now developed. Common Article 2 of the four 1949 Geneva Conventions provides for their implementation in "... cases of declared war or .... other armed conflict ... even if the state of war is not recognised by one [party]... also cases of partial or total occupation of ... territory ... even if [it] ... meets with no armed resistance". No reference is made to the lawfulness of any party's involvement in the conflict, the sole concern being with the protection of victims of a conflict which is in fact in progress. The legal issues arising from the commencement of the conflict do not in principle have any bearing upon the application of "Geneva Law" to it. The same is by and large true of the application of "Hague Law". This has been the case since the mid-19th century when both branches of the *jus in bellum* in their modern form originated and remains so despite major changes in the *jus ad bello* during the past 100 years. In the 1860s which were the period of genesis of the modern law, war as such was regarded as a legitimate means for the attainment of policy objectives. So far as the law of war was concerned in that era, war was accepted as a fact of international relations for which palliative measures should be sought. This view, reflective of the ethics of Palmerston and Bismarck, was overthrown by the impact of the First World War.

The post-war international legal order was intended to herald an era of peace in which the presumption would be very much against resort to armed force. Article 12 of the Covenant of the League of Nations accordingly provided that international disputes should be submitted to judicial or arbitral determination and that there should in no case be resort to armed force until a period of three months had elapsed from such determination. Article 16(1) added that resort to war contrary to the undertakings in the Covenant would "... *ipso facto* be deemed to [be] ... an act of war against all other Members of the League ...". provision was made for collective sanctions, possibly including armed force, in such cases. Armed force was not therefore specifically outlawed, instead the assumption was made that wars could be avoided if States were afforded a "cooling off" period before resort to armed force would be considered lawful. It is however arguable that aggressive use of armed force constituted, at least by implication, a contravention of Article 10 of the League Covenant which provided that Members of the League should:

> "... respect and preserve as against external aggression the territorial integrity and existing political independence of all Members of the League."(3)

A further step was taken with the General Treaty for the Renunciation of War(4) of 1928. The sixty-three States party to this treaty including all the major powers, renounced war "as an instrument of national policy in their relations with one another". It was this agreement which later formed the basis for the conviction of the government of the Third Reich for the planning and waging of aggressive warfare by the Nuremburg War Crimes Tribunal.(5)

The post-1945 international legal order took an unequivocal stance upon the matter. The Charter of the United Nations provides explicitly by Article 2(4) that:

> "All members shall refrain in their international relations from the threat or use of force against the territorial integrity of any state ....."

subject only to the reservation by Article 51 of an:

> "... inherent right of individual or collective self-defence if an armed attack occurs against a Member of the United Nations ..."

This reservation raises interesting questions not germane to the immediate issue such as the law fulness of "anticipatory self-defence" and "copenhagening" actions.(6) In general however it might reasonably appear that the *prima facie* effect of Article 2(4) is explicitly to outlaw the aggressive use of armed force subject to some inevitable argument upon the actual limits of the "inherent" right of self-defence. It should be added parenthetically that Article 51 may in certain circumstances impinge upon the *jus in bello* insofar as definition of the legitimacy of military response to a given situation may also set proportional limits to particular actions within such response. Clearly therefore Article 51 may not except certain actions from the effect of Article 2(4) which would not in themselves contravene any provision of the *jus in bello*. This is not however a true conflation of the *jus ad bellum* and *jus in bello*. It remains the case that the *jus ad bellum* determines the legitimacy of resort to armed force and in some cases to the detail of its exercise, but within the legitimate, and indeed the illegitimate, use of armed force the primary regime continues to be that of the *jus in bello*. It is important to remember that even if an armed conflict were to be wholly lawful (e.g. coincident mutual expression?) the *jus in bello* would continue to apply within the conflict without being added to by the operation of Article 51. Paradoxically however, in parallel with the gradual hardening of the positive legal restrictions upon the use of force - which led Herczeg to favour the usage *jus contra bellum* there has been also a gradual doctrinal development which has produced a partial renaissance of the theory of the "just war" or *bellum justum*.

2. The Idea of "Just War"

This conventionally much execrated theory was described by Jean Pictet as:

> "... the well known and malignant doctrine of the "just war", ... embraced by St. Thomas Aquinas and a host of casuists .... [which] did nothing less than provide believers with a justification for war and all its infamy."(7)

It cannot be denied that the doctrine of the "just war" came in its heyday to be abused as in effect a war-mongers' charter. That however was a consequence entirely alien to its original purpose. The doctrine of the "just war" was a minor aspect of a classical "naturalist" jurisprudence the roots of which lie in both ancient Judaic and classical Greek thought. The two strands of Judaeo-Christian and Hellenistic thought were fused when in 313 AD Constantine the Great made Christianity the official religion of the Roman Empire through the promulgation of the Edict of Milan. From this point an "official" Christian jurisprudence developed which reached its classical stage of development with the medieval scholasticism of St. Thomas Aquinas (1225- 1274).

It had been accepted by the early medieval period that war between Christian states was in principle an abomination. This indeed was a simple extension of the disapprobation of dissension within the community of the faithful found in the teaching of the Apostle Paul[8] as also in the Judaic thought upon which Christian ideas were founded. At the same time armed conflict both amongst Christian States and between Christian and non-Christian States remained all too evident a feature of international relations. The doctrine of the "just war" was contrived not to foster but to limit this situation. St. Augustine of Hippo (354-430) writing in the last days of the western Roman Empire taught that resort to War was permissible only when founded upon a "just" *causus belli*. By this was meant a resort to force for the restoration of a "proper" *status quo ante* between States which had been disrupted by an "unjust" wrong which the wrongdoer could not be brought to undo by any means short of war. Thus St. Augustine stated clearly that war as such was an evil, even if one which might on occasion be employed by Divine agency as a scourge for sin.[9]. This he then qualified by the argument that "injustice" meaning gross violation of the Divinely appointed, "natural" order between States, could impel a wise ruler to wage war in which case the injustice itself rather than the resort to force should be lamented as the origin of the resulting misery.[10]. This latter argument is somewhat parallel with that advanced by General Sherman in justification of the burning of Atlanta during the American Civil War. He argued that the fault lay not with him who gave the order but with the Confederacy which, by their rebellion, had created the stern military necessity in accordance with the dictates of which he acted. Thus Sherman said to the Confederate commander, General Hood:

> "... those who brought war into our country deserve ... maledictions [but] ... I had no hand in making this war......[11]

The actual requirements for a "just" war were set out clearly by Aquinas in his principal work, the "Summa Theologica". He set out three conditions for such a war being:

i. commencement as a legitimate exercise of authority by a ruler acting in defence of the interests of his State,

ii. a just cause, meaning that a wrong has been done which can be reversed only by resort to armed forces, and

iii. intention that military action be limited to the restoration of a "just" order between the belligerents.[12]

To this Aquinas added the qualification that even an originally "just" use of armed force may become iniquitous when pursued in a spirit of vendetta or to such excess as to constitute a wrong in itself, citing St. Augustine in *Contra Faustem.* Aquinas however laid much greater emphasis than had Augustine upon the immoral intention of the wrong doing State, in distinction from the mere fact of the wrongful act - in the terminology of English criminal law upon *mens rea* rather than *actus reus.* Aquinas did not it should in fairness be stressed, believe that forcible conversion of non-Christians, whether by armed force or otherwise, could be justified since faith is an act of will which cannot be coerced.[13] The scholastic argument upon the "just war" may, in short, be argued to have been propounded as a limited exception to a general principle that resort to armed force was morally impermissible rather than as a licence for warfare.

Unfortunately, as Pictet implies, the political use made of the doctrine of the "just war" was frequently far from reputable and it is here that certain alarming parallels with modern trends can begin to be discerned. Inevitably in the medieval political context, and in accordance with the basic - if much abused - Doctrine of the Two Powers associated with Pope Gelasius I (492-496), the question of what was and was not a "just" resort to armed force tended to be referred to the spiritual jurisdiction of the Papacy, rather than to the temporal jurisdiction of the Holy Roman Emperor, for determination. The result was a bizarre system of Papal sanction which amounted in truth to the granting of "licenses" for warfare. That this mechanism was open to flagrant abuse had become manifest even before the time of Aquinas. An example may be seen in the sanction given by Pope Alexander II (1061-1073) to William of Normandy for the conquest of England in 1066 upon the basis of an alleged assignment of inheritance to the throne made by Edward the Confessor with the concurrence of the future Harold II. From any objective viewpoint however the Norman conquest was a straightforward war of territorial aggression, the support of the Pope being readily explicable by his reliance upon Norman support against the pretensions of the pro-Imperial party and their anti-pope Honorious II.

This doctrine and system became impractical with the waning of the medieval world order and the Renaissance emphasis upon the independence of the nation State.[14] The process was brought to finality by the Reformation which shattered the European Catholic consensus and with it the spiritual hegemony of the Papacy.[15] The death knell for the "just war" approach is argued by many to have been sounded by the peace of Westphalia in 1648 which ended the 30 years of European war founded upon denominational division. The Treaty of Munster made by the Congress of Westphalia was made *ad Christianae Reipublicae salutem*, to the whole Christian polity but in adopting the principle *cujus regio ejus religio*, the religion of a State shall be that of its ruler,[16] ended the medieval order of international relations.[17] A point which was evident to Pope Innocent X (1644-1655) in the light of the highly critical Bull *Zel Domus* which he issued in 1648.

After 1648 the doctrine of the "just war" effectively disappeared and was replaced by a more complex structure of rules in a *jus ad bellum* in an era symbolised by the systematising work of Grotius. The end result was the 18th and 19th century view according to which, as Shaw puts it:

> "Whether the cause was just or not became irrelevant in any legal way to the international community (though, of course, important in political terms) and the basic issue revolved around whether in fact a state of war existed."[18]

Paradoxically, it was the transition from this era to that of the "peace" oriented League of Nations which signalled a renaissance of what can best be described as a "just war" doctrine manque.

3. The Modern Renaissance of "Just War" Thinking

The First World War was given the character of a great moral crusade in a manner which was at best, a gross over-simplification. The more extreme manifestations of this view, such as the post-1918 "hang the kaiser" campaign, can now be regarded as fortunately still-born, but still bore fruit in the distinctly vindictive Versailles Peace Settlement.[19] In the immediate context the most significant element was the famous "war guilt" clause of the Treaty of Versailles Article 231, which proclaimed the late war to have been wholly and exclu sively the fault and responsibility of the central powers. In fact the structure of dispute resolution set up by the League of Nations and outlined above, modelled as it was upon a concept of war by inadvertence, in itself revealed the dubiousness of this sweeping view. Nonetheless the "war guilt" verdict passed upon Germany and Austria-Hungary and their allies re-introduced the notion of "just cause" in warfare and was by no means discouraged by architects of the post-war settlement such as President Wilson and David Lloyd-George. In particular the principle of "self-determination" became a part of the international legal vocabulary. In origin it had been the conceptual basis for the dismemberment of the Austro-Hungarian Empire into its many component "national" parts. Its great defect, then and now however lies in the problem of determining exactly what demographic units have a "right of self-determination" and herein there is infinite room for disagreement. The doctrine is also readily capable of abuse as Hitler demonstrated in his reference to it in respect of the "claim" of the Sudeten Germans in Czechoslovakia for integration into "Gross Deutschland", which was in truth a preliminary ploy in the destruction of the Czechoslovak State whose fate was sealed at Munich.

At the same time as the Versailles Peace Settlement a new factor was appearing in international politics in the shape of the Soviet Union. The Russian monarchy had collapsed in 1917 and, after a period of chaos and a Nationalist Republic under the nominal headship of Prince Lvov but actual control by the Menshevik Kerensky, Lenin and the Bolsheviks had seized power and won through in the ensuing civil war and foreign interventions. The USSR took no part in the Versailles settlement, having reached a highly disadvantageous settlement with Germany at least as harsh as the settlement imposed upon Germany at Versailles, in the Treaty of Brest-Litovsk. The Marxist-Leninist policy makers and jurists of the USSR took a very sceptical view of the post-Versailles international order.

In fact use of force in this context fitted in well with basic Marxist (and Marxist-Leninist) political and historical analysis. The Marxist theory of social development through class struggle, punctuated by successive revolutions as the social "superstructure" is remoulded to reflect changes in a fundamental economic base and the use of literal "war" had an obvious place in this analysis. The resulting analysis has been well described by Geoffrey Best:

> "The international status quo after Versailles, for the marxist, was by definition a bourgeois imperialist one, wherein justice was all on the side of those who sought to overturn it. .... national self-determination was nowhere more just than for the oppressed and exploited peoples of the capitalists' colonial empires."(20)

It is perhaps worth adding in parenthesis that the inter-war administrations in the United States were by no means without sympathy for at least the "anti- colonialist" aspect of this view.

Although the U.N. Charter takes a more stringent view of the use of force than did the League Charter, both the circumstances of its origin and the pattern of its future development have in fact proved conducive to "just war" ideas. The Second World War has widely been treated as having become, if not having originated, as a war waged in the interests of "justice" - with vastly more justification than was the case with the 1914-1918 conflict. The existence of a "just" war in the origins of the United Nations together with a proliferation of new ex-colonial States, created a climate of opinion ripe for "just war" thinking. The war of independence in Algeria from 1954-1961 marked a decisive stage in this process. The independence movement, the F.L.N., succeeded in establishing before the U.N. General Assembly its claim to be fighting not in a "rebellion", however sympathetically regarded, but in an "international" conflict to recover a sovereignty unlawfully withheld from them by an occupying imperial power. The implications of this are again well stated by Best in his comment that:

> "The Algerian war of independence ... crystallized [the]... conception of the war of national liberation into the common one shared by the marxist and third worlds from the early sixties onwards. Thus ... armed conflicts indisputably "non-international" from [one] ... standpoint was represented as intrinsically international... and a merely defensive (and certainly "just") response to the imperial power's original aggression [from the other] ..."(21)

This view is essentially that "colonial" or racist rule is ex hypothesi a forceful repression of "national self-determination" against which armed force may be used as a defensive "war of national liberation" in full accordance with Article 51 of the United Nations Charter. This was essentially the view advanced by India in respect of the seizure of the Portuguese enclave of Goa,(22) which received a considerable measure of approval in the U.N. General Assembly.

Nonetheless the term "war of national liberation" remains unsatisfactorily ambiguous. The "Developed" World has not accepted the Marxist and Third World view and argues in contrast that armed struggle is permissible only where actual military repression of "national" aspirations is in progress. The *Consensus Definition of Aggression* adopted by the U.N. General Assembly in 1974 takes a rather unsatisfactory compromise stance between these views and provides by Article 7 that peoples forcibly denied rights of self-determination may "struggle to that end" and receive support in so doing in accordance with the U.N. Charter. Exactly how this relates to Articles 2(4) and 51 of the Charter is left unclear as is the exact status of external support for such "struggles". The ambigious state of the general law is a problem in itself and also exacerbates other more basic problems. There is of course recognised a right to "defensive" use of force under the U.N. Charter and there is no reason why this doctrine should not be extended to resistance to oppression nor why such resistance should be legitimate only in respect of "colonialist" repression. Within this argument there are however two profound difficulties which also arose in the medieval exerience of "just war" doctrine. There is firstly the general problem of subjectivity of interpretation within the *jus ad bellum*. The instances of Algeria and Goa perhaps represent clear cut cases. What however of the later absorption by India of the independent Himalayan Kingdom of Sikkim? This must seem at least a much more doubtful exercise. At present and in the recent past there are and have been many instances in which armed force has been used either in the name of self-determination or allegedly by "invitation" from states believing their sovereign integrity to be under threat. One may consider for example the situations in Sri Lanka, Afghanistan and Grenada as a mere sample. The interpretive difficulty is not one of uncertainty, on the contrary it is one of stridently conflicting certainties. The interpretive mechanisms, which tend in practice to be the Security Council and the General

Assembly rather than the International Court of Justice are placed in essentially the same invidious position as was the medieval Papacy in judging what is a "just" resort to armed conflict. Their "judgments'" like those of their Papal precursors, are inevitably "political" in nature and insofar as objectivity might be possible in such a context there is little evidence that it has been achieved. Indeed the evidence of partisan stridency upon some issues and pointed silences upon others from the various interested factions raises doubt that objectivity is even aimed at. Given the political will, an admittedly large demand, it is possible that these problems could be resolved. The concepts of "wars of national liberation" and "self-determination" are not in themselves intrinsically objectionable, far from it, the difficulty lies in definition and interpretation. Given an adequate "consensus upon aggression" and the establishment of a useful interpretive jurisprudence in the Security Council, with or without the aid of the Court, the concept could readily be incorporated in the U.N. dispute resolutions machinery. The requisite political will is however lacking.

4. "Just War" Doctrines and the *Jus in Bello*

If the reappearance of a form of "just war" doctrine has created potentially difficult ambiguities in the *jus ad bellum* it has the most alarming potentialities within the *jus in bello*. The modern i.e. post 1860s jurisprudence of this area of law has been founded upon a complete separation of the law relating to the use of force and the norms applicable within an armed conflict, however commenced. The best statement of the basic aim of the *jus in bello* in both its "Hague" and "Geneva" aspects, could not be better stated than in the 1868 Declaration of St. Petersburg a limitation agreement upon the use of explosive shells. The Declaration stated as general principles that,

> "... the progress of civilisation should have the effect of alleviating as much as possible the calamities of war .... the only legitimate object which states should endeavour to accomplish during war is to weaken the military forces of the enemy. .... in order to maintain the principles which they have established and to conciliate the necessities of war with the laws of humanity."

The legitimacy of the participation in the conflict of any

party is not here at issue, the point being the minimisation of the brutality of impact of conflict both upon combatants through weapons limitation and upon its victims whether *hors de combat* through injury, captured or civilian through "Geneva" protective provisions. The essence of this approach is enshrined in three of the formal principles of the International Red Cross, those of Humanity, Impartiality and Neutrality. To this extent the laws of armed conflict, and international humanitarian law in particular can be regarded as part of the general body of the law of Human Rights. This view is to some extent controversial. Herczeg[(23)] argues that no aspect of the laws of armed conflict can be regarded as a part of Human Rights law, although clearly inter-related with it. The basis for this view is that a law of armed conflict presupposes armed conflict which is in itself a breach of human rights. On the other hand, with all due respect to the logic of Herczeg's case, the very idea of human rights supposes the danger of breach and there seems no good reason why there should not even in War be a doctrine of "human rights" however limited. This seems in essence to be the view of another Eastern bloc writer Igor P. Blishchenko who argues in effect that both "Hague" and "Geneva" provisions are ultimately an expression of the right to life.[(24)] Be that as it may, these basic principles of Humanity, Impartiality and Neutrality are all potentially under threat from a renaissant "just war" doctrine. Alarming questions spring to mind; to what extent, if any, are the permissible means and methods of waging a struggle for national self determination limited? Is international terrorism to be counted a legitimate form of "struggle" and, if so how, if at all, are humanitarian norms to be applied to it?[(25)] Much the worst potential effects of a revival of "just war" doctrine would clearly lie in the area of international humanitarian law. It is a common although not perhaps a "necessary", concommitant of a "just war" doctrine that the enemy is regarded as "unjust" or even evil and therefore undeserving of humanitarian consideration. Elements of this type of thinking have begun to show themselves in a number of statements and incidents of recent years. Of these the most potentially alarming is the revival in Islamic thought of the idea of *jihad*. *Jihad* does not literally mean "holy war" but amounts to much the same thing as a conflict waged in the name of and for the greater glory of Allah. Such ideas have had at least a subtextual presence in the successive Arab/Israeli conflicts, on both sides it should be said, but have received their most pointed statement in the Gulf War. This unfortunately, should occasion no surprise. The most barbarous wars have always been fought between adherents of different forms of the same religion. The atrocious sack of Constantinople in April 1203 during the Fourth Crusade set the seal upon the enduring legacy of bitterness between the Eastern Orthodox and Roman Catholic traditions of Christianity which is only beginning to be broken down by modern ecumenism. The horrors of the inter-denominational Thirty Years War ended by the peace of Westphalia in 1648[(26)] are also much in point having been in many ways the midwife to the birth of modern public international law. The conflict between Shi'te Iran and largely sunni Iraq has taken on much of the bitterness of a war in which the enemy is seen not only as the national adversary but as a "heretical" enemy of God. Newspaper reports in 1986 suggested that Iran was contemplating denunciation of the 1949 Geneva Conventions as "unIslamic" and inapplicable in an Islamic "holy war". Fortunately this was not done and most recent public reports (1987) suggest that humanitarian observance in the Gulf War is showing some signs of improvement.

In a number of less dramatic ways however the substance of international humanitarian law has begun to be affected by the directional changes in the *jus ad bellum*. This is especially noticeable in the controversial 1977 Protocol I additional to the 1949 Geneva Conventions. One minor but significant step is to be seen in Article 47 of the Protocol which covers mercenaries. Article 47 effectively excludes mercenaries from the protection of the Geneva Conventions as either "combatants" or "prisoners of war". This is an overtly moral judgment inserted in Protocol I, primarily pursuant to Third World argument, to exclude those who are effectively "contract killers" to a great extent from humanitarian consideration. It could hardly be argued that "mercenaries" strictly so-called are deserving of much sympathy. There is however difficulty in definition as the complex six part definition given by Protocol I demonstrates. The most basic definition of a mercenary would be simply one who hires himself out to the highest bidder as a fighter, an activity which paradoxically, formed a significant part of the economic base of medieval Switzerland.[(27)] Article 47(2) specifies however:

a. special recruitment
b. actual participation in conflict
c. motivation by desire for private gain
d. foreign or non-resident status

e. non-membership of the foreign armed forces, and
f. not having been sent by another State on duty as a member of its armed forces.

As a matter of construction it must seem that all those conditions are required to be satisfied for the application of the article. If this is so those falling within Article 47 would indeed be limited to such as the British and American mercenaries in Angola or the British mercenaries involved in the attempted coup in the Seychelles in 1982, who were perhaps hardly in a position to claim favourable judgments. Without for a moment seeking to defend mercenaries however, there are two fundamental objections which may be made to Article 47. These are firstly the possibility of mischievous abuse of the provision and, secondly, the serious difficulties of application in the field. The former was illustrated on 20th May 1982 during a Security Council debate upon the attempted coup in the Seychelles when the representative of Argentina attempted to draw a parallel between "mercenaries" and the Gurkha regiments of the British Army. In terms of Protocol I any such analogy must clearly be excluded at least by Article 47(2)(e), which refers to persons who are members of the armed forces of a party involved in conflict. The United Kingdom representative, Mr. Whyte, made specific reference to this provision, interestingly in the light of the United Kingdom's current (January 1988) refusal to ratify Protocol I, in his statement that:

> "regiments of Gurkhas ... have a long and distinguished record of service with the British Crown in accordance with agreements ... with the Government of Nepal. ... [the Protocol I) definition excludes ... "[members] of the armed forces" ... The Gurkhas comprise units of regular troops; they form a fully integrated part of the United Kingdom forces. In no way can they be classified as mercenaries."(28)

The suggestion to which this was a response can no doubt be dismissed as part of the "cut and thrust" of U.N. politics but does cast the shadow of the threat of much more serious (ab)uses of Article 47 to the detriment of persons properly entitled to the protection of the Geneva Conventions. This potential is rendered more sinister by the possibilities of confusion in the field.(29) Article 47 provides that "mercenaries" are excluded from the scheme of "Geneva" protection. Since Article 5 of 1949 Geneva Convention III provides that prisoners of war are entitled to protection from the moment of capture, the possibility is raised of "mistaken" decisions made upon moral and ideological bases by forces in the field. It may be added that upon a broader perspective Article 47 is arguably not anyway an appropriate response to the problem of mercenary forces. Nothing in the "Geneva" legal regime precludes the punishment of offences committed prior to capture by prisoners of war, even if practical and political considerations militate against it. There is no good reason why mercenaries *strictu sensu* should not be accorded a status equivalent to that of *hostes humani generis*, as have been aerial hijackers since the established law of piracy proved an adequate means of dealing with them. This would be much the preferable course to a "just" exception to the full regime of "Geneva" protection since later trial and punishment through due process would not anyway be precluded by the Conventions and could be undertaken without implicit subversion of the basic principles of humanity, impartiality and neutrality.

5. "Terrorists", Combatants and Humanitarian protection

Article 47 is, so far, the only overt inroad upon traditional "Geneva" jurisprudence upon a near "just war" basis. There have however been more subtle developments which, if anything, give rise to greater concern. The principal focus of these are the definition of "international" conflicts and the limits of combatant status. As to the first of these, common Article 2 of the 1949 Geneva Convention provides for their general implementation in:

> "... all cases of declared war or of any other armed conflict ... between ... High Contracting Parties, even if the state of war is not recognised by one of them ... also ... all cases of partial or total occupation of the territory of a High Contracting Party even if [it] ... meets with no armed resistance."

This compendious definition was intended in part to obviate the difficulties arising from the increasing technicality of the usage of the term "War". This was well illustrated in the case of *Kawasaki Kisen Kabushiki Kaisha v. Bantham S.S. Co. Ltd.*[(30)] which involved a charter party containing a cancellation clause operative "if war breaks out involving

Japan". In 1957 Japan having been militarily engaged in Chinese territory for some five years,[31] invaded South China perpetrating appalling atrocities in Nanking in particular. Accordingly the Bantham S.S. Co. sought to cancel the charter party and KKK objecting, the court in accordance with usual practice sought a Foreign Office certificate as to the prevailing state of Sino-Japanese relations.

The reply was given that:

> "I am directed by Mr. Neville Chamberlain to inform you that the current situation in China is indeterminate and anomalous..."[32]

The situation may have seemed "indeterminate" to H.M.G. in the person of Mr. Neville Chamberlain but can hardly have done so to anyone else. The Court of Appeal in fact decided that the interpretation of the charter party turned upon the dictionary rather than the technical Foreign Office usage of the term "war" and therefore determined that it was indeed cancelled.[33] The term "armed conflict" used in Common Article 2 is intended to be a purely factual and descriptive term which, at least so far as international conflicts are concerned, avoids such technical obfuscation. In pre-1977 "Geneva" law, provision for non-international armed conflicts within the territory of a High Contracting party was made by Common Article 3 of the 1949 Geneva Conventions in the form of certain "minimum provisions" whilst also urging the implementation so far as possible of the Conventions in full. Thus the 1949 provision was in effect for a general regime for international armed conflicts with a minimum "safety net" for non-international conflicts, the minimum concerned falling for the most part any way, into the category of basic "human rights". The 1977 Additional Protocols have taken this a little further and have unfortunately, arguably, been productive of further definitional ambiguity resulting from the modern revival of "just war" thinking. The original intention had been a new and stricter regime for non-international conflicts to be set out in Protocol II while Protocol I was to make additional provision for international conflicts. Ultimately Protocol II has emerged as a relatively uncontroversial provision with the more "difficult" issues having been removed into Protocol I. The most controversial provisions in the present context are Articles 1(4) and 44(3). It is primarily those provisions which have caused Protocol I to be stigmatised in British and American eyes as a "terrorists' charter", which is doubly unfortunate in that Protocol I contains much which is admitted to be both uncontroversial and useful. The more extreme fears expressed in relation to these provisions can reasonably be argued to be considerably exaggerated, but there is nonetheless some cause for genuine concern.

The origin of these articles lay in changes in patterns of warfare since 1949, linked to but not synonymous with the rise of the concept of "wars of national liberation". The historical argument is that in modern armed conflict confrontation between clearly identified armed forces of hostile States has to a significant extent been superceded by hostilities between a mixture of formal armed forces and also less formal "guerilla" forces of varying types of organisation, some of external origin, some internal "freedom fighters". Neither "guerilla" warfare nor "freedom fighting" were of course developments of the second half of the 20th century. The term "guerilla" originated in the Napoleonic Wars during Spanish resistance to French occupation and "freedom fighting" is as old as adverse occupation. Examples of current or recently past conflicts which have involved "guerilla" forces acting with varying degrees of credibility under banners of "national liberation" include, Korea, Vietnam, Afghanistan and Nicaragua. It must of course be added parenthetically that such "modern" wars have not ended historically "normal" warfare seen upon extreme ends of the scale in the Falklands conflict and in the Gulf War. A change in modern thinking has however come about in attitudes towards "guerilla" and "resistance" fights. Formerly they tended to be shot as *franc tireurs*(34) but have come to be regarded in some circumstances as having a claim to legitimacy as combatants. This is not in itself a new phenomenon and can certainly be seen in allied attitudes to resistance groups in Nazi-occupied Europe. The idea has gained force however with the notion of "wars of national liberation" and is reflected in 1977 Additional Protocol I. Articles 45(1) and 44(5) consequently make significant additions to the categories of persons considered "combatants" and entitled to "prisoner of war" status if captured.

Article 43(1) defines "armed forces" as including all units of a party to the conflict under responsible command (meaning one hierarchically structured and answerable to ultimate authority) and having an internal discipline which includes observation of the laws of armed conflict. Such "forces" are assumed to be uniformed or at least distinguished by some "uniform" identifying apparel. Article 44(5) provides further that although protection of civilians demands that combatants distinguish themselves from civilians, especially while engaged in military activity, there may be circumstances in which, "owing to the nature of the hostilities", this is not possible. Combatants in such circumstances are stated nonetheless to retain combatant, and entitlement upon capture to prisoner of war status provided that they carry arms openly (i) during each military engagement and (ii) when visible to the adversary while deploying in preparation for attack.

The argument that this is in itself a "terrorists' charter" can reasonably be argued to be an exaggeration. It must be remembered that Article 44(5), which does *prima facie* seem to remove almost all distinct meaning from the concept of an "armed force", does not stand independently. It is instead a qualifying provision additional to Article 23 applicable in, admittedly vaguely defined, exceptional circumstances. It is therefore required pursuant to Article 43(1) that recognised armed forces should be willing and able to comply with the laws of armed conflict which would clearly include 1949 Geneva Convention III on prisoners of war. To take examples not necessarily from the context of Protocol I, the F.L.N. in the Algerian War of Independence was able to convince the international community of its ability to act as a "provisional government" and to observe the laws of armed conflict thus forcing France to accord the same treatment to themselves, whereas, in contrast, the I.R.A. has demonstrated neither the required capacity nor the necessary will. Nonetheless Article 44(5) can be argued to represent a potentially dangerous muddying of the legal waters. The laws of armed conflict are not designed to be applied *ex post facto* by international lawyers but in the heat of combat by non-lawyers. The aim is not primarily to pronounce judicially upon war crimes committed but rather to obviate their "accidental" perpetration. The mere carrying of arms openly in the confusion of urban warfare such as is currently (January 1988) to be found in the Lebanon is not a very adequate distinguishing mark. This becomes especially so when Article 42(5) is read in conjunction with the, entirely laudable, aspirations of Part IV of 1977 Protocol I in respect of the civilian population. Article 48 states as a basic rule that:

> "... Parties to ... conflict shall at all times distinguish between the civilian population and combatants ... and accordingly shall direct their operations only against military objectives."

Application of this requirement, which already demands delicate judgments upon the nature of "military objectives"[35], is not rendered any easier by the potential for confusion inherent in Article 44(5). The sinister path down which such confusion might be a signpost is illustrated, *inter multos alios* by the reported harrying of (genuine) nuns in Belgium in 1939 following (false) reports that German fifth columnists had been parachuted into the country disguised in nuns' habits. The difficulty is impliedly recognised in Article 44(5) by the restatement of the general rule that:

> "In order to promote the protection of the civilian population from the effects of hostilities, combatants are obliged to distinguish themselves from the civilian population ...."

The implied ambiguity of the article's substantive provision remains nonetheless a cause for some legitimate concern.

The same is true in a slightly different way of Article 1(4) of 1977 Protocol I. This provides that the definition of international armed conflict to which the Geneva Conventions apply contained in Common Article 2 of the 1949 Geneva Conventions[36] shall be extended to include:

> "... armed conflicts ... against colonial domination and alien occupation and ... racist regimes in the exercise of [a] ... right of self-determination ...."

It has already been contended[37] that this type of provision is symptomatic of a general renaissance of "just war" thinking in the jurisprudence of armed conflict. There is however a more specific concern in connection with Article 1(4), which is that it introduces possible confusion between "international" and "non-international" armed conflicts in the context of "Geneva" norms. There is a separate humanitarian regime provided for non international armed conflicts in the "minimum", scheme of Common Article 3 of the 1949 Geneva Conventions and, more extensively in 1977 Additional Protocol II, which, as commented above, is largely uncontroversial. The endeavour to recategorise certain "just" internal conflicts as international conflicts introduces, as Best suggests[38], an ambiguity of application in certain circumstances which dangerously undermines the certainty of norms which already, and ex hypothesi, operate at the limits of international legal relations.

Much has been said in this paper which is expressly or impliedly critical both of modern quasi- "just war" doctrine and of its specific reflection in 1977 Protocol I additional to the 1949 Geneva Conventions. Before proceeding to a more general conclusion upon the state of the jurisprudence of the laws of armed conflict one classificatory point should be emphasised. It is not the concepts of "self-determination and "wars of national liberation" *per se* to which objection is made but the means of their advancement in the specific context of the laws of armed conflict. To this exception is taken upon two levels. At the broader level of abstraction the laws of armed conflict in general and international humanitarian law in particular have since the 1860s been determinedly a neutralist structure of norms designed to mitigate to the greatest extent practically possible the brutalities of armed conflicts, whatever the legal and moral issues attendant upon their inception. These latter being reserved for consideration in the distinct, if obviously related, legal context of the *jus ad bellum* rather than in that of the *jus in bello*. Once this distinction breaks down as certain modern trends appear to threaten, the way is opened for inhumane treatment of adversaries more or less subjectively deemed to be "unjust" in an ultimate subversion of the whole basis of this area of law. At the level of practical application too there is serious cause for concern. Whatever other qualities the laws of armed conflict must or should possess, it is unarguably imperative that its provisions should be capable of ready application in the field of non-specialists. This is the point of the comment made by Peter Rowe that:

> "[It must be questioned] ... whether the Protocols . really ... reflect a common human trait of making laws of war during times of peace and ... wandering into unreality. The danger is ... that once ... rules are perceived by those who have to carry them out as unrealistic, they, along with much else, will be abandoned."(39)

There is a balance to be struck between the urgings of unrestrained militarism and the aspirations of impractical humanitarian idealism, bearing in mind that the only fully "humanitarian" approach to armed conflict is its avoidance. It would be very unfortunate if the genuine advances made by 1977 Protocol I(40) were ultimately to be jeopardised because of certain ill-advised aspirations enshrined within it. It may reasonably be contended that the proper place for consideration of claims to self-determination lies in general public international law and possibly in the *jus ad bellum* as such, but certainly not in the *jus in bello* which can at best only be confused thereby and might at worst be utterly subverted.

6. Fundamental Issues

The specific issues raised by recent developments in the laws of armed conflict may ultimately be seen as reflective of the more fundamental philosophical difficulty at the root of the concept of laws of armed conflict to which reference was made at the outset of this paper. That is by way of repetition that, as Sir Hersch Lauterpacht maintained armed conflict is an ultimate breakdown of international legal order within which the existence of "laws" represents an irresolvable paradox. The point was put most graphically by von Clausewitz,

> "War is an act of force ... which theoretically can have no limits"(41)

This is one reason why as implied above, criticism of 1977 Protocol I must be approached with some care since, taken without severe qualification, it may open the doors to Clausewitz and, so to speak, cast out the legal baby with the conceptual bath water. To this most basic of issues the remainder of this paper will be addressed.

Notwithstanding Clauswitz, armed conflict is not now and has not for centuries past been generally regarded as a situation inherently involving an unqualified and unrestrained use of force. Some may have thought so and there have been, and continue to be, appalling barbarities in wartime but there has, equally long been a sense of the ethical appropriateness of some restraint in the conduct of armed conflict. The aim of the modern laws of armed conflict has since the 1860s been, in the words of the 1868 St. Petersburg Declaration, to limit the objectives and practice of armed conflict to an endeavour "to weaken the military forces of the enemy" without extension into brutality against persons *hors de combat* or civilians. The notion was not, however, an original insight of the mid-19th century, the contribution of that era was one of systematisation and institutionalisation. The basic idea can be seen in much earlier eras. In *De Civitate Dei* St. Augustine argued that Christian doctrine should be interpreted as having a palliative effect upon the barbarities of warfare(42), an aspiration which proved in fact rather illusory in practice. The Middle Ages too had, at least in theory, rules of war, many of them admittedly aspects of so-called "chivalry" which had more the air of a noble "game" than of systematic humanitarian concern. The full panoply of restrictive interpretation and "cheating" was also to be found in these early times. Bishop Odo of Bayeux with his mace at the battle of Hastings in 1066 was a famous example.[43] Nonetheless some more exalted concerns were evidently felt at least in retrospect. One example may be seen in the lingering unease felt by English commentators upon the killing of prisoners at the battle of Agincourt on St. Crispin's Day 25th October 1415. Fearing the danger posed by the large number of French prisoners in his ranks during a French counter-attack King Henry V ordered that they be killed. Many were killed before the order was countermanded when the perceived threat receded. In his account Shakespeare[44] chose to emphasise a possibly "unlawful" French attack upon the English baggage train and the "boys" guarding it, but even so felt bound to make wry comment upon the incident. Later writers such as Hume preferred to emphasise the apparent emergency during which the order was given and its swift cancellation upon the resolution of the misapprehension.[45] It is however clear that English commentators have felt marked unease about the proprieties of this affair from an essentially "humanitarian" viewpoint. The "gamesmanship" aspect of the traditional rules of the law of armed conflict in contrast were well illustrated in the action between H.M.S. *Shannon* and U.S.S. *Chesapeake* in 1813. The Captain of the *Shannon* ordered the detachment of a companion frigate, H.M.S. *Tenedos*, in order not to have an "unfair" advantage in a ship to ship "duel". The *Shannon* won in the event, but such an approach would have seemed bizarre by the time of the battle of the River Plate in 1939.[46] If, however, rather haphazard ideas of restraint in armed conflict long predated the modern law of armed conflict[47] it was clearly from the 1860's onwards that the modern systematised laws of armed conflict developed, symbolised on the "Geneva" side by the first Geneva Convention for the Amelioration of the Condition of the Wounded in Armies in the Field of 1864 and on the "Hague" side by such agreements as the 1868 St. Petersburg Declaration.

As matters now stand the *jus in bello* consists of such "Hague" and "Geneva" provisions, the relationship and standing of which are in themselves the ultimate subjects of jurisprudential enquiry in this area and directly or indirectly the origin of all other such speculations upon the laws of armed conflict. Strictly speaking "Hague" law limiting the means and methods of warfare and "Geneva" law, making provision for the protection of victims of armed conflict, are distinct in both function and structure. This is a position maintained up to a point by Pictet[48] and more strongly by Herczeg[49]. The latter maintains that "Hague" law presupposes that war will occur and merely provides rules for its conduct, "Geneva" law makes the same assumption but is distinct in making "humanitarian" provision for victims of armed conflict, whereas "human rights" law treats war in itself as a breach of basic rights and is a higher form of provision. This argument has been addressed in brief above[50] but becomes now of fundamental importance. In fact it may be contended that all such distinctions are unsatisfactory if treated as more than divisions of convenience and are found, upon examination, to rest upon semantic niceties which are unsound foundations for absolute categorisations. In reality both "Hague" and "Geneva" provisions ultimately share the objective, set out by Pictet in the context of international humanitarian law:

> "... to regulate hostilities in order to attenuate their hardship."[51]

Thus the 1868 St. Petersburg Declaration cited above[52] had an overtly "humanitarian" base. The same can be seen in the diplomatic note circulated in 1898 in preparation for the first Hague Peace Conference by the Imperial Russian Government which is worth quoting *in extenso*, not least for its rather depressing "modernity" nearly a century on:

> "The maintenance of general peace and a possible reduction of ... excessive armaments (is an) ... ideal towards which the endeavours of all governments should be directed. (And with which) the humanitarian ... views of His Majesty the Emperor ... are in ... accord ... [T]he Imperial Government believes that the present moment would be very favourable for seeking, by means of international discussion ... the benefits of ... lasting peace, and (the limitation of) ... progressive development of existing armaments".[53]

Equally "Geneva" provisions contain many statements of distinctly "Hague-like" tendency. As an example there may be taken the statement of Article 35 of 1977 Protocol I which commences from the proposition that:

> "In any armed conflict the right of the Parties to the conflict to choose methods or means of warfare is not unlimited."[54]

and proceeds to forbid methods of warfare causing "superfluous injury or unnecessary suffering"[55] or "widespread long-term and severe damage to the natural environment".[56] The "Hague" tendency of these latter provisions is obvious even without their use by some as an argument in the debate upon the lawfulness of the possession and use of nuclear weapons.[57] The same point may be made generally about the content of Part IV of 1977 Protocol I[58] which endeavours considerably to extend the protection of civilian populations against the effects of hostilities from the rather minimal provisions of 1949 Geneva Convention IV. Examples can be seen in Article 51 which seeks to ban attacks upon the civilian population as such (Article 51(2)) and "indiscriminate" attacks (Article 51(4) and (5)). These points are expanded in Articles 52 to 56. It had in fact originally been intended that Additional Protocol I should include much more specific restrictions upon the use of certain conventional weapons but agreement upon these points was not reached in time. Eventually the consideration was resumed in 1979 under the aegis of the United Nations Conference on prohibitions or Restrictions of Use of Certain Conventional Weapons which may be deemed to be Excessively Injurious or to have Indiscriminate Effects. The result in 1981 was the United Nations Convention bearing the same cumbrous title as the Conference which produced it, with three annexed Protocols.

The 1981 Convention was founded upon the well established principle that the means and methods of warfare are not unlimited and the specific ideas, also stated in 1977 Protocol I additional to the 1949 Geneva Conventions, that such means and methods "of a nature to cause superfluous injury or unnecessary suffering" or "widespread long-term and severe damage to the natural environment" are prohibited. The Convention itself is largely procedural and is stated to apply in the circumstances set out in Common Article 2 of the 1949 Geneva Conventions and in Article 1(4) of 1977 Additional Protocol I (Article 1). The substantive provision is made in the three annexed Protocols which deal respectively with fragments incapable of detection in the human body by X-ray; mines, booby traps and other devices; and incendiary weapons. The first of these are banned outright, in a concern which is in some ways the technological descendent of that with explosive shells reflected in the 1868 Declaration of St. Petersburg. The remaining two Protocols however, although imposing some general restrictions, lay emphasis upon the protection of civilian populations from the use of the weapons concerned.

Thus (eg) Article 5(2) of Protocol II provides that:

> "It is prohibited in all circumstances to direct weapons to which this article applies ... against the civilian population as such or against individual civilians."

Similarly Article 2(1) of Protocol III provides that:

> "It is prohibited in all circumstances to make the civilian population as such, individual civilians or civilian objects the object of attack by incendiary weapons."

The general points which can be made about the expanded regime of civilian protection provided for in 1977 Protocol I additional to the 1949 Geneva Conventions can also, by the same token, be made about the 1981 Convention. It is however obvious that here there is a provision which has, in almost equal measure a combination of "Geneva" and "Hague" concerns. This overlap is in fact inevitable since the only cause for rules and principles limiting the conduct of armed conflict is, in one form or another humanitarianism. In circumstances of modern "total" war the 19th century idea of rules concerning what combatants may do to each other (Hague law) and rules for the treatment of those *hors de combat* or *non-combatant ab inito* (Geneva law) becomes untenable upon any but the most technical grounds, even if, for convenience of study, such a technical separation remains useful.

It is not necessary to share the implicit view of von Clausewitz and Stalin, that limitations upon the conduct of armed conflict are synonomous with military inefficiency and intrinsically unrealistic to concede that there is a balance to be drawn between military practicality and considerations of humanity. This point was implicit to (eg) the 1868 Declaration of St. Petersburg it is also a point made by writers such as Rowe(59) and Draper.(60) The laws of armed conflict cannot make war "humane", it is by definition barbarous, the aim is rather to strike a balance which confines the incidence of barbarism within the narrowest practicable bounds pending a solution to the problem of conflict in general. In this sense the emphasis upon ultimate humanitarianism lies in development of the *jus ad bellum* into a true *jus contra bellum*, not unfortunately the current direction of new movement rather than upon either technical category of the *jus in bello*. Both "Hague" and "Geneva" law are in their own ways designed to mitigate the horrors of war which is not to say that war is "presupposed" in the pejorative sense implied by (eg) Herczeg. Again one returns to the issue of practicality of implementation. Some criticism is made of the civilian protection provisions of Protocol I on this basis. These include bans upon "indiscriminate" attacks (Article 51) and attacks upon "civilian objects" (Article 52). This is in itself un objectionable provided it is clear that "military" and "civilian" objects are not in practice quite so neatly separable as the language of some of these provisions might seem strictly to imply. The argument that such provisions impede military effectiveness is true but irrelevant since, in the crudest sense, that is implicit in any regime for the limitation of the conduct of armed conflict.

7. Conclusions

This argument however leads into the most general issue of all. Is it actually desirable that there should be a (or rather some) *jus in bello*? Some, like the novelist Tolstoy and playwrite G.B. Shaw, have argued that attempts to mitigate the horrors of armed conflict actually encourage war by making it more "acceptable". Upon a practical level such arguments may readily be dismissed. Were this view correct war would have ended long ago; even making allowance for the remoteness of "traditional" wars from the bulk of the populace it is difficult to see how it could have survived the 17th century Thirty Years War or in modern times the First World War Somme offensive. In so "classic" an armed conflict as the Falklands conflict a confrontation between professional armed forces for which the historical provision of international humanitarian law up to and including the 1949 Geneva Conventions were designed and in which its provision was well applied by both sides,[61] there was no dearth of suffering. Many men were killed and injured, such is the nature of armed conflict and the mitigation of its horror is in no "danger" of rendering it otherwise. In this however we return to the opinion expressed of law in general by Karl N. Llewellyn to which reference was made at the outset of this paper. Can a system of "law" regulating the conduct of armed conflict be jurisprudentially maintainable? The answer must be positive. The law of armed conflict does not set at nought the objective of peace. The opening words of the preamble to 1977 Protocol I additional to the 1949 Geneva Conventions:

> "The High Contracting Parties,
>
> Proclaiming their earnest wish to see peace prevail among peoples,
>
> ....
>
> Believing it necessary nevertheless to reaffirm and develop the provisions protecting the victims of armed conflict ...."

express the jurisprudential position of both "Geneva" and "Hague" law perfectly. Humanitarian mitigation of the horrors of armed conflict does not preclude endeavour for the ultimate humanitarianism of peace, arms limitation does not preclude the pursuit of ultimate arms abolition and may indeed be seen as a, necessarily and properly, careful step in that general direction. The ultimate aim is not, and should not be, "peace at any price", there are horrors other than those of armed conflict which all the peoples of the world have good cause to remember from the recent past and which also call for "humanitarian" consideration. This is not an argument for outright "just war" doctrines but for a rationally defined doctrine of "defence" upon which some of the arguments have been outlined above. In the end one may agree with such as SS. Augustine and Thomas Aquinas, without necessary reference to the broader theological implications, that armed conflict is symptomatic of an unhealthy world order, a "cure" for which is highly desirable. One may however at the same time urge without inconsistency that to pursue a medical analogy, palliative measures are in themselves desirable even if prophylaxis is ultimately to be preferred. To answer Llewellyn in the immediate context it may indeed be the function of law to obviate or safely to "channel" potentially damaging disputes but where this cannot be done, it is at least a respectable subsidiary function for legal norms to mitigate to the greatest extent possible the impact of conflicts. The present danger in this area of law lies not in the "encouragement" of war through humanitarian endeavour but in the confusion of the distinct roles of palliation and prophylaxis within one legal sector at the peril of its ultimate subversion and overthrow.

FOOTNOTES

1. See Karl N. Llewellyn, "The Normative, the legal and the Law jobs: the Problem of Juristic Method (1939-40)", 49 *Yale L.J.*, 1355.

2. Geza Herczeg, *Development of International Humanitarian Law*, (Akademiai Kiado, Budapest 1984, trans. Sander Simon ed. Lajos Czante), p. 56.

3. The view based on a "cooling-off" period proved naive in practice. It may, in fairness have been a reasonable contention in the case of European governments in 1914, many of which showed signs of "cold feet" - albeit too late to restrain the momentum of the military machine. It proved however a dangerous misapprehension in the era of Hitler and Mussolini as the saga of "appeasement" and the debacle of Munich amply demonstrated, admittedly beyond the ambit of the League of Nations although this is in itself a not insignificant point.

4. Commonly known as the Pact of Paris or the Kellogg-Briand Pact.

5. See 41 AJIL 1947, p. 172 *et seq.*

6. I.e. the destruction or seizure of forces of a neutral or "allied" power believed to be about to join an enemy. The term is derived from the Battle of Copenhagen in 1801 in which a British fleet under Admiral Sir Hyde Parker, his second-in-command - Nelson - famously "seeing no signal", destroyed the Danish fleet which was feared to be about to be employed in Napoleon's "continental system". A more recent example may be seen in the attack upon the French Fleet in Toulon following the French capitulation in 1940.

7. J. Picket, *Development and Principles of International Humanitarian Law*, (Martinus Nijhoff, 1385), p. 13 citing C. Draper, *The Conception of the Just War*.

8. See Corinthians 1:10 - 11.

9. *De Civitate Dei* Bk.V:22 and XIX:7.

10. *Ibid.*, Bk. XIX:7.

11. Cited by Michael Walker in his discussion of the burning of Atlanta in *Just and Unjust Wars* (Allen Lane, 1978), pp. 32-33.

12. St. Thomas Aquinas, *Summa Theologica*, 2a2ae, 40.

13. *Ibid.*, 2a2ae, 10.

14. This too led to a more overtly "amoral" appreciation of resort to armed force of which Maciavelli's account in *The Prince* (Il Principe) was symptomatic.

15. Strictly it should be added that those parts of Europe adherent to the Eastern Orthodox persuasion or under Islamic rule were not, of course, anyway subject to Papal jurisdiction.

16. A formula taken from the 1555 Peace of Augsburg.

17. An analysis of the impact of the Peace of Westphalia can be found in Leo Cross's account, "The Peace of Westphalia, 1648-1948", 42 *AJIL*. 1948, p. 20.

18. Malcolm N. Shaw, International Law (2nd ed. Grotius, 1986) p. 541.

19. There is in fact an uncomfortable element of truth in the satirical assertion of W.C. Sellar and R.J. Yeatman (*1066 and all That*) that the war to end war was followed by "the Peace to end Peace".

20. G. Best, *Humanity in Warfare* (University Paperbacks Methuen 1983) p. 310. 21.

21. *Ibid.*, p. 312.

22. An interesting discussion of this incident can be found in Wright, "The Goa Incident", 56 *AJIL* 1962, p. 617.

23. *Op.cit.* at note 2.

24. Igor P. Blishchenko, *Humanitarian Norms and Human Rights*, in *Modern Wars, the Humanitarian Challenge* (ed. Bedjaoui), p. 142.

25. For an interesting discussion of this issue, see S.K. Chatterjee, "Terrorism and Certain Legal Aspects of Human Rights" (1980) Vol. VI, *International Relations*, p. 749.

26. *q.v. ante.*

27. Two Swiss "mercenary" forces survived into the modern era. The Swiss Guard of the Kings of France, massacred during the Revolution, and the Papal Swiss Guard. The latter is still extant but has long ceased to be a "mercenary" force, having become very much an appointment of honour.

28. See 53 *BYIL*, p. 418.

29. The affair of Captain Astiz (actually a Frigate-Captain of which Lieutenant Commander is the closest equivalent R.N. rank) during the Falklands Conflict provided an instructive instance of this problem. For an account of the issues arising see Michael A. Meyer, "Liability of Prisoners of War for Offences Committed prior to Capture: the Astiz Affair", 32 *ICLQ*, 1983, p. 948. It should be added that following the establishment of civilian government in Argentina Captain Astiz was tried for alleged human rights violations and the case was dismissed by reason of the effluxion of time under a statute of limitations. At the time of writing (January 1988) Captain Astiz is again the centre of controversy within Argentina having been proposed for promotion in the Argentine Navy.

30. (1939) 2KB 544.

31. In 1932 Japan set up the puppet state of Manchukuo in Manchuria with the Manchu ex-Emperor of China, Henry Pu Yi, as nominal head of state.

32. (1939) 2KB 546.

33. This was of course a decision upon municipal commercial law without comment upon the prevailing public international law. A discussion of the case can be found in Lord McNair and A.D. Watts, *The Legal Effects of War* (4th ed., 1966) at p. 36.

34. Famously recorded in Napoleonic Spain by Goya.

35. Which is not to say that those judgments are impossible or should not be demanded.

36. " ... all cases of declared war or... any other armed conflict which may arise between two or more of the High Contracting Parties, even if the state of war is not

recognised by one of them. (And) ... all cases of partial or total occupation of the territory of a High Contracting Party, even if the said occupation meets with no armed resistance."

37. See *ante*, p. 38 *et seq.*

38 *Op.cit.* p. 306 *et seq.*

39. Rowe, *Defence: The Legal Implications* (Brassey's Defence Publishers, 1987) p. 150.

40. For a general consideration of the significance of Protocol I see George H. Aldrich "New Life for the Laws of War", 75 *AJIL* 1981, p. 764.

41. Karl von Clausewitz, *On War* (Vom Kriege, 1932) Ch-1, p. 1. Trans. Col. J.J. Graham, ed. Col. F.N. Maude (1908), Penguin Abridgement 1982.

42. St. Augustine, *De Civitate Dei*, Bk V:24.

43. Ecclesiastics were forbidden to shed blood so Bishop Odo used a mace which shed no blood, or at least, not much but still wrought destruction very effectively.

44. See Shakespeare, King Henry V.

45. An interesting discussion of this incident can be found in Walker, *op. cit.*, pp. 17-19.

46. In December 1939 the commerce raiding German pocket battleship *Graf Spee* was damaged in action with H.M. Cruisers Exeter, *Achilles and Ajax* and took refuge in Montevideo. After the period permitted for repairs under prevailing law the Captain of the *Graf Spee*, anticipating the arrival of overwhelming force in the form of the aircraft carrier *Ark Royal* and the battlecruiser *Renown*, took his ship into the River Plate and scuttled her on 17th December 1939.

47. The arguments for the antiquity of "humanitarian" concern in armed conflict advanced by Pictet (*op. cit.*, Ch. 1) may, however, reasonably be argued to represent a somewhat selective view.

48. *Op.cit.* Ch. 1.

49. *Op.cit.* pp. 65-73.

50. *Ante* p. 41.

51. Pictet *op. cit.* p.1.

52. *Ante*, p. 41.

53. Circulated in the name of Tsar Nicholas II by Count Muraviev, the Russian Foreign Minister, and dated 12th August 1898.

54. Article 35(1).

55. Article 35(2).

56. Article 35(3).

57. It may be reckoned with near certainty that any United Kingdom ratification of Protocol I would be subject to a reservation excluding any such implication from Article 35.

58. Articles 48 - 58.

59. See *ante*.

60. "The Emerging Law of Weapon Restraint" (1977) 19 *Survival* 9, 15. Cited by Rowe, *op. cit.* p. 150.

61. See the I.C.R.C. Report rendered by Silvie-Stoyanka Junod *(Protection of the Victims of Armed Conflict Falkland/ Malvinas Islands (1982))*.

HUMAN RIGHTS AND HUMANITARIAN LAW IN INTERNAL CONFLICTS

Francoise Hampson

1. Introduction

Recent experience in internal conflicts such as those in Nigeria, Kampuchea, Sri Lanka and El Salvador, might suggest that there are no rules of international law setting limits on the conduct of hostilities. The object of this paper is to examine whether that is the case or whether there are in fact legal rules binding on the parties to such conflicts and regulating their treatment of individuals within their jurisdiction. Internal conflict is used here to describe armed struggles within the frontiers of one State. The question of foreign involvement will be considered below.

At first sight, since the conflict is internal, one would assume that there cannot be any rules of international law applicable. Article 2(7) of the UN Charter provides that the United Nations cannot "intervene in matters which are essentially within the domestic jurisdiction of any State or require the Members to submit such matters to settlement under the ... Charter". Both State practice and international obligations entered into by States suggest, however, that there are at least two exceptions to that rule. Alternatively, if they are not exceptions one can say that certain matters occurring within the land territory of one State may not necessarily be within the exclusive jurisdiction of that State and outside the international domain. Those two areas are international human rights law(1)* and humanitarian law(2). This does not, of itself, establish that those bodies of rules will be applicable in an internal armed conflict. It merely shows that some international law can apply to a situation within one State. It might be the case for example that human rights law only applies in peacetime and that international humanitarian law only applies

* For footnotes see p. 72.

during conflicts between two or more States. In that event, there would be a legal vacuum with regard to internal armed conflicts. Is that, in fact, the case?

2. Applicability of international human rights law during internal armed conflicts

The years since 1945 have seen not only the emergence of customary law principles[(3)] in the field of human rights but also the elaboration of specific texts.[(4)] Many States are parties to both an international and a regional human rights treaty. For the purposes of this paper attention will be focused on the International Covenant on Civil and political Rights (ICCPR)[(5)] and the European Convention on Human Rights (ECHR)[(6)]. The first is the most relevant of the international texts and the second the regional treaty with the most developed case-law. The combination of the two therefore provides a useful model.

Both treaties provide for derogation in the event of public emergencies and armed conflicts. In other words they define situations in which the obligations imposed on States may be modified. This must be distinguished from, on the one hand, reservations[(7)] and, on the other, limitations[(8)] attached to the rights themselves. In the case of reservations a State has indicated at the time of ratification that it does not accept one or more provisions in the treaty. Limitations attached to rights represent the qualifications which must often attend the exercise by A of a right in the face of B's competing rights. Thus, A's right to freedom of expression may be limited by the need to protect B from the invasion of his privacy and defamation. Derogation however, has the effect of modifying the scope of rights under the terms of the treaty itself but only in certain situations, defined by the treaty and not by the individual States parties.

Both the ICCPR and the ECHR provide certain rights from which no derogation is possible. In other words, they apply in peacetime and in all armed conflicts. The State party is obliged never to violate the rights in question. An examination will be made of those non-derogable rights before turning to the situations in which derogation is possible and the effect this may have on other treaty provisions.

A. Non-derogable human rights

The list of rights which do not admit of derogation in the International Covenant and the European Convention overlap. All those in the latter come within the former, which also includes certain other rights. Thus under both texts, no one shall be subjected to torture or to inhuman or degrading treatment or punishment (Article 7 ICCPR and Article 3 ECHR). The right to life shall be protected by law. Certain deprivations of life are defined as not being in breach of that right such as death resulting "from the use of force which is no more than absolutely necessary ... for the purpose of quelling a riot or insurrection" (Article 2(2)(c) ECHR). No derogation at all is permitted under Article 6 ICCPR and only in relation to deaths resulting from lawful acts of war under Articles 15(2) and 2 ECHR. No one shall be held in slavery or servitude (Article 8 ICCPR and Article 4 ECHR) which does not include the performance of any military service required. No retroactive penal legislation may be introduced (Article 15 ICCPR and Article 7 ECHR). These are the only non-derogable rights common to both texts. In addition the International Covenant proscribes derogation from the following rights: No one is to be imprisoned for debt (Article 11), everyone has the right to recognition as a person before the law (Article 16) and protection is accorded to freedom of thought, conscience and religion (Article 18). Furthermore, measures cannot be taken in derogation of the obligations under the treaty if they "involve discrimination solely on the ground of race, colour, sex, language, religion or social origin" (Article 4(1)). In other words, derogation may be permitted from the non-discrimination provision (Article 2(1)) but only if it concerns distinctions based on political or other opinions national origin, property, birth, or other status.

Clearly two of the non-derogable rights are of fundamental importance during an internal armed conflict; the protection of the right to life and freedom from torture or inhuman or degrading treatment. This will, for example, inhibit the measures a State may take in interrogating "terrorists", "freedom fighters", lawful or other combatants or whatever the State chooses to call its opponents.[9] It will restrict measures which can be taken for riot control. Certain types of equipment otherwise lawful in international law during an armed conflict, may be too likely to result in unnecessary civilian deaths to be permitted.[10] Very relevant areas of international human rights law clearly, therefore apply during an armed conflict but the question arises of whether they remain pure theory or whether they apply in practice. In very many cases, they clearly are not so applied; the reports of Amnesty International testify to that.[11] This still, however, leaves the question of whether the treaty obligations are respected in the case of State parties to the two texts chosen as a model, the ICCPR and the ECHR. Western Europe may not recently have undergone the upheavals of Central and Latin America, and the Middle East or South-East Asia, but it has seen the overthrow of democratically elected regimes in Greece and Turkey, the invasion and occupation of part of Cyprus by Turkey, serious civil disorder accompanied by terrorist activity in Northern Ireland and more sporadic terrorist problems in West Germany and Italy. The question is whether non-derogable provisions in the two human rights texts have been respected in those situations. The answer appears to be that it varies with the extent of the upheaval. In both the Greek[12] and Turkish[13] cases only when allegations of torture were notorious did other States invoke the enforcement mechanism under the ECHR. The regime of the Greek colonels gave the Commission certain facilities for its investigations but later set up obstructions, necessitating the departure of the Commission from Greece. In its report,[14] the Commission found violations of many Provisions of the Convention including Article 3, the prohibition against torture. Immediately before a vote was to be taken on the expulsion of Greece from the Council of Europe, she chose to withdraw from the organisation. At first sight, one might be tempted to see this solely as a failure of the Convention system. There are, however, two points worthy of note: firstly Greece did originally co-operate with the Commission and, secondly, one of the first international acts of the government which replaced that of the colonels was to rejoin the Council of Europe and to reaffirm its acceptance of the European Convention on Human Rights. This suggests that the invoking of the enforcement system under the Convention did make a difference to Greece but the mere existence of the treaty obligation was not sufficient to prevent torture. Again, in the case of Turkey, there was considerable delay between the publication of reports alleging torture and the introduction of a case against her by other States. In this instance a "friendly settlement"[15] was arrived at between the parties. Turkey gave certain assurances to the applicant States and the Commission and has subsequently accepted the right of individual petition. In return, the case was struck off without the Commission reaching an opinion on whether Article 3 had been violated. Here again the existence of the treaty obligation may not have been sufficient to prevent the alleged violations but the invoking of the enforcement system did make a difference. In the case which the government of Eire brought against the UK concerning events in Northern Ireland the enforcement system again had a significant effect. This time, both the Commission(16) and Court(17) were involved. The UK gave an assurance that it would no longer use the five techniques which, taken together, were held to constitute torture by the Commission but "merely" inhuman and degrading treatment by the Court even though the crisis said to have justified them was continuing, albeit on a lesser scale. The existence of the prohibition against torture and inhuman or degrading treatment had not, however, prevented the measures from being taken in the first place. In cases involving anti-terrorist measures in Germany and Italy, other considerations apply. Different Convention provisions were at issue. The compatibility of practices under the Italian system of criminal justice with the European Convention had been called into question not merely in the context of its trials of suspected terrorists.(18) In the case of Germany(19) the domestic courts were aware of the issue of compatibility with the Convention as it can be raised before them. From these cases, three propositions emerge.

1. The more serious the domestic upheaval the less likely it is that the State party's obligations under the Convention will prevent violations from occurring.

2. The invoking of the Convention's enforcement machinery does have some effect, varying in degree in accordance with the State's perception of the gravity of the domestic situation.

3. Where the right of individual petition to the Commission exists and/or the Convention may be invoked before domestic courts, there is a greater likelihood of abuses being prevented. This proposition can only be advanced tentatively as in the most notorious cases (Greece, Turkey and the Turkish invasion of Cyprus) the right of individual petition did not exist. In the case of Northern Ireland, it did. It is only possible to speculate as to why possible breaches of the Convention have not occurred!

It has therefore been established that certain provisions of human rights law, most notably the protection of the right to life and the prohibition against torture and inhuman or degrading treatment, continue to apply in their entirety during an armed conflict but that the extent to which they will be observed varies in inverse ratio to the gravity of the domestic upheaval as perceived by the State party.

There are other difficulties of a practical rather than a legal nature in securing the observance of non-derogable rights. The first is the understandable reluctance of States to bring actions against other contracting parties unless they have something to gain politically in so doing.[20] Where a State has not accepted the right of individual petition, the enforcement system can only be triggered off by other States. Once a case is brought before the Commission an independent examination of the issues ensues. It is the Commission and not the defendant State which defines the scope of terms such as "torture"[21] and which examines the facts and establishes its opinion. Where the jurisdiction of the Court may be invoked, its conclusions take the form of a binding judgment. Other problems concern the responsibility of insurgents. Firstly, if the State is bound by its obligations in the field of human rights but the people against whom it is seeking to act are not, the State is being required to fight with one hand tied behind its back. In a different context, the Commission has said that the Convention obligations are not based on reciprocity.[22] It might well be unwilling to allow a State to take measures in breach of the Convention merely because its opponents were doing so. The provisions against abuse of the Covenant and Convention (Article 5(1) ICCPR and Article 17 ECHR)[23] will not come into play as a complainant is not claiming the right to torture others but is rather objecting to being tortured himself. It appears to be irrelevant what acts he is himself alleged to have perpetrated. The second problem arises where a State has to deal with two or more groups within its jurisdiction who are fighting one another. Is the State to be held responsible for not adequately protecting the right to life of those within its jurisdiction on account of its failure to prevent killings by such groups or by one group in conflict with the State? A similar issue would arise where an individual contested his deportation or expulsion from State A to State B on the grounds that he is likely to be subjected to torture not by the government but by an opposition group. Whilst the State can only be held responsible for torture which its agents commit, it has been held that a State may have positive duties in relation to the protection of the right to life.[24] The attitude of the Commission appears to be that nothing can "justify" torture. None of the European cases has come before the Human Rights Committee set up under the ICCPR. Where that body has been confronted with issues arising out of internal armed conflicts, it has been by virtue of regular State reports or individual applications under the Optional Protocol. It has then faced practical problems of a nature different from those under the European Convention. In many such cases, for example the respondent government has failed to reply either in specific detail or at all.[25] The Committee has then had to reach its conclusion on the basis of the evidence before it.

It has been shown that there are major difficulties in securing the observance of rights regarded as so fundamental that no derogation is permitted to them. Nevertheless, in many cases the invoking of the enforcement machinery provided has made a difference.

B. Derogable human rights

We are concerned here with obligations which may be modified by virtue of a situation existing which entitles the state to derogate. It is therefore necessary to establish in what circumstances a State may derogate and then what difference it makes.

Derogation is only permitted "in time of war or other public emergency threatening the life of the nation" (Article 15(1) ECHR; Article 4(1) ICCPR omits the reference to war). It is not for the State itself to determine whether such a situation exists but, according to the constant jurisprudence of the Commission it is for the enforcement mechanisms set up under the Convention to do so. Those bodies have allowed States a "margin of appreciation"[28] but it is unclear whether that only extends to the State's appraisal of what measures are necessary or whether it also extends to the State's analysis of the crisis as constituting a "public emergency". Professor Higgins[27] is of the view that it should be confined to the former determination. The European Court of Human Rights in the *Lawless* case,[28] understood the phrase in Article 15(1) to "... refer to an exceptional situation of crisis or emergency which affects the whole population and constitutes a threat to the organised life of the community of which the State is composed". The Commission, in the Greek case, elaborated the analysis further and said that the following elements had to be present:

1. an actual or imminent emergency;
2. involving the whole nation;
3. threatening the continuance of the organised life of the community;
4. the normal measures or restrictions permitted by the Convention for the maintenance of public safety, health and order being inadequate.[29]

In relation to the second criterion, it is interesting to note that both parties in the case Eire brought against the UK[30] accepted the existence of an emergency even though it only affected a discrete part of the UK land territory. In only one case, that involving Greece, has the Commission determined that the domestic crisis was not such as to warrant a derogation on the part of the State. This does, however, demonstrate the importance of independent fact-finding and adjudication. It was not for Greece to determine whether it could derogate. This could bring into question the validity of the French reservation to Article 15 which appears to reserve that decision to itself.[31]

An internal armed conflict is almost certain to be a "public emergency" even if confined to only part of the State's territory. The European text, in contrast to the International Covenant also speaks of "war". This has been interpreted as meaning a *de facto* armed conflict,[32] rather than a legal state of war with all its legal consequences. A further difficulty concerns the reliance of a revolutionary government on a derogation provision; is it entitled to invoke an emergency which it has created itself to justify derogating from human rights obligations? The Commission, by a majority, in the Greek case concluded that the State's rights and obligations under the Convention were not removed by the revolution and that, if the conditions of Article 15 were met the Greek government could rely on it.

A further limitation on the power of derogation arises from the obligation of notification in Articles 4(3) ICCPR and 15(3) ECHR. A State party must indicate "the provisions from which it has derogated" (ICCPR) or "the measures which it has taken" (ECHR) and the reasons why. In various cases the sufficiency of the notification has been challenged[33] and the question of the inter-relationship between a breach of that obligation and the right to derogate raised. In the Greek case, the Commission examined the facts under Article 15(1) even though it had found a breach of Article 15(3). The Greek government had provided some information. This still leaves open the question of whether the State may invoke the right to derogate during Commission proceedings where it has provided no notification at all. Following the invasion and occupation of part of Cyprus by Turkish armed forces, not only was the Secretary-General of the Council of Europe not informed of measures in derogation and of the need for them, but there was no formal public act of derogation, such as the declaration of a state of emergency by the Turkish authorities. The Commission held[(34)] that where a government proclaims no such act, although it was not prevented from doing so, Article 15 could not be invoked. It remains unclear what the effect of non-communication to the Secretary-General would be where the State had taken some public measure domestically. The *Cyprus v. Turkey* case shows that the notoriety of the facts will not of itself constitute notification.

A further limitation on derogation is that the measures must not be inconsistent with the State's other obligations under international law. It could be argued that a State bound by both the ECHR and ICCPR could not, under the former, derogate from non-derogable provisions of the latter. It will be recalled that the list of such provisions was longer in the case of the International Covenant. Again, it could be argued that the State could not derogate in a fashion inconsistent with its obligations under the Geneva Conventions and the Protocols if applicable.[(35)] This could give rise to both practical and legal problems. Imagine that X is killed in detention during an internal conflict in circumstances which require the State to provide a report to the International Committee of the Red Cross (ICRC). Imagine further that his widow brings an action under Article 2 ECHR (protection of the right to life). If the State is entitled to derogate it may invoke Article 15(2) which provides that a death resulting from a "lawful act of war" is not a breach of the Convention. It is not clear how the Commission should determine what constitutes a "lawful act of war". It would perhaps use the criteria established under the Hague and Geneva Conventions. Even so, the Commission might reach a conclusion different from that of the ICRC on the facts. The Commission would presumably not be bound by the report of the ICRC. In effect, the Commission would be applying and interpreting the rules of humanitarian law, even if it was in the context of the ECHR. As will be seen below a State's obligations under humanitarian law are very limited in the case of internal armed conflicts thus reducing the scope for overlap. Before the notion is dismissed, however it should be remembered that such problems could have arisen out of the Falklands/Malvinas conflict, an inter-State one. Under the ECHR, a State is responsible for the acts of its agents, even acting extra-territorially.[36] An Argentine prisoner of war was killed in South Georgia.[37] The investigation suggested that the death resulted from an understandable mistake of fact. If the next-of-kin of the POW had brought an otherwise admissible application under the ECHR, the UK would firstly have needed to establish that it could derogate from the Convention. No notice had been sent to the Secretary-General of the Council of Europe. Secondly, it would have had to show that death resulted from a "lawful act of war". A similar problem could have arisen in relation to the sinking of the *Belgrano.* The question of the application of the Hague and Geneva Conventions by human rights bodies is not, therefore, merely hypothetical.

Once a State has established that it may derogate from its obligations under human rights conventions such derogation is limited "to the extent strictly required by the exigencies of the situation". There appears to be a margin of appreciation both with regard to the measures taken and the manner of their application.[38] The element of discretion is probably greater with regard to the latter. The evaluation of the necessity of the measures will depend on the facts. There is only space here to repeat that, again, the ultimate decision is for the Commission and Court but, in situations in which they have accepted the right of a State to derogate, they have shown a reluctance to find that the measures taken exceeded the margin of appreciation with regard to those rights from which derogation is possible. So, in the Greek case, the Commission did not accept the existence of an emergency. In the *Irish State* case the alleged breach of Article 3 was unaffected by the derogation. In that case and in the *Lawless* case, articles from which derogation is possible, such as Article 5, were found not to have been violated.

It has been shown that some human rights can never be derogated from at all, even during an internal armed conflict, and that others can only be derogated from in defined circumstances and to the extent "strictly required by the exigencies of the situation". The determinations fall to be made by the institutions set up by the ICCPR and ECHR and not the State. In an internal armed conflict there are likely to be problems of responsibility in relation to the insurgents. Where the Hague and/or Geneva Conventions are applicable, the enforcement agencies may face the task of applying those rules. What was seen at the outset as a potential legal vacuum therefore contains substantial human rights protections, in theory at least. It remains to be seen whether and to what extent humanitarian law might be applicable.

3. Applicability of humanitarian law during internal armed conflicts

Humanitarian law is that body of rules which applies to the victims of armed conflicts and which, under the 1977 Protocols to the Geneva Conventions of 1949, also limits the way in which the fighting is carried on.[39] The first question is whether humanitarian law applies in an internal armed conflict and the second, the scope of its content.

A. Field of application

The Geneva Conventions apply to all cases of declared war or any other armed conflict which may arise between two or more of the High Contracting Parties, even if the state of war is not recognised by one of them. At first sight, this suggests that they do not apply in internal armed conflicts or civil wars as those conflicts are not between two States capable of being High Contracting Parties. There are three situations, however, in which the Conventions apply even if the conflict takes place within the frontiers of only one State. Firstly, common Article 2 of the Conventions states that they also apply to all cases of partial or total occupation of the territory of a High Contracting Party, even if it meets with no armed resistance. This raises the question of when troops are occupation troops and when they are merely "assisting" the domestic armed forces. Such a problem of characterisation arises for example, in the cases of Kampuchea and Afghanistan. The resolution of the issue is important - it determines which parts of humanitarian law apply to the situation - but, in practice, it is always a highly-charged political question. If for example, the Russians represent an army of occupation in Afghanistan the whole body of humanitarian law applies to the conflict. If, on the other hand, they are merely assisting the Afghan government, only those provisions of humanitarian law applicable in an internal armed conflict apply and as will be seen below, these are much more limited in scope. Secondly, a situation could arise in which the armed forces of a State A were assisting "rebels" in State B fighting against the established government. This raises the question as to the meaning of an "armed conflict ... between two or more High Contracting Parties" (emphasis added). Such a situation arose in the case of India's assistance to Bangladesh when it asserted its independence from Pakistan. That also raised the politically controversial question of the right to self-determination. The third situation in which the Conventions apply in their entirety, even though the conflict is within the land territory of one State, was added by Article 1(4) of Protocol I. Conflicts in which peoples are fighting for their right to self determination and against colonial domination, alien occupation and (which should apparently be read disjunctively) racist regimes, come within the scope of the Conventions. In selecting these criteria the Third World had very specific situations in mind. They understood Article 1(4) as applying to the then Portuguese colonies of Angola and Mozambique, the Israeli-occupied West Bank territories and Namibia and South Africa. This was not seen as a secessionist charter. UN practice makes it clear that when General Assembly Resolutions or international treaty texts, such as the ICCPR, speak of "nations" and "peoples", they do not mean all nations or all peoples. They mean rather those of whose struggle for independence the majority in the UN approve.[40] The Biafrans the Eritreans have not, for example, received that approval and support for the struggle in East Timor, as reflected in voting patterns in the General Assembly, is waning. Article 1(4) of Protocol I is probably best viewed as applying only to the conflicts listed above. Where it does apply, the Geneva Conventions and Protocol I are said to apply in their entirety, subject to ratification of the Protocol if the principle is not part of customary international law.

In the three situations discussed above, the rules of international law applicable to inter State armed conflicts may apply even though the fighting takes place within the land territory of one State and thus constitutes an internal conflict as defined at the outset. It is outside the scope of this paper to examine the content of those rules which are designed to protect the wounded, sick and shipwrecked, those *hors de combat*, prisoners of war and civilians. It is sufficient to note that one possible cause of a legal vacuum in internal conflicts, the applicability of humanitarian law only to inter-State conflicts involving two or more territories, is subject to three possible exceptions in which the full range of humanitarian law applies.

It needs to be examined whether there are, in addition, rules designed to apply in any internal conflict and not just those coming within the three exceptions. Article 3 common to all four Geneva Conventions applies to an "armed conflict not of an international character occurring in the territory of one of the High Contracting Parties" and binds each "party to the conflict". Protocol II was designed to develop and supplement Article 3 but its field of application may be more limited. It applies to all armed conflicts not covered by Protocol I between the armed forces of a High Contracting Party and dissident armed forces or groups provided that the latter are under responsible command and "exercise such control over a part of its [the State's] territory as to enable them to carry out sustained and concerted military operations and to implement this Protocol" (Article 1(1) Protocol II). It is not clear whether the dissident armed forces must manifest the ability to apply the Protocol by doing so or if it is sufficient that they have the capacity or ability to do so. The Protocol specifically does "not apply to situations of internal disturbances and tensions, such as riots, isolated and sporadic acts of violence and other acts of a similar nature, as not being armed conflicts" (Article 1(2), Protocol II, emphasis added). Nothing in Common Article 3 requires that the dissident armed forces satisfy organisational requirements or hold territory. Nor is there any minimum threshold of violence to trigger off its application. It would appear therefore that in some situations both Article 3 and Protocol II will be applicable whereas in others, if the conditions of Protocol II are not satisfied, Article 3 alone will be applicable as it applies to all armed conflicts not of an international character. This appears, at least, to be the understanding of the ICRC as to the field of application of the the provisions.[41] It is, however, necesary to sound a note of caution. Common Article 3 speaks of armed conflicts and does not define them. Protocol II, designed to develop and supplement that article, defines the term negatively by excluding certain types of violence. This might suggest that Article 3 could not apply to such situations either, as it applies to armed conflicts and "isolated and sporadic acts of violence" are not armed conflicts. It is submitted that the practice of assuming that Article 3 applies to all situations of a non-international character whatever the level of violence is to be preferred on humanitarian grounds if no other. Most importantly, it would make the ICRC's "right of initiative" (see below) applicable in all non-international disturbances.

The lawfulness of the resort to force is irrelevant to the

application of humanitarian law[42] (with the possible exception of Article 1(4) of Protocol I).[43] It has been shown that, in an internal armed conflict, not only are certain rules of international human rights law applicable but there are also provisions of humanitarian law designed expressly to deal with such situations and, in certain circumstances, the full range of the Geneva Conventions and Protocol I will be applicable. It remains to be seen what protection Common Article 3 and Protocol II in fact afford the individual.

B. The scope of humanitarian law provisions designed to apply to internal armed conflicts

Protocol II was originally envisaged as a more comprehensive system of protection than that which finally emerged from the negotiation process. The "socialist" States had never wanted it and, once the Third World had secured the adoption of Article 1(4) of Protocol I they lost interest in the regulation of any other type of civil war. Certain European States were a little cautious as they have within their frontiers groups which have resorted or might resort to violence, such as groups seeking autonomy in the UK and France. This helps to account for the limited scope of the Protocol. It provides certain fundamental guarantees for non-combatants, military personnel *hors de combat* and prisoners. There are for example, rules about internment, penal prosecutions and medical care. The Protocol also provides certain basic protections for the civilian population: forced movement of civilians cannot be ordered other than for their safety or imperative military reasons and objects dispensable to their survival are not to be made objects of attack. Violence to life, health and physical or mental well-being, including murder and cruel treatment such as torture or mutilation, is prohibited as are collective punishments, the taking of hostages, pillage and outrages upon personal dignity. This last includes "humiliating and degrading treatment, rape, enforced prostitution and any form of indecent assault".[44] The list of prohibitions resembles closely that contained in common Article 3 but is slightly more specific. Protocol II, it must be remembered, only applies to those States which have ratified it. It would appear premature to regard as customary international law those provisions which go beyond common Article 3, which does have that status. Furthermore, the Protocol only applies if the dissident armed forces satisfy the criteria outlined above. As already indicated, it is unclear whether such forces need themselves to implement the Protocol or whether it is sufficient if they are capable of so doing.

Common Article 3, which is of more general application as a treaty obligation for 165 States and as customary international law, covers broadly similar ground. Each party to the conflict must treat those not taking an active part in the hostilities humanely. In particular violence to life and to the person including murder, mutilation, cruel treatment and torture, the taking of hostages and outrages upon personal dignity in particular humiliating and degrading treatment, are prohibited. It will be recalled that many of the acts prohibited under both Article 3 and Protocol II also represent individual rights from which the State cannot derogate under human rights conventions. Thus the arbitrary taking of life and torture or inhuman or degrading treatment are prohibited under both codes.

The great weakness of both Protocol II and Article 3 is the enforcement system. Common Article 3 is not based on reciprocity,[45] whereas Protocol II may be, as seen earlier. Experience, in both inter-State and internal conflicts, does however suggest that enforcement of humanitarian law is likely to depend on primitive reciprocity and fear of reprisals.[46] One party to the conflict may apply the law for fear of the consequences for its own forces if it does not do so. Where there is no reasonable prospect of one side applying the law, whether from a lack of the particular resources called for, unwillingness or just plain ignorance, the other side is less likely to feel so inhibited. In such conflicts it may be difficult for the ICRC to work within the territory. It is all the more important for it to find some way of working with the non-State party to the conflict to educate the fighters in the principles of humanitarian law. This strengthens its hand in urging the government to respect its obligations by increasing the likelihood of some form of reciprocity however limited. One case in point is the work of the ICRC in giving basic training in first-aid and the principles of humanitarian law to Afghan nationals in Pakistan who then return to their own country.[47] The non-State party to a conflict may have practical difficulties, in for instance caring adequately for captured members of the State's armed forces. The non-State party may not share the technological advantages of the State. Without aeroplanes it cannot be tempted into indiscriminate aerial bombardment! Where the obligation imposed on the parties is negative rather than positive, for example the proscription of torture, each side is equally able to implement it. The experience of the two parties in implementing the provisions of humanitarian law may be very different but each is capable of refraining from acts which would violate those rules.

Common Article 3 does contain one provision of very great practical importance in securing at least a minimum of respect for the law. It provides that an "impartial humanitarian body, such as the International Committee of the Red Cross, may offer its services to the Parties to the Conflict". This is the basis of the so-called "right of initiative" of the ICRC. The ICRC has often been able to gain access to prisoners and interned persons by invoking this provision in situations in which Protocol II would not be applicable. The UK, for example maintained consistently throughout the negotiation of the Protocol that it did not and would never have applied to the situation in Northern Ireland because that consisted of "isolated and sporadic acts of violence". ICRC delegates were nevertheless able to obtain access to prisoners in the Maze prison by invoking their right of initiative. It implied no recognition of any particular status for the prisoners. The Government had nothing to lose by granting such access but rather had something to gain: it was implying that it had nothing to hide. No government[48] cares to be known as denying access to the ICRC. In the conflict in Afghanistan, the status of which is a matter of controversy, the ICRC was authorised to return to the country in January 1987 at around the same time as the announcement of a programme of national reconciliation and two months before the Special Rapporteur of the UN Human Rights Commission was allowed to visit the country. The same reluctance to be seen to be excluding ICRC delegates was, again, seen recently in the case of South Africa. The application of this "right of initiative" in all non-international armed conflicts is a further reason why Protocol II should not be construed as limiting the field of application of Common Article 3. The visits by the delegates may take place without publicity and the reports to the State may be confidential but their efficacy was demonstrated when the Secretary-General of Amnesty International said "The reports which the ICRC send to governments after visits by its delegates to prisoners are often more effective in stopping torture than any other action".[49] The fact that the visits and reports take place behind the scenes is one reason for their effectiveness but it also makes it difficult to evaluate that effectiveness. Paradoxically, another method of enforcement of humanitarian law is publicity. Reports by independent and impartial organisations, such as Amnesty International may cause the issue of respect for human rights in a particular country to be put on the international agenda for example by the UN Human Rights Commission. The only organisation which expressly and exclusively deals with humanitarian law is the ICRC. Compliance with the Geneva Conventions may, however, come within the sphere of interest of other groups concerned with human rights on a broader scale. Amnesty International[(50)], for example, seeks to ensure compliance with the prohibition against torture contained in the Universal Declaration of Human Rights and the ICCPR. Its concern with torture leads it to examine activities which are also in breach of the Geneva Conventions, if the torture takes place during the course of an armed conflict. The substantive overlap between human rights law and humanitarian law therefore serves to contribute towards the enforcement of both bodies of rules. Publicity regarding alleged violations of humanitarian law must be distinguished from the dissemination of knowledge of its provisions, referred to earlier. The latter seeks to prevent breaches by instructing persons involved in an armed conflict, or who may become so involved in the principles of humanitarian law. The former attempts to use the pressure of international public opinion to shame the participants into complying with their obligations. Both have their part to play in the enforcement of humanitarian law, as do crude principles of reciprocity and the fear of reprisals and the visits of ICRC officials.

The striking feature of humanitarian law in internal conflicts is that there is no independent enforcement machinery. There is no body, equivalent to the European Commission of Human Rights or the Human Rights Committee, capable of making objective determinations of fact. There is no mechanism by which a State can be compelled to account for its conduct during an internal conflict.[(51)] The International Court of Justice whose jurisdiction has occasionally been invoked to deal with issues arising out of inter-State conflicts,[(52)] has only the most limited role to play in internal conflicts. A dispute might be submitted to it by States parties in conflict within one land territory but *locus standi* would present grave difficulties in a case arising out of a conflict between a State and a non-State.[(53)]

4. Conclusion

Experience suggests that it is in internal armed conflicts or civil wars that we see some of the most flagrant violations of fundamental human rights. This does not arise from a legal vacuum. Some international human rights law continues to remain applicable, even during armed conflicts, and certain provisions of humanitarian law are applicable in internal conflicts. The reasons for such violations lie beyond the reach of the law but effective enforcement systems for such rules as are applicable can make a difference. In addition to formal procedures, such as the investigations and reports of the Human Rights Committee and the European Commission and Court of Human Rights other mechanisms have a part to play.[54] The quiet diplomacy of the ICRC and public reports of organisations such as Amnesty International also serve to show parties to a conflict that, even in the case of civil wars, they are not free to wage war with a total disregard for the sufferings of the affected population. There nevertheless remains much work to be done in securing the enforcement in practice of agreed rules of international human rights and humanitarian law in internal armed conflicts.

FOOTNOTES

1. For the purposes of this paper, international human rights law means that body of rules accepted by a State which require it to deal in a certain way with those who come within its jurisdiction, including its nationals. It is this last which makes human rights law unusual in the context of international law which for the most part regulates the dealings of States *inter se*. The form of human rights law is not unusual: the paper deals with treaties of either an international or a regional character and customary international law as evidenced by the Universal Declaration of Human Rights.

2. For the purpose of this paper, humanitarian law includes not only the four Geneva Conventions of 1949 ("Geneva Law") but also those elements of the Hague Conventions of 1907 ("Hague Law") which were up-dated and incorporated into the two 1977 Protocols additional to the Geneva Conventions.

3. e.g. Articles 1, 55 and 56 of the United Nations Charter: Universal Declaration of Human Rights, GA Resn 217A (III) - Mrs. Eleanor Roosevelt, US representative to the General Assembly and Chairman of the United Nations Commission on Human Rights whilst the Declaration was being drafted, said it "is not, and does not purport to be a statement of law or of legal obligation"; it is rather "a common standard of achievement for all peoples of all nations". 19 *US Dept. of State Bulletin* 751 (1948).

4. e.g. International Covenant on Civil and Political Rights and the Optional Protocol 1966; International Covenant on Economic, Social and Cultural Rights 1966; Convention on the Prevention and Punishment of the Crime of Genocide 1948; International Covenant on the Elimination of all forms of Racial Discrimination 1966; Convention on the Suppression and Punishment of the Crime of Apartheid 1973; UN Convention against Torture or other Cruel, Inhuman or Degrading Treatment or Punishment; European Convention on Human Rights and Fundamental Freedoms 1950 and Protocols; American Convention on Human Rights 1970; African Charter on Human and Peoples' Rights 1981. See generally Brownlie, I (ed.), *Basic Documents on Human Rights*, Oxford, 2nd ed. 1981.

5. For text, see Brownlie, *op.cit.* It is beyond the scope of this paper to analyse in detail the system of implementation of the Covenant. Briefly, the contracting parties undertake to submit periodic reports to the Human Rights Committee on the measures they have adopted giving effect to the rights. The Committee consists of eighteen members elected by the contracting parties. They sit in their personal capacity - i.e. not as representatives of their home States. The Committee may make "general comments" on the reports. A contracting party may accept the right of the other parties to bring a claim against it, alleging a violation of the Covenant, before the Committee, on condition of reciprocity. The Committee makes available its "good offices". A long process of attempted conciliation ensues. If unsuccessful, the Commission produces a report stating the facts and indicating "its views on the possibilities of an amicable settlement", which report is not binding. The Covenant makes no provision for petition by individuals. Under the Optional Protocol, however, the Committee may receive such applications subject to procedural requirements similar to those under the European Convention (see

note 6 below). The Committee simply forwards its views to the State and individual. It has no power of execution nor is any other body provided with such powers.

6. For text, see Brownlie, *op.cit.* It is, again, beyond the scope of this paper to analyse in detail the system of implementation of the European Convention. Briefly, any contracting party may refer to the European Commission of Human Rights an alleged breach of the Convention by any other party. The Commission consists of a number of members equal to that of the contracting States and they sit in their individual capacity. A State may accept to have complaints brought against it by individuals to the Commission, subject to procedural requirements in Articles 25-27. The Commission examines the facts and seeks a "friendly settlement" between the parties on the basis of respect for human rights. If a solution is not found, the Commission draws up a report on the facts and states its opinion as to whether they disclose a breach of the Convention. The report is transmitted to the Committee of Ministers of the Council of Europe. If no other action is taken, that Committee decides whether there has been a violation. The parties are bound by the decision. Alternatively, if the State has recognised the jurisdiction of the European Court of Human Rights, within three months of the transmission of the Commission's report to the Committee of Ministers, the Commission or the defendant State (or the applicant State in the case of an inter-State case) may refer the case to the Court. The individual applicant has no such right. The members of the Court must possess the qualifications required for appointment to "high judicial office or be jurisconsults of recognised competence". The Court delivers a judgment binding on the parties, the execution of which is supervised by the Committee of Ministers.

7. "A unilateral statement, however phrased or named, made by a State, when signing, ratifying, accepting, approving or acceding to a treaty, whereby it purports to exclude or to modify the legal effect of certain provisions of the treaty in their application to that State". Article 2(1)(d) Vienna Convention on the Law of Treaties 1969. For validity and effect of reservations, see Vienna Convention, Articles 19-23.

8. Human rights treaties provide both general and specific limitation provisions. Articles 47 ICCPR and 16 and 18 ECHR are examples of general provisions. The specific ones are attached to the relevant articles. See further, P. Sieghart *The International Law of Human Rights*, Oxford, 1983, pp. 87-90; R. Higgins "Derogations Under Human Rights Treaties", 48 *BYIL* (1976-77) 281 at p. 283-286; 307-315.

9. e.g. *Denmark, Norway, Sweden and the Netherlands v. Greece*, 3321-3/67; 3344/67; YB 12 *bis; Ireland v. UK*, 5310/71, Report of the Commission, 25th January 1976; Judgment of the Court, Eur.Ct.HR, Series A No. 25. For an account of what constitutes torture or inhuman or degrading treatment, see P. Sieghart, *op.cit.* p. 162 *et seq.*

10. The use of rubber bullets in Northern Ireland has caused concern in the Parliamentary Assembly of the Council of Europe. The use of force "which is no more than absolutely necessary" has also been examined in *Farrell v. UK* 9013/80, 30 D & R 96. A "friendly settlement" of the case was concluded, under which the British government made a substantial ex gratia payment - see 38 D & R 44.

11. Recent AI reports on States in which some form of internal conflict as defined is taking place include Afghanistan, Nicaragua and Kampuchea.

12. *Denmark et al. v. Greece, supra* note 9.

13. *France Norway Denmark Sweden Netherlands v. Turkey* 9940-9944/82, 35 D & R 143.

14. *Denmark et al. v. Greece, supra* note 9.

15. HRLJ, Vol. 6 (1985), p. 331. Under ECHR Article 28: in the event of the Commission accepting a petition referred to it ... (b) it shall place itself at the disposal of parties concerned with a view to securing a friendly settlement of the matter *on the basis of respect for human rights ...*" (emphasis added). For text of Turkish declaration under Article 25 ECHR recognising the right of individual petition for 3 years, see European Human Rights Reports, Vol. 9, p. 235.

16. *Ireland v. UK, supra*, note 9.

17. *Ireland v. UK, supra*, note 9.

18. *Foti and others v. Italy* Eur Ct HR Series A No. 56 in which the unusual political and social climate in Reggio Calabria was relied on by the government. *Guzzardi v. Italy*, Eur Ct HR, Series A Vol. 39 - kidnapping; but see also *Goddi v. Italy* Eur Ct HR, Series A, No. 76; *Colozza v. Italy*, Eur Ct HR, Series A No. 89.

19. e.g. *Klass v. Federal Republic of Germany*, 5029/71, Eur Ct HR, Series A, Vol. 28 involving availability of an effective remedy (ECHR Article 13) in relation to surveillance measures.

20. In cases brought by Greece, Austria, Ireland and Cyprus against the UK, Italy, UK and Turkey respectively, it was to the applicant governments' political advantage domestically to be seen to be taking a stand. In only two inter-State cases has there been no apparent political advantage for the applicant governments other than satisfying the domestic human rights lobby. Significantly, both those cases involved many applicant States acting together (i.e. the cases brought against Greece and Turkey).

21. P. Sieghart, *op. cit.* note 8, p. 162 *et seq.*

22. *In France, Norway, Denmark, Sweden, Netherlands v. Turkey*, 9940-9944/82, 35 D & R 143 at 169, the Commission reaffirmed its view that the obligations under the European Convention on Human Rights are "essentially of an objective character, being designed rather to protect the fundamental rights of individual human beings from infringement by any of the High Contracting Parties than to create subjective and reciprocal rights for the High Contracting Parties themselves".

23. The provisions are designed to make it impossible for groups or individuals to invoke a Convention right so as to perform an act aimed at destroying for others the rights and freedoms in the Convention. However Article 17 ECHR is negative in scope and cannot be construed so as to deprive a person of the rights guaranteed by, for example, Articles 5 and 6 ECHR e.g. *Lawless v. Ireland*, 322/57, Eur Ct HR, Series A, Vol. 3.

24. *Association X v. UK* 7154/75, 14 D & R, 31.

25. See the Reports of the Human Rights Committee, A/32/44, A/33/40, A/34/40, A/35/40, A/36/40 *et seq.*

26. e.g. *Greece v. UK*, Ybk 2 (1958-9), p. 174 and R. Higgins, *op. cit.* note 8, at p. 296.

27. *ibid.* at p. 299.

28. *Lawless v. Ireland*, 322/57, Eur Ct HR, Series A, Vol. 3.

29. Ybk, 12 (1969) p. 72, para. 153.

30. *Ireland v. UK, supra*, note 9.

31. *France, Norway, Denmark, Sweden, Netherlands v. Turkey*, 9940-9944/82, 35 D & R 143 at p. 168.

32. *Cyprus v. Turkey* 6780/74 & 6950/75, Report of 10 July 1976, declassified following Committee of Ministers Resolution DH(79)1 of 21 January 1979.

33. e.g. *Lawless v. Ireland*, 322/57, Eur Ct HR, Series A, Vol. 3. *Denmark et al v. Greece, supra*, note 9. *Ireland v. UK, supra*, note 9.

34. *Cyprus v. Turkey*, 6780/74 & 6950/75, Report: 10 July 1976.

35. See Paragraph 3A of this paper at p. 65.

36. *Cyprus v. Turkey*, 6780/74 and 6950/75, 2 D & R 125 at p. 136, para. 8.

37. M. Arthur. *Above All Courage*, Sphere (1985) p. 62.

38. See R. Higgins, art cit.note 9 *supra*, at p. 296 *et seq* and especially at p. 300.

39. Historically, the Hague Conventions of 1907, notably the Annex to Convention IV Respecting the Laws and Customs of War on Land, regulated the means and methods of warfare. In up-dating the Geneva Conventions of 1949, it was recognised that potential victims of an armed conflict needed to be protected against certain means and methods of waging war e.g. indiscriminate use of lawful weapons; use of weapons which by their nature are indiscriminate.

Some elements of "the Hague Law" were therefore up-dated and incorporated into the 1977 Protocols additional to the Geneva Conventions.

40. e.g. GA Resn 1514 (XV); GA Resn 2621 (XXV); GA Resn 2525(XXV) ICCPR Art. 1(1); International Covenant on Economic, Social and Cultural Rights, Art. 1(1).

41. Teaching Guidelines for "Ideals in Action" course on Red Cross Principles and International Humanitarian Law, British Red Cross Society, 1985. Also see the *Commentary on the Additional Protocols* published by the ICRC (Geneva, 1987) at p. 1350. Strictly speaking, although this Commentary was written by members of the ICRC, it is not a commentary of the ICRC.

42. Common Article 2 of the Geneva Conventions of 1949 defines the factual situations in which they apply - i.e. "all cases of declared war or of other armed conflict ..." and "all cases of partial or total occupation ...". See also G. Best, *Humanity in Warfare*, 1980.

43. See e.g. D.E. Graham, "The 1974 Diplomatic Conference on the Law of War: A Victory for Political Causes and a Return to the "Just War" Concept of the Eleventh Century", *Washington & Lee Law Rev.* Vol. XXXII (1975), p. 25.

44. Article 4(2)(e) of Protocol Additional to the Geneva Conventions of 12th August 1949 and Relating to the Protection of Victims of Non-International Armed Conflicts (Protocol II).

45. " ... each Party to the conflict shall be bound to apply; as a minimum, the following provisions: ...", Article 3, Geneva Conventions of 1949.

46. Col. G.I.A.D. Draper, "The Implementation of the Modern Law of Armed Conflicts", Lionel Cohen Lectures, Hebrew University of Jerusalem, 1973. The law of reprisals is highly contentious. There are two situations in which the term is used: firstly, a resort to armed force by way of reprisal. This forms part of the *ius ad bellum*. Secondly, there is the issue of reprisals during the course of an armed conflict, part of the *ius in bello*. We are only concerned here with the second of these. Reprisals were lawful, if they satisfied certain criteria, in customary international

law. See the *Naulilaa* Case, *Portugal v. Germany*, 1928, 2 RIAA 1072. Various types of reprisals are prohibited under Protocol I to the Geneva Conventions (e.g. Article 51(6): "Attacks against the civilian population or civilians by way of reprisals are prohibited"). There is profound disagreement in the international community as to whether reprisals represent a form of barbarity which must be banned or whether, within limits, they are an effective deterrent. It is also argued that, whatever the law, resort will be had to reprisals and it is therefore more in the interests of humanity to recognise that and set limits to the reprisals that may be lawfully undertaken.

47. "Dissemination", No. 7, August 1987, ICRC, p. 7.

48. The notorious exceptions are the States parties to the Iran/Iraq conflict. They are parties to the Geneva Conventions. On two occasions the ICRC has publicly had to ask the other High Contracting Parties to bring pressure to bear on Iran and Iraq to respect their obligations under the Conventions.

49. Quoted in Teaching Guidelines for "Ideals in Action" course, *op. cit. supra* n. 41, in Session 4, p. 9.

50. Statute of Amnesty International, clause 1, in *Amnesty International Handbook*

51. Under Protocol I, Article 90, States may accept, on the basis of reciprocity, the competence of an independent fact-finding commission to investigate alleged grave breaches and to facilitate "the restoration of an attitude of respect for the Conventions" and Protocol. Twenty such declarations are required to bring about the establishment of the Commission. As of May 1988, there were only 11 declarations.

52. *Trial of Pakistan Prisoners of War, Interim Protection, Pakistan v. India*, ICJ Rep, 1973, p. 328 and discontinuance order, p. 347: Case concerning military activities in Nicaragua, *Nicaragua v. USA*, ICJ, XXV ILM, No. 5, September 1986.

53. e.g. *locus standi* problem of Ethiopia and Liberia in *South West Africa* Cases, Second Phase, ICJ Reports, 1966, p. 6.

54. In addition to the effect of enforcement on victims or potential victims discussed earlier, one may speculate on the effect on the armed forces themselves. This may be most effective if it takes place during the conflict e.g. court-martials for breaches of military law. In a novel based on experiences in the Vietnam war, it is suggested that non-enforcement contributed to a lack of respect for and subsequent further breaches of humanitarian law. Only those who have been placed in such a situation can confirm or refute the hypothesis but it does have the ring of truth about it. See D.A. Dye, *Platoon*, Grafton, 1987, pp. 143-8, based on a screenplay by Oliver Stone. See also W.T. Mallison, *Studies in the Law of Naval Warfare*, Naval War College, 1966, pp. 20, 27; P. Karsten, *Law, Soldiers and Combat*, Greenwood Press, 1978, pp. xv; 161;164.

SOME LEGAL ISSUES CONCERNING RATIFICATION OF THE 1977 GENEVA PROCOTOLS

*Hans-Peter Gasser**

On 8th June 1977, when the two Protocols additional to the Geneva Conventions of 12th August 1949, and relating to the Protection of Victims of Armed Conflicts[1], were adopted by consensus a sense of relief pervaded the representatives of more than a hundred States, several liberation movements and other organizations seeking to strengthen the humanitarian law applicable in armed conflict. That day marked the successful outcome of exacting work which took much longer than is generally realized.[2] Indeed, the foundation-stone for a new chapter of humanitarian law was laid some time in the early fifties when the International Committee of the Red Cross (ICRC) started to consider supplementing the 1949 Geneva Conventions with a set of rules for the protection of the civilian population against the effects of hostilities: the Draft Rules for the Limitation of the Dangers incurred by the Civilian Population in Time of War. But at that time, governments were not prepared to follow the proposed text through in particular because the draft included a rule which in effect would have prohibited the use of nuclear weapons.[3]

It took the wars of the sixties (Vietnam, Nigeria the Middle East) and the confrontations which characterized the period of decolonization to induce governments to take a real interest in the further development of international humanitarian law. The Twentieth International Conference of the Red Cross (Vienna, 1965), the International Conference on Human Rights (Teheran, 1968), and Resolution 2444 (XXIII) adopted by the United Nations General Assembly in 1968 and entitled "Respect for Human Rights in Armed Conflicts" are the successive phases which prompted the Twenty-first International Conference of the Red Cross (Istanbul, 1969) to request the ICRC to propose "concrete rules which would

* For footnotes see p. 99.

supplement the existing humanitarian law" (Resolution XIII). The United Nations General Assembly adopted in 1970 the very explicit Resolution 2675 (XXV) which is a kind of simplified draft for the subsequent rules on the protection of the civilian population. Convened by the ICRC, the Conference of Government Experts at its two sessions discussed in detail the ICRC's drafts.[4] Finally, at the invitation of the Swiss Federal Council, the Diplomatic Conference held four sessions in Geneva from 1974 to 1977 to negotiate the final texts which were adopted by consensus on 8th June 1977.[5] Each year the progress of the Diplomatic Conference was discussed by the United Nations General Assembly.

This brief look at the history of the 1977 Protocols is meant to demonstrate that these treaties were not hammered out on the spur of the moment at a hastily convened international conference and pushed through by an "automatic majority". They are sound in content and in structure because they matured over many years. In the course of that lengthy process governments had frequent occasion to take cognizance of the issues involved and the solutions suggested, and ample time to influence its progress and development. Today, however, the debates on ratification of the Protocols quite often give the impression that legal and military experts seem to be talking about a completely new, strange, if not totally alien product. Has it been forgotten that the two Protocols after all were drawn up by State representatives and not by a few inexperienced individuals?

The many difficulties encountered in the debate on ratification and the general ignorance with regard to the two Protocols are clear evidence of the need to write over and over again about the various legal issues which stand in the way of ratification. By identifying some of the major problems this paper tries to make some of them better understood. The space available is not sufficient, however, for a comprehensive discussion of all the issues. Reference to the relevant literature should assist the reader to explore the problems further.[6]

1. A glance at the content of the Protocols

It may be useful to call to mind, very briefly, the main contribution of the two Protocols to international humanitarian law:

Protocol I - on international armed conflicts

- increases the protection of the civilian population against the effects of hostilities by codifying and supplementing the rules of what is known as the "Law of The Hague". The reaffirmation and simultaneous incorporation into treaty law not only of the obligation to distinguish between combatants and civilians between military objectives and civilian objects, but also of the prohibitions on attacks against civilians are of great significance. Several specific provisions make the general rule operational;

- reaffirms and develops some rules of customary law regulating methods and means of warfare. Indeed, in these latter years of the twentieth century, governments have again committed themselves to the long-established principle that the right to choose methods or means of warfare is not unlimited. Weapons which cause superfluous Anjury or unnecessary suffering are prohibited, a principle which the 1981 Weapons Convention[7] has started to transform into specific prohibitions;

- has extended the scope of application of the law on international armed conflicts to "armed conflicts in which people are fighting against colonial domination and alien occupation and against racist regimes in the exercise of their right of self-determination", thereby strengthening the protection of victims of such conflict. In the same context, Protocol I has brought guerrilla warfare into the ambit of international law;

- has updated a considerable number of rules of the traditional "Law of Geneva" (e.g. obligation to account for missing persons, new rules on relief operations, a protected status for civil defence).

Protocol II - on non-international armed conflicts

- brings a welcome advance in the protection of victims of non-international armed conflicts by developing the existing law (Article 3 common to the four Geneva

Conventions, and customary law). For the first time it likewise places parties to a non-international conflict under the explicit obligation to respect and protect the civilian population.

After adoption by the Diplomatic Conference, Protocol I was signed by 62 States, and Protocol II by 58. They entered into force on 7th December 1978, with two States party to them. As at 30th April 1988, Protocol I was binding on 76 States and Protocol II on 66 States, some through ratification and some through accession.[8] Several States made reservations with regard to one or other of the provisions; others filed declarations of interpretation on specific issues. Ten States have made the declaration provided for in Article 90 of Protocol I, thereby recognizing the competence of the International Fact-Finding Commission. Only a very limited number of governments have explicitly rejected one or other of the two Protocols.

2. Controversial issues: an overview

The two Protocols deal with humanitarian problems arising in armed conflict. Each provision has to strike a balance between humanitarian considerations and military exigencies: quite a difficult endeavour, more often than not! Before addressing the controversial issues or the unsettled problems it must be recalled that the large majority of all provisions definitely do solve difficult issues and do settle tough problems, to the satisfaction of all. A look at some open issues should not make the observer forget what is considered by all as remarkable progress in the protection of war victims.

The following controversial issues merit examination in this paper:

- protection of the civilian population: extent of the protection against effects of hostilities and the meaning to be given to some key notions,

- prohibition of reprisals against civilians and the civilian population, and against civilian objects;

- the law of Protocol I and nuclear weapons;

- extension of the applicability of the law on international armed conflict to wars of national liberation;

- new criteria for combatants in exceptional conflict situations ("guerrilla warfare");

- the decision to strengthen the protection of victims of non-international armed conflict: Protocol II.

To compile this list of problems, the author has drawn on the publications available on the topic on the declarations and reservations made by States on signing or ratifying the Protocols and on his own experience gained in discussions with officials all over the world. It is revealing to note that virtually all these problems were already the subject of controversy at the Diplomatic Conference. That means, among other things that none of the controversial issues have been done away with since 1977. It could be thought that governments might have solved some problems by reaching a mutual under standing, by suggesting a particular State practice or by some other means of resolving disputes. That does not seem to be the case: the old problems are still with us. Military and legal experts, especially from the Defence Ministries, but also from the Ministries for Foreign Affairs and other governmental agencies, should therefore continue to put forward their comments on the unresolved issues, for only then can a commonly accepted interpretation of the instruments - the pre-requisite for harmonized implementation by States - ultimately be achieved. In this connection the views of military commanders are of particular importance for an understanding of the rules relating to the conduct of military operations.

The ICRC too, endeavours to bring about a clearer understanding of the new rules. First and foremost, the ICRC conducts an active campaign to promote the Protocols and to convince governments to ratify them.(9) It has also published a Commentary on the Protocols,(10) drawn up by members of its legal staff, and it gives legal advice, especially to governments examining them with a view to their ratification. But as a neutral institution whose *raison d'etre* is humanitarian action, i.e. assistance to victims of armed conflict, the ICRC has to be somewhat reserved about taking a stand on differences in interpretation, in particular on questions concerning the "Law of The Hague". Since the making of international law is the prerogative of States it is their duty to clarify the tenor of the rights and obligations incumbent upon them. The ICRC has no assigned part to play in that process; it is not competent to give mandatory interpretations of the humanitarian law treaties.

We no longer deal with a criticism voiced here and there that the Protocols (in particular Protocol I) have "politicized" humanitarian protection through international law. This is completely unfounded. Is it really necessary to point out that any armed conflict is not only the outcome of a failure of a political process but is also embedded in a highly political context, and that political considerations therefore inevitably have to be taken into account when elaborating realistic standards? The people who drafted the Protocols had to do this without falling into the trap of introducing such political considerations into the law itself. They succeeded. Indeed, none of the new rules of 1977 contravenes the general principle of non-discrimination and impartiality as stated again in the fifth preambular paragraph of Protocol I:

> "Reaffirming further that the provisions of the Geneva Conventions of 12th August 1949 and of this Protocol must be fully applied in all circumstances to all persons who are protected by those instruments, without any adverse distinction based on the nature or origin of the armed conflict or on the causes espoused by or attributed to the Parties to the conflict ...."

3. Some issues relating to the protection of the civilian population

Section I of Part IV with its rules on the protection of the civilian population against the effects of hostilities is the very core of Protocol I. Although hardly any provisions break major new ground - they rely on the firm basis provided by the customary law prohibition of attacks on civilians as such - some of them have given rise to controversy through the mere fact of translating general principles into specific rules. The following questions in particular have been raised in this context:

A. "Military objectives"

The definition of the term "military objective" (Article 52,para. 2) has raised some questions. One controversial issue has always been to know whether a specific area of land may or may not be a legitimate target for a military operation. Italy and the Netherlands, on ratification of Protocol I, both made an almost identical declaration according to which a specific area of land may be a military objective if (among other criteria) "its total or partial destruction, capture or neutralization in the circumstances ruling at the time, offers a definite military advantage".[11] The Government of the United Kingdom also made a declaration to the same effect on signing Protocol I.[12]

This interpretation seems to be reasonable. As no objection has been voiced against it either in the formal procedure by a State party to Protocol I or in literature, it is deemed to be generally acceptable.

Other doubts as to the value of this first explicit definition of the term "military objective" are difficult to understand. The concept is sufficiently clear, and it is the task of national authorities to translate the legal definition into operative language (by means of manuals, instructions, etc.), for the benefit of those who have to plan, decide or implement military operations.

B. Presumption of civilian status

Article 50, para. 1 requires that "in case of doubt whether a person is a civilian" that person shall be considered to be a civilian - and shall therefore not be attacked; Article 52, para. 3 makes the same stipulation in the case of civilian objects, e.g. buildings. This presumption is considered to be an "impossible requirement" in view of the uncertainties of information available on the battle field.[13]

The rule under discussion here gives tangible form to the principle of distinction, i.e. the obligation, in the conduct of hostilities to differentiate between military objectives (which may be attacked) and civilian persons or objects (which may not). The military commander may therefore under no circumstances escape the obligation (or the order) to distinguish between legitimate targets and protected persons or objects. Articles 57 and 58 remind him of his duties. Under the heading "precautions in attack" Article 57 para. 2 enjoins "those who plan or decide upon an attack" to "do everything feasible to verify that the objectives to be attacked are neither civilians nor civilian objects ...". Article 58 imposes similar obligations in other circumstances.

The keyword is feasible: the law does not expect the impossible, but it asks the commander or the staff officer to do what he can do. The United Kingdom's declaration on signing Protocol I gives appropriate indications for the interpretation of this notion: "the word 'feasible' means that which is practicable or practically possible, taking into account all circumstances at the time including those relevant to the success of military operations".(14) This statement puts into operational terms the general rule according to which the law has to be given an interpretation in good faith. Nobody asks a military commander to spare "civilians" recognized as being soldiers in civilian disguise and about to attack his position.(15)

The issue discussed here raises yet another problem, namely how far does a commander have to go in collecting information on which to base his decision, provided that he intends to respect the law in good faith? Several States, among them the United Kingdom when signing Protocol I, have given their views on the issue by way of an interpretative statement which says that "military commanders and others responsible for planning, deciding upon or executing attacks necessarily have to reach decisions on the basis of their assessment of the information from all sources which is available to them at the relevant time".(16) This clarification should exclude the danger of judging by hindsight and is thus particularly important for those who might be involved in penal proceedings for violation of the law during military operations.

Both declarations of interpretation play a welcome part in defining the extent to which commanders must endeavour to ensure respect for the civilian population and civilian objects during military operations. By setting up workable standards they should lay to rest possible controversies on the wisdom of the law.

C. "Military advantage"

Somewhat similar remarks can be made with respect to the meaning of the expression "military advantage" (Articles 51 and 57). A proper understanding of this notion is of crucial importance for the principle of proportionality to take due effect, for it is stipulated that in an attack on a military objective, civilian casualties shall not "be excessive in relation to the concrete and direct military advantage anticipated" (Article 51, para. 5(b)).

Several governments have declared on signing Protocol I (among them the United Kingdom) or on ratification thereof that "military advantage refers to the advantage anticipated from the attack considered as a whole and not only from isolated or particular parts of the attack".(17) This clarification does not require further comment; it seems to be acceptable, no objection having been made to it.(18)

D. Protection of cultural objects

With the adoption of Article 53 the Diplomatic Conference introduced into Protocol I a provision on the protection of cultural objects and places of worship, although the former are the object of a special treaty, the 1954 Hague Convention for the protection of cultural property in the event of armed conflict. On ratifying Protocol I, Italy and the Netherlands made a reservation to Article 53 saying that "if and for so long as the objects and places protected by this Article in violation of paragraph (b), are used in support of the military efforts, they will thereby lose such protection".(19) This reservation is probably meant to bring the obligations under Article 53 in line with those stipulated by the 1954 Hague Convention. That Convention explicitly permits the protection of cultural objects to be waived if "military necessity imperatively requires such a waiver" (Article 4, para. 2). The idea is therefore not new. As long as it remains clear that the limits set by Articles 48 *et seq.* of Protocol I remain applicable, in particular the rule of proportionality, it is difficult to object to the Dutch and Italian reservation.(20) But the fact remains that there is now controversy over the degree of protection to be accorded to cultural objects and places of worship.

E. Dangerous installations

Article 56 introduces the prohibition, under certain circumstances, of attacks against certain installations containing dangerous forces - among them dams, dykes and nuclear power stations - "if such attack may cause the release of dangerous forces and consequent severe losses among the civilian population". This is a major contribution to better protection for the civilian population as a glance at the dykes in the Netherlands, the high dams in the Swiss Alps or the Chernobyl nuclear power station quite easily brings home. But its wisdom has been put in doubt. It has been said that its standards are operationally unworkable. Furthermore, as the strategic value of such installations is so great the very concept of protection has been attacked.[21]

The opposition to this novel attempt to protect the civilian population from particularly ugly dangers seems unfounded, as the rule has several inbuilt limits: the protection is of course not absolute, and military considerations are taken into account. The sole purpose of the rule is to safeguard civilians from the effect of hostilities in this case from flooding or being exposed to radiation - and not to protect such installations from destruction. Consequently, they may be attacked if their destruction does not cause "severe losses" among the civilian population. Such an installation may also be put out of operation by means other than wholesale destruction, with all its catastrophic effects. In conclusion, the rule strikes an acceptable balance between military considerations and the need to safeguard civilians.

F. The weapon of hunger

It has also been said that Article 54 on the "protection of objects indispensable to the survival of the civilian population", which prohibits the starvation of civilians as a method of warfare, goes too far, as well as the provisions relating to relief actions (Article 70), for it is claimed that the obligation to allow the passage of relief supplies to the civilian population in need would undermine the effectiveness of any siege or blockade.[22]

There is no doubt about the fact that humanitarian law requires only civilians to be provided with relief goods. The detailed provisions of Article 70 (on relief actions) authorizes parties to a conflict which allow the passage of relief consignments to a place under blockade to take all necessary measures to ensure that the relief is destined for civilians only. The distribution of such relief may take place under the supervision of the Protecting Power (if any) or the ICRC (which has some experience in such types of operations). It is therefore possible to guarantee that civilians, and not members of the armed forces, will be beneficiaries of the relief operation. Under these circumstances it is hardly understandable why the outlawing of starvation as a means of warfare, and the concomitant obligation to provide for relief to those who are in need, should be incompatible with legitimate military exigencies.

The question of blockades raises another interesting - and controversial - issue: the extent to which Protocol I affects the law of naval warfare. For lack of space it cannot be explored here.(23) It seems, however, that this doctrinal issue is not an obstacle in the way of Protocol I's ratification by governments.

G. Protection of the environment

Articles 35, para. 3, and 55 introduce concern for the protection of the natural environment into humanitarian law: military operations shall not do "widespread, long-term and severe damage" to the natural environment.(24) Whereas this rule did not give rise to much controversy during the Diplomatic Conference, some criticism has subsequently been voiced against it. Questions have been asked e.g. whether an attack against oil tankers and ships carrying hazardous chemical cargoes is now prohibited,(25) or whether it is allowed under the law to attack a nuclear submarine! The answer depends on the interpretation of "widespread, long-term and severe damage". The *travaux preparatoires* shed some light on the matter.(26) It would seem that the spilling of oil into the sea and on to the shores does not normally cause such damage as to fall under the strict criteria of Article 55. The legitimacy of an attack on a chemical cargo has to be judged by the facts: if those chemical substances destroy everything in the vicinity of the event for the next fifty years such an attack will be illegal (and certainly also unwise from a military stand- point). The possibility of attacks on nuclear submarines is another matter altogether. Since the use of nuclear submarines for military purposes has never been prohibited, it is also legal to attack them (subject to the rules of the law of war). The new law introduced by Articles 35, para. 3, and 55, does not change the situation.

H. Reprisals

The prohibition of attacks against the civilian population, or individual civilians, and against civilian objects by way of reprisals may well be the most far-reaching innovation in the law on the conduct of military operations.(27) While the prohibition of reprisals against wounded and sick on the battlefield or shipwrecked on the high sea, and against prisoners of war or civilian persons in the hands of the enemy, is now part of the undisputed core of humanitarian obligations, the outlawing of such reprisals in the domain covered by the "Hague Law" remains controversial.

At the Diplomatic Conference "[i]t proved impossible to reconcile the different points of view".(28) One view was that reprisals - or the threat thereof - were the most efficient way (or the only way) of inducing the other side to respect its own obligations. Others did not believe in this effect and thought that the possibility of resort to reprisals only opened the door for the worst abuses, with their victim inevitably being the civilian population. The adoption, by the Diplomatic Conference, of the new provisions prohibiting reprisals quite clearly did not settle the controversy.

This is not the place to pursue further this extremely important debate. Suffice it to say that commentators on the Protocol disagree on the wisdom of this innovation,(29) as did the diplomats and military experts at the Diplomatic Conference. It is well known that the reprisal issue plays an important role in the evaluation of Protocol I for many governments. But no reservation has been made to this day against any of the individual provisions prohibiting reprisals.

The Italian Government, however, accompanied ratification of Protocol I by a declaration or reservation which seems to touch on the reprisal issue. That declaration reads:

"Italy will react to serious and systematic violations by an enemy of the obligations imposed by Additional Protocol I and in particular its Articles 51 and 52 with all means admissible under international law in order to prevent any further violation".[30]

Having accepted the ban on reprisals against the civilian population the Italian Government thereby seems to be notifying potential enemies that, in the event of serious and systematic attacks on the civilian population, e.g. through bombardment of urban centres, it will feel free to react in such a way as to have these illegal attacks stopped. Can this be achieved by resorting to "all means admissible under international law" as the Italian statement says? Or will the reaction consist in an attack on the enemy's own civilian population, in violation of the obligation to spare civilians and civilian objects? The statement is ambiguous.

The moral dilemma caused by the wish (which may well become a political necessity) to respond to severe attacks on civilians by attacking the enemy's own civilian population, and conversely the determination to uphold the law prohibiting such acts, is a most serious one for those who have accepted the prohibition of reprisals against civilians and civilian objects. The Italian statement seems to say that there are limits beyond which a government may not be expected to exercise restraint; in extreme situations, it may well feel compelled to take exceptional measures, capable of preserving its own population. It is not within the scope of this paper to find an answer to this dilemma. Further thought is necessary, whilst avoiding the old pitfall of regarding reprisals as the panacea for achieving compliance with the provisions of the "Hague Law".[31]

4. Protocol I and nuclear weapons

Belgium, Italy and the Netherlands, which are all members of the NATO alliance, made a declaration on ratification of Protocol I, saying that (in the words of the Italian statement) "the rules relating to the use of weapons introduced by the Additional Protocol I were intended to apply exclusively to conventional weapons. They do not prejudice any other rule of international law applicable to other types of weapons".[32] The representatives of the United States, France and the United Kingdom made similar statements when signing

Protocol I.[33] The Soviet Union has never expressed its views on the subject. The Soviet delegation, however, did not object to the Western position but according to a testimony by the head of the US delegation at the Diplomatic Conference, "privately agreed with those statements".[34]

Those declarations say that, by adopting Protocol I, the Diplomatic Conference did not create new obligations with respect to the use of nuclear weapons. Insofar as Protocol I merely codifies existing obligations, and since the Diplomatic Conference did not intend to change them either, those obligations do not apply to nuclear weapons. Protocol I does not alter the law pertaining to nuclear weapons, at least in the view of the great majority of the Geneva law-makers.

This interpretation of a sometimes controversial issue seems to be shared by most commentators.[35] No party to Protocol I has taken the opposite view, either by way of a declaration of understanding or by objecting to the statements made by Belgium, Italy or the Netherlands on this subject. On the legal side, the controversy seems to have been laid to rest.

5. Wars of national liberation

Article 1, para. 4 of Protocol I incorporates "armed conflicts in which peoples are fighting against colonial domination and alien occupation and against racist regimes in the exercise of their right of self-determination, as enshrined in the Charter of the United Nations and the Declaration on Principles of International Law concerning Friendly Relations and Co-operation among States in accordance with the Charter of the United Nations" into the category of international armed conflict. By shifting wars of national liberation from the legal category of non-international conflict to that of international armed conflict, at the suggestion of Third World countries, Protocol I considerably tightens the humanitarian law regime applicable to such conflicts. What many observers, notably in the Third World, consider an important step forward, others view as a "prostitution of humanitarian law".[36]

This important innovation of humanitarian law created considerable controversy during the first session of the Diplomatic Conference. The adoption of the new rule by a clear majority three years later at the end of the Conference namely by 80 in favour, 1 against (Israel) and 11 abstentions (Western countries) seemed to show that "the war was over". However, the United States" decision not to ratify Protocol I is prompted mainly by rejection of Article 1 para. 4 (and also of the new rules on guerrilla warfare).(37) The Presidential message to the Senate says that the new rule "elevates the international legal status of self-described 'national liberation' groups that make a practice of terrorism". But this is not so, as Protocol I quite clearly does not affect the legal status of any group. It provides only, and under very limited conditions for the authority representing a people engaged in such a war to make a declaration to the effect that the whole body of humanitarian law shall become applicable to that conflict.(38) Expressing the views held by members of the Western Group (and others) that only liberation movements which are recognized as such by the respective regional governmental organisation should be qualified to make such a declaration, Belgium and the Republic of Korea made a declaration of understanding to that effect.(39) Furthermore, the prohibition of terrorist acts is a central concern of the Geneva Conventions and Protocol I.(40) This prohibition, with its provisions on criminal sanctions will become applicable in its entirety to wars of national liberation, thanks to Protocol I and its Article 1, para. 4. Therefore, humanitarian law neither legitimizes any kind of armed conflict, nor does it weaken the ban on terrorism. The fears of the US Executive Branch would therefore seem to be unfounded.

Article 1, para. 4 has given rise to some doubts in Third World countries, where it is feared that political opponents could misuse the new provision for propaganda purposes. It appears, however that Article 1 para. 4, is confined to the narrow concept of the right of self-determination by a people. Internal opposition against the authorities of a State by a minority group or other political opponents does not come within this concept. A declaration of understanding may be the appropriate means of clarifying that interpretation.

6. Guerrilla warfare

It is not surprising that the debate on Article 44, which redefines the criteria for entitlement to combatant and prisoner-of-war status, went on even after the end of the Conference. According to the new law a combatant may in very limited circumstances, omit to comply with his obligation to distinguish himself from the civilian population: he may resort to the technique of guerrilla warfare. The moot point is how far this exception goes. The *travaux preparatoires* and since 1977, the relevant literature give some guidance for interpretation of the much discussed Article 44 para. 3. It is generally accepted that a combatant may avail himself of this exception only in occupied territory and during a war of national liberation.(41) With that very limited scope of application (and taking into account the scant probability that the provision on wars of national liberation will ever be come operational) the new rule has become acceptable to most governments. Following the position taken by members of the Western Group during the negotiations, Belgium, Italy, the Netherlands and the Republic of Korea placed on record at the moment of ratification their understanding of the words "engaged in a military deployment". It is taken to mean (in the words of the Dutch declaration) "any movements towards a place from which an attack may be launched".(42) No objection has been raised, either by governments or by writers, against these declarations of interpretation, which give a useful clarification of a controversial issue.

Argentina has also made a declaration of understanding on this clause.(43) That declaration is a welcome contribution to the understanding of Article 44; its substance does not give rise to any controversy.

The United States however has rejected Protocol I also with the argument that the new rule weakens the protection of civilians to an unacceptable degree. The President's Letter of Transmittal says that Article 44, "would grant combatant status to irregular forces even if they do not satisfy the traditional requirements to distinguish themselves from the civilian population and otherwise comply with the laws of war".(44) Only one point will be taken up here. It is difficult to understand why it should be inferred that combatants (i.e. members of armed forces, never irregulars) taking advantage of Article 44, para. 3 need not comply with the laws of war in such exceptional situations. On the contrary, they have to. They have in particular to respect the prohibition of attacks on civilians. The new law does not advance the cause of terrorism.

A reasonable interpretation of Article 44, para. 3 could have brought the difficulties of this new provision under control. The reaction by the United States makes it harder to achieve that goal.

7. Non-international armed conflict

The inception of Protocol II was not particularly easy.[46] Whereas negotiations started on the basis of a rather modest draft elaborated by the ICRC, the delegates at the Diplomatic Conference put more and more into the text, with the laudable intent of strengthening the rules protecting victims of non international armed conflict to the maximum degree possible.[47] However, in the last few days of the Conference, governments, realizing what had happened with the original draft, came to the conclusion that the outcome of their deliberations placed too much strain on their concept of State sovereignty. After severe cutbacks Protocol II was ready for adoption by consensus.

Opposition to Protocol II in its final form has not subsided. Indeed, whereas 76 States are party to Protocol I, only 66 States have ratified Protocol II, i.e. ten States less. None of them has explained its refusal to endorse the development of humanitarian rules applicable in internal armed conflict. It seems, however, that the reason for their reluctance to do so is not so much a lack of enthusiasm for one or other of the provisions of Protocol II which appear to be well-balanced. These governments seem to reject the very idea of creating international rules relating to events considered to be internal affairs of sovereign States.

It is difficult to accept such an argument in view of the subject matter of Protocol II, namely rules of a purely humanitarian character designed to ease the plight of war victims. Protocol II does not introduce any major innovation into international law, as Article 3 common to the Geneva Convention already deals with humanitarian aspects of civil wars. Protocol II merely develops and strengthens the rules by making the general principles of Article 3 more specific, more operational. It adds but one new dimension to traditional law by introducing a prohibition of attacks on the civilian population and individual civilians, and certain categories of civilian objects.[48] Furthermore, Protocol II is applicable only in situations of high-intensity internal armed conflicts. Situations of internal disturbances and tensions, such as riots or isolated and sporadic acts of violence, are not included in its scope of application.[49] To allay any fears that government officials might feel, Article 3 common to the Geneva Conventions had already made it plain that respect, by the government, of humanitarian obligations in an internal conflict does not amount to recognition of the insurgents or of their claims. Furthermore, Protocol II states explicitly that none of its rules "shall be invoked for the purpose of affecting the sovereignty of a State" (Article 3, para. 1). The same Article goes on to say that governments retain their right to maintain or re-establish law and order "by all legitimate means" and that the Protocol may not be invoked as a justification for intervening in the internal affairs of any State. In other words, agreeing to comply with humanitarian obligations in internal armed conflicts can never and must never be understood as a sell-out of a country's sovereignty but much more as "a step towards universal protection of the victims of armed conflict".[50]

8. Final observations

Problems of interpretation are quite often a direct consequence of the fact that the given rule is the result of a compromise. Resolved issues have also left their mark on the two Protocols.

The following remark points to one of the contradictions which had to be overcome at the Diplomatic Conference: "On the one hand there were those humanitarian idealists who apparently wanted to make war a matter of such legal complexity that the military would be unwilling (or unable) to engage in it ... On the other side there were those who were perhaps more realistic and who wanted the Protocol to contain simple rules easily understood by those who actually participate in battle .... Neither faction entirely succeeded".[51] Other difficulties arose from the universal participation at the Diplomatic Conference: east and west, north and south were all represented, and all blocs and groups of countries managed to have some of their requests included in the Protocols. That is definitely a positive factor since only thus can an international treaty become the expression of universal concern. And the fact that, eventually, all States settled down in 1977 and agreed on the two Protocols has already been called a miracle.

Some arguments put forward against ratification do not really concern the Protocols as such but are political considerations going beyond humanitarian law: the doubts as to the status of wars of national liberation, the problem of terorrism and the nuclear question.

Protocol I cannot provide adequate solutions for these problems. A certain amount of self constraint is necessary. International humanitarian law is neither *jus ad bellum* nor a set of rules for arms control, nor a blueprint for peace: it is *jus in bello* intended to answer humanitarian needs caused by armed conflict.

Now that they have been ratified by almost half of the community of nations, the Protocols have become a reality to be reckoned with. Difficulties with interpretation of some of the new provisions are no reason to withhold consent to the treaties as a whole. As the former head of the British delegation said in his final statement after adoption of the Protocols by the Diplomatic Conference, "taken as a whole, the Protocols represented a significant advance in international humanitarian law applicable in armed conflicts".[52] Governments must now have the courage to settle open problems through interpretation if necesary after consulting each other, and to make their views public. States which have not yet ratified both Protocols should do so soon. The goal of these instruments - to bring a little bit of humanity to the victims of war - makes every effort worthwhile.

FOOTNOTES

* The views expressed are personal and do not necessarily reflect those of the International Committee of the Red Cross.

1. 1125 *UNTS* 3 and 609 - see also 16 ILM 1391 and 1442 (1977); Roberts and Guelff, *Documents on the Laws of War*, Oxford 1982, 387 and 447; *Protocols additional to the Geneva Conventions of 12th August 1949*, text edition published by the International Committee of the Red Cross, Geneva 1977.

2. Sandoz, Swinarski, Zimmermann (ed.), *Commentary of the Additional Protocols*, International Committee of the Red Cross and Martinus Nijhoff Publishers, Geneva 1987 (hereinafter: ICRC Commentary), "General Introduction", XXIX-XXXV.

3. *Draft Rules for the Limitation of the Dangers incurred by the Civilian Population in Time of War*, International Committee of the Red Cross, Geneva 1958 (2nd ed.).

4. *Reports on the Work of the Conference of Government Experts on the Reaffirmation and Development of International Humanitarian Law Applicable in Armed Conficts*, First and Second Session, International Committee of the Red Cross, Geneva 1971 and 1972.

5. *Official Records of the Diplomatic Conference on the Reaffirmation and Development of International Humanitarian Law Applicable in Armed Conflicts* Geneva (1974-1977), Vol.I - XVII.

6. *ICRC Commentary* [Footnote 2]; Bothe, Partsch, Solf, *New Rules for Victims of Armed Conflicts, Commentary of the Two 1977 Protocols Additional to the Geneva Conventions of 1949*, The Hague/Boston/London 1982; Aldrich, "New Life for the Laws of War", 75 *AJIL* (1981) 764-783; Cassese (ed.), *The New Humanitarian Law of Armed Conflict*, Naples 1979; Herczeg, *Development of International Humanitarian Law*, Budapest 1984; Kalshoven, "Reaffirmation and Development of International Humanitarian Law Applicable in Armed Conflicts, Parts I and II", *Netherlands Yearbook of International Law*, vol. 8 (1977) 107-135 and vol. 9 (1978) 107-171 - see also "Armed Forces and the Development of the Law of War", Proceedings of the 9th International Congress of the International Society of Military Law and Law of War, *The Military Law and Law of War Review*, vol. XXI (1982); *Studies and Essays on International Humanitarian Law and Red Cross Principles*, in honour of Jean Pictet, Geneva/The Hague 1984.

7. Convention on Prohibitions or Restrictions on the Use of Certain Conventional Weapons Which May be Deemed to be Excessivley Injurious or to Have Indiscriminate Effects, adopted by the United Nations General Assembly on 12.12.80, reprinted in Roberts and Guelff [Footnote 1] 467.

8. The *International Review of the Red Cross* regularly publishes the state of ratification of (or accession to) the 1977 Protocols.

9. *Annual Reports* of the ICRC; by the present author: "Die Genfer Zusatzprotokolle vom 8. Juni 1977; von der Diplomatischen Konferenz zur Ratifikation durch die Staaten", in *Studies and Essays* [Footnote 6] 147-165.

10. See Footnote 2.

11. According to the Dutch declaration, reprinted in the *International Review of the Red Cross* 1987, 425/6.

12. The declaration of understanding made by the United Kingdom on signing the Protocols is reprinted in Roberts and Guelff [Footnote 1] 461/2.

13. Guy B. Roberts, "The New Rules for Waging War: The Case Against Ratification of Additional Protocol I", 26 *Virginia Journal of International Law* (1985) 109-170 - see the reply to Roberts' article by the former head of the US delegation at the Diplomatic Conference: Aldrich, "Progressive Development of the Laws of War: A Reply to Criticisms of the 1977 Geneva Protocol I", 26 *Virginia Journal of International Law* (1986) 693-720.

14. See Footnote 12.

15. As it has been argued: Carnahan, "Additional Protocol I: A Military View" 19 *Akron Law Review* (1986) 544.

16. Dutch declaration [Footnote 11] - see also the British declaration [Footnote 12].

17. Dutch declaration [Footnote 11].

18. According to the *ICRC Commentary*, at 685, this statement seems redundant.

19. Dutch declaration [Footnote 11].

20. *ICRC Commentary* 648.

21. Roberts [Footnote 13] 156 - and the answer by Aldrich [Footnote 13] 714.

22. Roberts [Footnote 13] 155.

23. See in particular Rauch, *The Protocol Additional to the Geneva Conventions for the Protection of Victims of International Armed Conflicts and the United Nations Convention on the Law of the Sea: Repercussions on the Law of Naval Warfare*, Berlin 1984; Meyrowitz, "Le Protocole additionnel I aux Conventions de Geneve de 1949 et le droit de la guerre maritime", *Revue Generale de Droit International Public*, vol. 89 (1985) 243-298: Rauch, "Le droit contemporain de la guerre maritime, Quelques problemes crees par le Protocole additionnel I de 1977", *Revue Generale de Droit International Public*, vol. 89 (1985) 958-976.

24. On the relation of the Protocol's prohibitions to the 1976 UN Convention on the Prohibition of Military or any other Hostile Use of Environmental Modification Techniques (reprinted in Roberts and Guelff [Footnote 1] 379) see *ICRC Commentary* 414-418.

25. Roberts [Footnote 13].

26. *ICRC Commentary* 410 (Article 35, para. 3) and 662 (Article 55).

27. Articles 51(6), 52(1), 53(c), 54(4), 55(2) and 56(4) - see *ICRC Commentary* 982-987 (on the general issue) and the commentaries to the various provisions; Bothe, Partsch, Solf [Footnote 6] 317-375.

28. ICRC Commentary 985.

29. E.g. Bothe, Partsch, Solf [Footnote 6] 315; Roberts [Footnote 13] 139: Aldrich [Footnote 13] 710 and Aldrich [Footnote 6] 782; Kalshoven, *Constraints in the Waging of War*, Geneva 1987, 102; Nahlik, "Le probleme des represailles a la lumiere des travaux de la Conference diplomatique sur le droit humanitaire", *RGDIP vol. 82 (1978) 130-169; Matt, "The Laws of War and Belligerent Reprisals Against Enemy Civilian Populations", 21 The Air Force Law Review* (1979) 397-431.

30. *International Review of the Red Cross*, 1986, 113.

31. For an interesting comment on the problem see Meyrowitz, "Die Repressalienverbote des 1. Zusatzprotokolls zu den Genfer Abkommen vom 12. August 1949 und

das Reziprozitatsprinzip", *Neue Zeitschrift fur Wehrrecht* (1986) 177.

32. *International Review of the Red Cross* 1986, 113 - see also for Belgium, *ibid*, 172, and for the Netherlands, *Review* 1987, 425.

33. For the United Kingdom's declaration see Roberts and Guelff [Footnote 1] 462.

34. Aldrich [Footnote 13] 719.

35. See *ICRC Commentary* 589-596; Bothe, Partsch, Solf [Footnote 6] 188-192; Aldrich [Footnote 6] 780 - contrary opinion: Graefrath, "Die Bedeutung des Erganzungsprotokolls fur den Schutz der Zivilbevolkerung", *Studies and Essays* (Footnote 6] 167, 174; Fischer, *Der Einsatz von Nuklearwaffen nach Art. 51 des 1. Zusatzprotokolls zu den Genfer Konventionen von 1949*, Berlin 1985.

36. See for a broadside attack on this rule (and on Art. 44(3)): Feith, *Law in the Service of Terror - The Strange Case of the Additional Protocol*, The National Interest 1985 - 36-47.

37. Letter of Transmittal of President Reagan to the Senate of the United States (of 29th January 1987), reprinted in Agora: "The U.S. Decision not to Ratify Protocol I to the Geneva Conventions on the Protection of War Victims", 81 *AJIL* (1987) 910-912; see the comment by this author: "An Appeal for Ratification by the United States", 81 *AJIL* (1987) 912-925.

38. Art. 96(3).

39. *International Review of the Red Cross*, 1986, 174, (Belgium) - see the United Kingdom's declaration to the same effect made on signing: Roberts and Guelff [Footnote 1] 462.

40. See by the present author: "Prohibition of terrorist acts in international humanitarian law", *International Review of the Red Cross*, 1986, 200.

41. See *ICRC Commentary* 529; Bothe, Partsch, Solf [Footnote 6] 253; Aldrich [Footnote 6] 773.

42. Dutch declaration [Footnote 11] - The United Kingdom made the same declaration on signing Protocol I, Roberts and Guelff [Footnote 1] 462.

43. *International Review of the Red Cross*, 1987, 110.

44. See Letter of Transmittal [Footnote 37].

45. See the present author's reply to the Letter of Transmittal [Footnote 37].

46. *ICRC Commentary* 1325-1336; Rosemary Abi-Saab, *Droit humanitaire et conflit interne*, Geneva/Paris 1986.

47. See the very interesting comparative presentation of the various drafts of Protocol II in Abi-Saab [Footnote 46] 213-280.

48. Art. 13-18 of Protocol II.

49. Art. 1(1) and (2).

50. Bedjaoui, "Humanitarian law at a time of failing national and international consciousness", *Modern Wars, The Humanitarian Challenge*, A Report for the Independent Commission on International Humanitarian Issues, London 1986, 19 and also 31/32.

51. Sir David Hughes-Morgan, Intervention at the 9th International Congress of the International Society of Military Law and Law of War, *The Military Law and Law of War Review*, vol. XXI (1982) 327.

52. Sir John Freeland, in his capacity as head of the United Kingdom's delegation at the Diplomatic Conference, *Official Records* [Footnote 5] vol. VII, 302 (CDDH/SR.58): final statement after adoption of the two Protocols.

PART II

PERSONS COVERED BY THE 1977 GENEVA PROTOCOLS

COMBATANT AND PRISONER OF WAR STATUS

*M.H.F. Clarke, T. Glynn, A.P.V. Rogers**

1. Combatant Status before Protocol I of 1977[1]

A. Combatants and Non-Combatants

Perhaps one of the most basic distinctions in the law of armed conflict is that between combatant and non-combatant.[2] Put simply, acts of hostility cannot be committed by just anybody. The matter has been put more elegantly as follows:

> "Private individuals who take up arms and commit hostilities against the enemy do not enjoy the privileges of armed forces, and the enemy has, according to a customary rule of international law, the right to treat such individuals as war criminals. But they cease to be private individuals if they organise themselves in a manner which, according to the Hague Convention, confers upon them the status of members of regular forces."[3]

Thus war is a matter for States and their armies. If private individuals commit acts of hostility they are liable to trial as war criminals not because what they do necessarily infringes the laws governing the conduct of hostilities, but because the waging of war by private individuals is itself unlawful.[4]

The law therefore recognises two classes, the combatants, who:

- can wage war,
- can themselves be attacked by the enemy,
- but who on capture are not liable to be tried as ordinary criminals but are accorded the special status of Prisoners of War (PW):[5]

* For footnotes see p. 126.

and the non-combatants:

- who cannot lawfully be attacked,
- but who cannot themselves commit acts of hostility or if they do will be liable to trial as war criminals.[6]

Thus the two classes have distinct privileges, duties and disabilities. The 1929 edition of the *British Manual of Military Law* commented:

> "It is one of the purposes of the law of war to ensure that an individual must definitely choose to belong to one class or the other, and shall not be permitted to enjoy the privileges of both; in particular that an individual shall not be allowed to kill or wound members of the army of the opposing nation and subsequently, if captured or in danger of life, pretend to be a peaceful citizen."[7]

It is interesting that this was repeated in the 1958 edition of the same *Manual*, but with the following addition:

> "Subject to the fact that the distinction between combatants and non-combatants has become increasingly blurred."[8]

and there's the rub!

B. Members of Armed Forces

In considering first who is in fact entitled to combatant status it might be better to begin with the most obvious, and probably the most numerous group in this category that being members of the armed forces themselves. They are, of course, usually referred to as regular combatants.

It would seem to be generally accepted that a State has the exclusive right to determine the method of recruitment of its armed forces whether by conscription or voluntary enlistment. Further a State is also at liberty to determine the composition of its armed forces, whether they be regular, part-time volunteer or militia troops. This follows from Article 1 of the Hague Rules of 1907 which provides that in countries where militia or volunteer corps constitute the army or part of it they are included in the denomination "army".[9]

Criticism has been directed however at the integration into national forces of colonial troops. France for instance protested at the use by Germany of colonial troops during the First World War.[10] In more recent times, Canada, before sending conscripted troops into battle overseas, put the matter to a popular referendum on 27th April 1942.[11] In the event, incidentally, the principle was accepted by 2,744,653 votes to 1,481,345, or about 2 to 1 for. However, insofar as colonial troops are concerned there would not seem to be any evidence that such troops were ever denied PW status.

At this stage it seems necessary to note that the granting of PW status is not synonymous with combatant status. At least since the Hague Rules the law has accorded the right to PW status to certain persons who are non-combatants, for example the civilians accompanying armed forces, the so called "followers" and war correspondents.[12] Also a State is of course at liberty to grant PW status as a matter of good-will. Thus there will be more persons entitled to or granted PW status than the combatants themselves.

However, returning to regular armies, the question of colonial troops and colonies is now some thing of the past.[13] A more modern problem arises from the inclusion in a State's armed forces of persons who are not nationals of the State concerned. In this regard a distinction must be drawn between volunteers and conscripts.

Individual volunteers in regular armies, in themselves, present no real problem. The concept of foreign "volunteers", and (at this stage the use of the word "mercenaries" is probably premature), in the ranks of the armies of the more wealthy nations is not a new one. It is perhaps interesting that the Swiss, who we now think of as the classic neutrals, formed a large part of the French Army from about 1480 to 1884,[14] and indeed Napoleon's Grand Army of 700,000 men consisted of 300,000 Frenchmen and 400,000 foreigners.[15] In more modern times the existence of the French Foreign Legion or the British Brigade of Gurkhas would seem to be accepted internationally. Nor would the participation by its nationals in someone else's war seem to affect the neutral status of the country concerned, for example the participation of numerous British volunteers in the Spanish Civil War did not affect the United Kingdom's neutrality in regard to the two sides of that particular conflict.

Here one is referring to individual volunteers in the true sense; that is those individuals who, motivated by conscience or whatever travel abroad to join a foreign army. The organisation or recruitment in one State of so-called "volunteer" corps for the benefit of another State would be a violation of Article 4 of the Vth Hague Convention of 1907[16] dealing with neutrality. Many States had in any event, before 1907, banned by domestic legislation this practice of recruitment of foreign armes within their own territory, for example, the Swiss Law of 30th June 1859 and the English Foreign Enlistment Act of 1870.[17]

Thus individual volunteer foreigners are not a problem. The same however cannot be said of conscription, which involves the different consideration of the enforced participation in national defence by foreigners already resident in the State concerned. Recently, particularly during the Vietnam War, States appear to have abandoned this practice.[18]

Whilst this action may have been more diplomatic than legal, it would seem to have led to the practice becoming moribund, if not dead.

In summary therefore, members of the armed forces of belligerents, who will in most cases form the great majority of combatants, will have combatant status. Further it seems that States have effective control over combatant status because they are generally omnipotent in the recruitment and composition of their armed forces. The one exception is the conscription of resident aliens who are subsequently sent into battle, but this is a relatively minor problem.

Before leaving the subject of regular combatants it is important to note that not all members of regular forces are combatants. This has been evident at least since 1907 when Article 3 of the Hague Rules recognised that the armed forces of belligerents could consist of combatants and non combatants.[19] The vast majority of course will be combatants but it will be recalled that in modern times the Geneva Conventions of 1949 accorded a special non-combatant standing which is restricted to medical personnel and chaplains.[20] Thus like civilians they cannot take an offensive part in battle, are not themselves legitimate military objectives and have a special standing on capture they are in effect "retained"[21] rather than being PW, and thus must be repatriated if they are superfluous to the religious or medical needs of PW also held. The term "medical personnel" here, incidentally, includes not only doctors and nurses but also embraces a wide range of specialist technicians, maintenance staff, drivers, cooks and administrators, providing they are exclusively assigned to medical units.[22]

C. Irregular Forces

Non-regular combatants, that is those combatants who are not members of the regular armed forces, are usually called "irregular combatants".

Historically these fall into two groups; the *levee en masse* and the *franc-tireur*.

The origin of the term *levee en masse* would seem to lie in France and related to the requirement for the whole population to join the army, in fact conscription or mobilisation of everybody irrespective of age. The term was so understood by Cornot's decree of 1793.[23]

Today the expression is more generally understood to mean the taking up of arms by the population of a territory to resist or repel occupation, such action occurring before the occupation is accomplished and whether such rising happens spontaneously or possibly also at the call of the authorities of the country to be occupied.

This interpretation is certainly the connotation given to the term by Article 2 of the Hague Rules of 1907. This provides that:

> "the inhabitants of a territory[24] which has not been occupied,[25] who, on the approach of the enemy, spontaneously take up arms to resist the invading troops without having had time to organize themselves in accordance with Article 1 shall be regarded as belligerents if they carry arms openly and if they respect the laws and customs of war."

So it is clear that irregular troops in these circumstances forming a *levee en masse* would be accorded combatant status if they complied with the two conditions namely the overt carrying of arms and respect for the laws of war.[26]

No such recognition has however been accorded to the second category of irregular combatant, the *franc-tireur*. This term has never been precisely defined but would seem to signify every individual who, without being a part of the regular forces, voluntarily takes part in wartime operations, whether by patriotic motives or otherwise.

The term was certainly so understood by the Prussians who rose as irregulars against Napoleon's army.(27) However, in their turn the Prussian Government in 1870, when faced with *francs-tireurs* acting on behalf of France executed them.(28) When it was pointed out that the *francs-tireurs* were only doing what the Prussians had done in the previous war, Bismarck is reported to have replied, "True, and we can see the trees on which you hanged them".(29)

Nothing very much had changed in more modern times at least up to 1942. The so-called "case of the German Saboteurs" was heard by the US Supreme Court in that year.(30) This concerned a clandestine operation in which a group of German sympathisers were landed by submarine in both Florida and Long Island with a view to committing acts of sabotage. The Court held:

> **"By universal agreement and practice the law of war draws a distinction between lawful combatants who on capture are subject to detention as PW, and unlawful combatants, who are subject to trial and punishment by military tribunals for acts which render their belligerence unlawful. By the Rules of Land Warfare our government has recognised those who during war pass surreptitiously from enemy territory into our own, discarding their uniforms before entering for the commission of hostile acts, involving the destruction of life and property, have the status of unlawful combatant."**

These *francs-tireurs* were condemned to death, albeit for unlawful belligerency.(31)

The British Government would seem to have taken a similar line. In a war crimes trial after the Second World War,(32) relating to the execution of four captured nurses, two WAAF and two FANYs,(33) who had been sent to France with a mission of establishing communications between London and the Resistance movement, the prosecution admitted that had the nurses been tried by a competent court and lawfully executed, the case would not have been brought.(34) This would point to the fact that their activities were regarded as possibly falling within the *franc-tireur* category and as such that they might not have been entitled to combatant status.

So the golden rule, at least in those days, would seem to have been, if you are going to be an irregular combatant make sure you fall into the relatively restricted category of a *levee en masse* and not that of *franc-tireur.*

In studying the problem from a legal point of view however, the real difficulty is that there is little authority on the standing of irregular combatants between 1907 and 1949, the year of the present Geneva Conventions, nor really any consensus among jurists. Such opinion as there was, related to the conduct of partisan resistance fighters in guerilla fighting against the German Armed Forces in occupied terrories during the Second World War.

D. Partisan Resistance Fighters

This was, in its way, a new problem. Clearly partisan troops could not be considered a *levee en masse.* For a start the territory concerned was already occupied and in any event the partisans were not generally such a large part of the population really to be considered, as it were, "en masse". This was obviously an unsatisfactory state of affairs if you were a partisan resistance fighter as, however laudable your motives, you were clearly heading for categorisation as a *franc-tireur* and possible execution.

Certain steps were therefore taken on the allied side to try and overcome this problem.

If the French resistance movement is taken as an example, Article 10 of the Franco-German Armistice Agreement of 22nd June 1940,(35) admittedly drawn up by the Reich on something perhaps of a take it or leave it basis, specifically required the French Government to ban French resistance against Germany, and stipulated that French nationals who did not comply with the ban would be treated as *francs-tireurs.*

This unequivocal statement complicated the legal position of General de Gaulle's "Forces francaises libres" (FFL).

There seems to have been uncertainty as to their legal standing, even on the German side. On the one hand the Germans threatened to execute 2,000 French prisoners, captured in North Africa in 1942, even though they formed part of the British, regular, 8th Army.[36] On the other hand however, the Axis Powers would seem to have recognised as regular combatants later elements of the FFL particularly those forming part of the Allied Expeditionary Forces which ultimately liberated France. Whilst it is true that there had by then been set up a French Provisional Government, which had assimilated the FFL into its army,[37] this change of view by the German authorities might have had more to do with the fact that the tide of the war was by then running against them, rather than any clinical reappraisal of the legal position.

However, this is a slight digression because the FFL were in a different category from the partisans referred to initially, namely the resistance movements, who unlike the FFL were resident in the occupied territories. The doctrine of the German High Command had been expressed before the War in paragraph 3 of the Ordinance of 17th August 1938.[38] This text laid down the death penalty "for activities as *franc-tireur*" for anyone who, without being part of enemy forces, carried arms or engaged in acts of combat against members of the German Army. In applying this text, underground resistance fighters were generally executed, at least in the early stages. It was only after the allied landings in Normandy that the so-called "Forces francaises de l'interieur" (FFI) were, given some sort of legal status by the ordinance of the "Comite francais de liberation nationale" dated 9th June 1944.[39] That Ordinance stated that the FFI formed an integral part of the French Army. Members of the FFI then wore distinctive armlets stamped and distributed on behalf of the Supreme Headquarters Allied Expeditionary Force, were trained by officers parachuted in for the purpose, and placed under the nominal command of a French Army Officer. These were all obvious steps taken to try and vest the resistance fighters with the status of membership of a regular army and therefore combatant status. Germany did not however immediately change its practice of executing them. An exchange of notes followed between the Provisional Government of the French Republic, which had by then been set up, and the Government of the Reich, dated 14th June and 31st July 1944,[40] but without outcome. Later the Reich gave a verbal assurance that the FFI would be treated as PW, but it has never been possible to verify whether this was effectively complied with.

E. Third Geneva Convention of 1949

This rather unsatisfactory state of affairs of resistance movements obviously did not go unnoticed in Geneva in 1949. Although the Third, Prisoner of War, Convention does not seek directly to extend the categories of those entitled to combatant status under the Hague Rules,(41) as it is principally concerned with humanitarian considerations relating to PW rather than the regulation of armed conflict, that effect has perhaps been indirectly achieved. This is done by "repeating, reframing and extending"(42) the categories of those entitled to PW status laid down in the Hague Rules.

This was done in Article 4A(2) of the 1949 Convention as follows:

> "Members of other militias and members of other volunteer corps, including those of organized resistance movements, belonging to a Party to the conflict and operating in or outside their own territory, even if this territory is occupied, provided that such militias or volunteer corps, including such organized resistance movements, fulfil the following conditions."

Then follow the four conditions in Article 1 of the Hague Rules applying to militia and volunteer forces that they must:

1. be commanded by a person responsible for his subordinates

2. have a fixed distinctive sign recognisable at a distance.(43)

3. carry arms openly and

4. conduct their operations in accordance with the laws and customs of war.

Some believe(44) that the last of these conditions, which with the requirement to carry arms openly is one of the two requirements for combatant status as a *levee en masse*, has made it reasonably clear that those specified in Article 4A(2) as entitled to PW status have in fact been accorded combatant status. Whether or not this is correct, there would certainly seem to be a tendency in more modern times, not soundly supported in law, of identifying PW with lawful combatant status. This tendency would seem to date from the 1949 Convention. If so this would mean that the Geneva Conventions have, albeit obliquely, amended and extended the class of lawful combatants in the Hague Rules. The real practical difficulty of this new provision is however obvious. Most resistance fighters in occupied territory are unlikely to be able to distinguish themselves so as to take advantage of the provision without risking almost certain discovery and capture, which for practical purposes will put an end to the resistance.[45]

F. Guerillas and Mercenaries

However, the Conventions of 1949, to that extent at least, had attempted to sort out problems which had arisen in World War II. But the law of armed conflict seems to be something akin to the Sorcerers Apprentice; no sooner is one problem solved than two more present themselves. The major problems since 1959 have included those of guerillas, mercenaries and freedom fighters, generally involved in armed conflicts, or more usually liberation struggles of one sort or another in the third world, even if the international character of such conflicts has not been evident.

Not that there is anything new about guerillas, of course. This phenomenon dates back to ancient times and made a modern re-appearance in the popular Spanish uprising against Napoleon's armies. In recent years however guerilla fighting would seem to have been characterised by

1. the fact that the activities of guerillas are generally co-ordinated with a regular army.

2. the diversity of training of the fighters.

3. the mixed nature of the composition of forces used, whether made up of nationals or foreigners, or even renegades and deserters.

4. the diversity of their methods of combat going from clandestine actions to open fighting, with very often every excess imaginable for example sabotage, assassination, the taking of hostages and attacks against the civilian population.

In all, therefore, this amounts to a form of non-conventional warfare which corresponds neither to the classic forms of war nor the framework of the Hague Regulations and the Geneva Conventions.

Mercenaries too have many of the characteristics of guerillas. They are not new either, making a modern re-appearance in liberation struggles in such places as Angola, Biafra and Katanga after a relative eclipse in the 19th century. It is perhaps of sad note that the United Kingdom seems to have been something of a recruiting ground for mercenaries, leading to the Diplock Commission which reported on 3rd August 1976[46] and pointed to the inapplicability of the Foreign Enlistment Acts of 1819 and 1870 to civil wars.

It was of course with a view to regulating these new problems, and others, that the Diplomatic Conference was arranged in Geneva from 1974 to 1977.[47]

2. Combatant Status after Protocol I[48]

A. Rule of Distinction

The distinction between members of the armed forces and civilians, combatants and non-combatants, has become increasingly blurred in recent conflicts through the participation of civilians as part-time combatants.[49] Nevertheless it remains one of the purposes of the law of armed conflict to ensure that an individual who belongs to one class or the other shall not be permitted to enjoy the privileges of both. The necessity to draw a distinction between civilians and combatants has been reaffirmed by Protocol I.[50]

B. Combatants and Non-Combatants

In the past the expression combatant has been used in several senses but the expression has now acquired a technical meaning under Protocol I which defines combatants as being those who have the right to participate directly in hostilities.[51] Persons who do not have this right are non-combatants. It is as simple as that - or perhaps it is not so simple!

The Hague Rules[52] method of allowing states to decide which members of its armed forces should be treated as non-combatants was thought likely to cause confusion under modern conditions of warfare and has been abolished.[53]

Protocol I provides that all members of the armed forces of a party to a conflict are combatants, with the exception only of medical personnel and chaplains.[54] Members of the armed forces who are permanently assigned and exclusively devoted to civil defence organisations are prohibited from participating directly in hostilities and accordingly must also be considered as being non combatant.[55] However, if they fall into the power of an adverse party, they are entitled to PW status.[56]

A civilian, that is to say, a person who does not belong to the armed forces is always a non-combatant. He has no right to participate directly in hostilities unless taking part in a *levee en masse.* Any civilian who does participate by committing hostile acts is liable to punishment after a proper trial. Equally liable to trial and punishment, should they take part in hostilities, are medical personnel and chaplains and other members of the armed forces who have lost their combatant status, such as personnel permanently assigned to civil defence duties. However, non-combatant members of the armed forces are legally permitted to defend themselves against acts of violence directed at themselves personally and for this purpose the use of firearms may be justified.[57] Indeed medical personnel specifically do not lose their protection by being armed and by using arms in their own defence and in the defence of the wounded and sick in their charge.[58]

C. The Armed Forces

As we have seen, under the Hague Rules and Geneva Conventions, distinctions were made between regular, volunteer and irregular armed forces. Any such distinctions in international law have now been abolished by Protocol I.[59] Membership of the armed forces is unaffected by gender, race, manner of joining or nationality. Essential pre-requisites for recognition of an armed force are that it must be:

a. an organised armed force, group or unit; and

b. under a command responsible to a Party to the conflict for the conduct of its subordinates, even if that Party is represented by a government or authority not recognised by an adverse Party; and

c. Subject to an internal disciplinary system which *inter alia*, enforces compliance with the rules of international law applicable in armed conflict.

The requirement that an armed force should be under a command responsible to a Party to the conflict for the conduct of its subordinates is clearly satisfied if the commander is properly commissioned as an officer, or is otherwise recognised as a commander by the Party concerned. However, particularly in the case of resistance movements in occupied territory, formal State recognition is not necessary and an organisation may be formed spontaneously and appoint its own officers. The essential feature of this requirement is that the commander should accept both responsibility for the acts of his subordinates and equally his responsibility to, and his duty of obedience to, the orders of the Power upon which he depends. Partisans acting on their own individual responsibility do not comply with this requirement, so they are not members of an armed force. In the case of national liberation movements there must be both recognition by the appropriate regional intergovernmental organisation[60] and a declaration to be bound by the Geneva Conventions and Protocol I.[61]

To ensure that armed forces comply with the international law of armed conflict, they must be subject to an effective disciplinary system which enables compliance to be enforced. Any force, group or unit which in the course of its operations, regularly fails to obey the law would clearly be regarded as not being subject to an effective disciplinary system and it would not be a legally recognisable armed force under international law. The members of such a force would not be entitled to combatant status and would be liable to trial and punishment in the same way as other non-combatants who participate directly in hostilities.[62]

D. Loss of Combatant Status

Persons who do not belong to the armed forces as defined in Protocol I and who are not part of a *levee en masse*, can never acquire combatant status. On the other hand, combatant members of armed forces[63], cannot as a general rule lose their combatant status. Protocol I[64] makes it clear that this status is retained even if the individual concerned violates the rules of international law applicable in armed conflict.[65]

Article 44(3) of Protocol I provides both a general rule and an exception. Under the general rule and in order to promote the protection of the civilian population from the effects of hostilities, combatants are obliged to distinguish themselves from the civilian population while they are engaged in an attack or in a military operation preparatory to an attack. This rule supersedes the conditions contained in the Hague Rules[66] and in the Third Geneva Convention[67] which require the carrying of arms openly and having a fixed distinctive sign. The Diplomatic Conference which adopted Protocol I considered that the observance of those stringent conditions was impracticable in certain circumstances of modern warfare. Nevertheless, the need for combatants to be distinguished from civilians remains a central aim of the law of armed conflict. Failure on the part of combatants to distinguish themselves from civilians can only result in a real risk that civilians will be taken to be combatants. While that might benefit some irregular fighters, it gravely adds to the dangers of war for civilians.

This was one of the most difficult problems that the Diplomatic Conference had to resolve. On the one hand there was a desire among the majority of delegations to increase the legal protection of guerillas. However if guerillas were to take advantage of any relaxation of the rules so as to pose as harmless civilians until moments before the attack, this would seriously undermine the principle which is so important for the protection of the civilian population, namely the presumption that apparently unarmed persons in civilian clothes pose no threat and should not be attacked, leaving the regular forces to concentrate on attacking enemy combatants who should be identifiable as such. The development of guerilla warfare has severely increased the risks for the civilian population.

Protocol I does not specify the manner in which combatants should distinguish themselves. Certainly there is no difficulty in the case of regular troops whose uniform should in itself provide sufficient distinction.[68] Irregular non-uniformed forces must, however, take some positive steps to identify themselves as being combatants rather than civilians. The open carrying of arms and the wearing of a fixed distinctive sign visible at a distance would clearly suffice but on occasion something less than this might be acceptable. The criterion is whether members of the adversary forces are able to recognise that the person concerned is in fact a combatant, and therefore a legitimate target, rather than a civilian who is protected under international law. So, essentially the question of whether adequate distinction has been made is a matter of fact which may have to be determined by the tribunal before whom a person accused of violating the rule of distinction is brought.

It should be noted that the general obligation for a combatant to distinguish himself from the civilian population now applies when the former is engaged in an attack or in a military operation preparatory to an attack. In order that the civilian population should be adequately protected the expression "military operation preparatory to an attack" must be given a wide meaning; this could in certain circumstances include operations of a logistic nature. Accordingly, irregular forces should ensure that they at all times continue to be regarded as having combatant status by carrying their arms openly, wearing flak jackets, steel helmets and armbands and any other item of equipment which will clearly distinguish them from the civilian population. Members of armed forces who, in contact with the enemy, do not wear uniform or an adequate distinctive sign and whose sole arm is a pistol, hand grenade, or dagger concealed about the person or a sword stick or similar weapon or who hide their arms on the approach of the enemy, may all be considered as having lost their combatant status.[69] Protocol I does not specifically provide that a member of an armed force who fails to distinguish himself from the civilian population while engaging the enemy or deploying for an engagement shall forfeit his combatant status. Nevertheless, this result may be inferred from wording of paragraphs 2 and 3 of Article 44.[70] Equally, it would seem in strict legal terms that such a person would forfeit his right to be a PW although he should be awarded equivalent protection.[71]

E. Special Exception to the Rule of Distinction

However, Protocol I, in Article 44(3), recognises that there are situations in armed conflicts where, owing to the nature of the hostilities, an armed combatant cannot so distinguish himself. This is the "special exception" mentioned above. In such situations, a special rule applies and status as a combatant is retained provided that the person concerned carries his arms openly:

a. during each military engagement, and

b. during such time as he is visible to the adversary while he is engaged in a military deployment preceding the launching of an attack in which he is to participate.

Thus, in such situations[72] there is no obligation for a combatant to distinguish himself from the civilian population at any other time. The combatant is permitted, in effect, to disguise himself as a member of the civilian population and thereby seek to obtain the protection from attack given to the latter.[73]

As has already been suggested, wide application of this special rule would reduce the protection of civilians to vanishing point. Members of the opposing armed forces would come to regard every civilian as likely to be a combatant in disguise and, for their own protection, would see them as proper targets for attack. Accordingly, use of this special rule must be exceptional and limited to those situations where a combatant is truly unable both to operate effectively and to distinguish himself in accordance with the requirements of the general rule. The United Kingdom with certain other States, made a declaration on signature that these situations can only arise in occupied territory or during a "liberation conflict".[74] Even in these cases, there may be situations in which combatants are able to comply with the general rule and in such cases the special rule would have no application.

The special rule permits a combatant to retain his status as such only if he carries his arms openly in specific situations. The first situation is during a military engagement, that is when he is in contact with the enemy. The second situation is during such time as he is visible to the adversary while engaged in a military deployment preceding the launching of an attack in which he is to participate. The word "deployment" was perhaps unhappily chosen since it has a number of meanings and is clearly inappropriate to an individual acting by himself. Bearing in mind the fundamental need to protect innocent civilians, "deployment" must not be given a narrow meaning. It was for this reason that on signing Protocol I, the United Kingdom together with other States, made a declaration that the expression "military deployment" means "any movement towards a place from which an attack is to be launched". The requirement to carry arms openly during any such movement is limited to such time as the combatant is visible to the adversary. In the light of modern technical developments, "visible" cannot be construed as meaning only 'visible to the naked eye'. A combatant is accordingly required to carry his arms openly if he is visible through binoculars or during the night visible by the use of infra-red or image intensification devices. The criterion would appear to be whether the enemy, using such devices is able thereby to distinguish a civilian from a combatant carrying a weapon. If such distinction can be made, the combatant is "visible to the adversary". The wide availability of these devices seems to require that combatants who are operating under the special rule should carry their arms openly well before they are actually in contact with the enemy.(75)

F. Spies

The obtaining of information through the employment of spies is lawful but that does not prevent the punishment, under certain conditions, of individuals captured while procuring intelligence in other than an open manner. Under the Hague Rules as amplified by Protocol I,(76) a spy is any person who, when acting clandestinely on or false pretences, obtains or endeavours to obtain information in the zone of operations of a belligerent or in territory controlled by a belligerent with the intention of communicating it to a hostile party. A person so acting is engaged in espionage. Civilians in occupied territory, even outside the zone of operations, who furnish information to the enemy, while not being 'spies' nevertheless usually contravene security laws introduced by the Occupying Power(77) and may be tried and punished accordingly.

Any member of the armed forces of a party to the conflict, who falls into the power of an adverse party while actually engaging in espionage may be treated as a spy and is not then entitled to the status of PW.(78)

He is nevertheless to be treated humanely and his trial is to respect established judicial safeguards.(79) A spy may not be punished without first having been tried and convicted.(80)

On the other hand a member of the armed forces of a party to the conflict who gathers or attempts to gather information in territory controlled by an adverse party while wearing the uniform of his own armed forces is not to be regarded as a spy.(81) In wearing uniform, he would not be "acting clandestinely or on false pretences".

Similarly, where a member of an armed force (presumably belonging to a resistance group) who is a resident of territory occupied by an adverse power, gathers or attempts to gather military intelligence for his own side within that territory, he is not to be treated as a spy unless:

a. he acts through false pretences or deliberately in a clandestine manner, and

b. he is captured while actually engaging in espionage.(82)

From this it follows that a spy who is a resident of occupied territory who has been identified as such but not captured at the time and who is subsequently captured, does not then forfeit any entitlement to PW status on account of his earlier activities.

A member of the armed forces of a party to the conflict who has engaged in espionage and who is not a resident of the territory occupied by an adverse party, will not be treated as a spy unless he is captured before he has rejoined the armed forces to which he belongs.(83)

In the United Kingdom, spying is dealt with by the Official Secrets Acts 1911-1939. This legislation enables a wide range of establishments to be declared prohibited places. It is an offence to approach or inspect such places or prepare or disclose information about them for any purpose considered to be prejudicial to the safety or interests of the State. During large-scale armed conflicts, Parliament usually enacts special legislation to deal with espionage, such as the Treachery Act 1940.

G. Mercenaries

Within the definition contained in Protocol I,(84) mercenaries are not entitled as of right to be combatants or PWs but could be accorded PW status if the party to the conflict capturing them so desired.[85]

A mercenary is any person who:

a. is specially recruited locally or abroad in order to fight in an armed conflict;

b. does, in fact, take a direct part in the hostilities;

c. is motivated to take part in the hostilities essentially by the desire for private gain, and in fact is promised by or on behalf of a Party to the conflict, material compensation substantially in excess of that promised or paid to combatants of similar ranks and functions in the armed forces of that party;

d. is neither a national of a Party to the conflict nor a resident of territory controlled by a Party to the conflict;

e. is not a member of armed forces of a Party to the conflict; and

f. has not been sent by a State which is not a Party to the conflict on official duty as a member of its armed forces.

Thus, any member of the armed forces of a State party to the conflict or any member of the armed forces of any other State who is sent by that first State, is not a mercenary. For example, observers or advisers who are members of the armed forces of States other than those engaged in hostilities are not mercenaries.[86]

H. Trial and Punishment of Unlawful Combatants

Persons who participate directly in hostilities when they have no right so to do, for example non-combatants, mercenaries and members of armed forces who have lost their combatant status, are under international law liable to trial. Until their trial, these persons although not PWs are nevertheless to be given equivalent protection.[87]

The death penalty may be imposed although a lesser penalty may be provided by the regulations establishing the court of trial. Under no circumstances may punishment be imposed without trial and the recognised principles of judicial procedures must in all cases be followed.[88]

FOONOTES

* The views expressed in this Article are those of the authors and do not necessarily reflect Ministry of Defence or Government policy.

1. Protocol Additional to the Geneva Conventions of 12th August 1949 and Relating to the Protection of Victims of International Armed Conflicts (Protocol I), 1125 *U.N.T.S.* 3 published by HMSO in Cmnd. 6927, in this Article referred to as Protocol I.

2. For an interesting account of the history of combatant status, see Draper, "Combatant Status, an Historical Perspective", *Military Law and Law of War Review*, 1972, p. 136; and Conrad, "Combatant and Prisoner of War Status in Classical Islamic Law", *Military Law and the Law of War Review*, 1981, p. 271. A very readable account is to be found in Glover, *The Velvet Glove*, published by Hodder in 1982, Chapter 3. A detailed study of the legal aspects of guerilla warfare is in Veuthey, *Guerilla et Droit Humanitaire*, ICRC, 1983.

3. Oppenheim, *International Law* 7th Edition (1952) Vol.II, p. 574.

4. Keith, the editor of *Wheaton's International Law* (Stevens) 7th edition, p. 171, writing in some despair in 1943, referred to the rule of distinction as the greatest triumph of international law and went on to say "... all that need be said is that the progress of events has nullified the triumph, and that, probably it is just as well to abolish a distinction, in itself, illusory and immoral. The idea of war, as affecting only certain elements of the population, is probably an incentive to war". While one can understand these sentiments given the situation in 1943, this is a very pessimistic view. It seems to be based on a

misunderstanding of the purpose of the law of war which is aimed at reducing so far as possible the sufferings of war.

5. The letters "PW" may be used, under Article 23 of the Third Geneva Convention of 1949, to indicate prisoner of war camps. The letters "PW" will be used throughout this article as an abbreviation for prisoners of war.

6. But in the case of sieges, civilians who assisted in the defence have traditionally been spared, see Wheaton, *op.cit.* p. 171.

7. *The Manual of Military Law*, 1929, HMSO, Amendment No. 12, January 1936, Chapter XIV, para. 17.

8. *The Law of War on Land* being Part III of *The Manual of Military Law*, 1958, HMSO, para. 86 (*MML* part III).

9. Regulations Annexed to the International Convention No. IV concerning the Laws and Customs of War on Land, The Hague, 1907. See, e.g. Roberts and Guelff, *Documents on the Laws of War*, Oxford, 1982, p. 48.

10. Rousseau, *Le droit des Conflits Armes*, Pedone, 1983, p. 69.

11. Rousseau, *op.cit.*, p. 69.

12. See Article 4 of the Third Geneva Convention of 1949.

13. Early concerns with "use of semi-barbarous troops" in, e.g. Wheaton, *op.cit.*, p. 176, now seem extremely out moded.

14. See Clover *op.cit.*, p. 83; or Rousseau, *op.cit.*, p. 70, who refers to the period 1474-1830.

15. Rousseau, *op.cit.*, p. 70.

16. See Roberts and Guelff, *op.cit.*, p. 63.

17. See Rousseau, *op.cit.*, p. 71. The text of the Act of 1870 can be found in Halsbury's *Statutes of England and Wales*, 4th edition, Vol. 12, p. 130. The Act is subtitled "An Act to regulate the conduct of Her Majesty's subjects during the Existence of Hostilities between Foreign States with which

Her Majesty is at peace" and was brought into force at the time of the Franco-Prussian War. Among other things, the Act makes it an offence without licence to engage in the Armed Forces of any foreign State at war with any foreign State at peace with Her Majesty.
It has been held to apply to British subjects everywhere and to foreign subjects within the Queen"s dominions (*R v. Jameson* 1896 2 QB 425). This Act replaced an earlier statute of 1819. In addition, a soldier who absented himself from his own armed forces to enlist in the armed forces of another State would be guilty of desertion.

18. Rousseau, *op.cit.*, p. 71.

19. Although, in theory, Article 3 of the Hague Rules is still extant, it seems to have little relevance today having regard to Article 43, para. 2 of Protocol I. According to Detter de Lupis, *The Law of War*, Cambridge 1987, p. 107, the ambiguity in Article 3 was cleared up by Article 4A(1) of the 1949 PW Convention. For an explanation of the non-combatant categories covered by Article 3 of the Hague Rules, see Wheaton, *op.cit.*, p. 173.

20. First Geneva Convention of 1949, Articles 22, 24, 28.

21. *Ibid*, Article 28; Third Geneva Convention of 1949, Article 33.

22. See Pictet, *Commentary on the First Geneva Convention of 1949*, ICRC 1952, p. 219.

23. Rousseau, *op.cit.*, p. 72.

24. The reference to "territory" does not need to be interpreted as referring to the whole of a country.

25. According to Draper, "The Status of Combatants and the Question of Guerrilla Warfare", *British Year Book of International Law*, 1971, p. 192, occupation occurs when, under Article 42 of the Hague Rules, the territory is placed under the authority of the occupying power. He discusses the difficulty of assessing when this ceases, especially if there is regular activity by resistance movements.

26. According to Baxter, the *levee en masse* is an anomaly which has lost any real significance, see Baxter, "So-called

"Unprivileged Belligerency": Spies, Guerrillas and Saboteurs, *British Yearbook of International Law*, 1951, p. 335.

27. Rousseau, *op.cit.*, p. 73. According to Glover, *op.cit.* p. 55, the Prussians raised an irregular force, known as the Landsturm, which was under military control but was specifically enjoined not to conform to the customs of war and when the French caught any of its members they executed them immediately. For the origin of the term *"franc-tireur"*, see Glover, *op.cit.*, p. 58. For a comparison of the Landsturm and The British Home Guard raised in 1940, see Stone, *Legal Controls of International Conflict*, Stevens, 1954, p. 569.

28. Rousseau, *op.cit.*, p. 73.

29. Glover, *op.cit.*, p. 55.

30. *Ex Parte Quirin* (1942) 317 U.S.1.

31. It is of interest that Lauterpacht in Oppenheim's *International Law*, 7th edition, p. 425 refers to the case as authority for the proposition that spies are unlawful belligerents, while Baxter, *op.cit.*, p. 340 says that spies are not punishable as unlawful belligerents but as contravening the security of the capturing power. However, Draper casts some doubt on this theory of "privileged belligerency", in Draper, "The Status of Combatants, etc." *op.cit.*, p. 176.

32. *The trial of Werner Rohde and others*, Law Reports of Trials of War Criminals, UNWCC, 1947, Vol.V, p. 54.

33. Women's Auxiliary Air Force and First Aid Nursing Yeomanry.

34. See *trial of Rohde, op.cit.*, p. 57. In fact, the captives had been summarily killed by the injection of a lethal drug, and then cremated.

35. See note 8(b) p. 32 of *MML* part III; Pictet, *Commentary on the Third Geneva Convention of 1949*, ICRC 1960, p. 62; Rousseau, *op.cit.*, p. 73.4.

36. See Pictet, *Third Convention, op.cit.*, p. 62. In the event, following an intervention by the International Committee

of the Red Cross, the executions did not take place, Rousseau, *op.cit.*, p. 75.

37. See note 8(a) p. 32 of *MML* part III; Rousseau, *op.cit.*, p. 75.

38. Noted in Baxter *op.cit.*, p. 338, note 4.

39. Rousseau *op.cit.*, p. 76.

40. Rousseau, p.cit., p. 76.

41. Articles 1 and 2, i.e. armies; militia and volunteer corps fulfilling certain conditions; and members of a *levee en masse* fulfilling certain conditions.

42. Quoted from Draper, "The Status of Combatants", *op.cit.*, p. 190.

43. According to Draper, *op.cit.*, p. 202, this provision would not preclude the irregular fighter from using the ruse of camouflage.

44. e.g. Draper, *op.cit.*, p. 189. Of course, the civilian followers specified in Article 4A(4) of the Third Geneva Convention of 1949 cannot claim combatant status. The NAAFI employee who took over a machine gun during the Falklands War of 1982 was entitled to take a direct part in hostilities since he was, in fact, not a civilian at all. He had been pre-enlisted and became a petty officer on active service. In the same way, in the Army, members of NAAFI's Expeditionary Forces Institute, NAAFI staff attested to the Royal Army Ordnance Corps who provide uniformed and combatant service, are members of the armed forces.

45. Stone, *op.cit.*, p. 567, puts forward the interesting proposition that "guerillas, even when they are unprivileged belligerants, are (like spies) merely left by international law to punishment by the enemy state under its own law, or that of the occupied territory, and are not criminals under international law".

46. Cmnd. 6569.

47. Before proceeding to examine the 1977 Protocols, it is, perhaps, worthwhile to add a few words about spies, saboteurs and defectors all of whom may be serving as regular or irregular combatants. Spies, and saboteurs acting clandestinely, and not in uniform, have traditionally been denied combatant and PW status, see *MML* part III *op.cit.*, pp. 105-109. The *Manual* is equally emphatic, p. 37, about defectors. This stance is supported by The Privy Council decisions in the cases of *Public Prosecutor v. Koi* (1968) 1 AER 419 and *Mohamed Ali and Another v. Public Prosecutor* (1968) 3 AER 488. See also, Bothe, Partsch and Solf, *New Rules for Victims of Armed Conflicts*, Nijhoff, 1982, p. 256.

48. See note 1 above. By the time of writing (June 1988) the United Kingdom had not ratified the Protocol. On signature, and subject to the declarations which were deposited on signature, the United Kingdom was to be regarded as bound by the provisions of the Protocol which were declaratory of customary law. But it was not bound in respect of provisions containing new law. However, under Article 18 of the Vienna Convention on the Law of Treaties (published in, e.g. Brownlie, *Basic Documents International Law*, 3rd ed. Oxford, p. 349) the United Kingdom was obliged to refrain from any action which would defeat the object and purpose of the Protocol.

49. This is in addition to the catalogue of reasons set out in note 2(a) p. 30 of *MML* part III.

50. Article 48 - "... the Parties to the conflict shall at all times distinguish between the civilian population and combatants and between civilian objects and military objectives ...."

51. Article 43, paras. 1 and 2. In defining what is meant by Armed Forces, this article assimilates regular and irregular forces.

52. Article 3.

53. See note 21 above.

54. Article 43, para. 2.

55. Articles 61 and 67.

56. Article 67, para. 2.

57. With the possible exception of chaplains for whom no special dispensation equivalent to Article 22 of the First Geneva Convention of 1949 is granted.

58. Article 22, *ibid*. According to Article 13 of Protocol I, these must be light individual weapons.

59. Article 43, para. 1.

60. At least, according to the statement of understanding made by the United Kingdom at the time of signature. A similar statement was made by the Republic of Korea on ratification.

61. Article 96, para. 3.

62. For a full discussion of this problem, see Draper, "The Status of Combatants etc." *op.cit.* p. 198 et seq. Unless i controls territory, a liberation movement or other armec faction would find it extremely difficult, if not impossible to comply with its obligations under the PW Convention That would seriously undermine its prospects of being recognised as a legitimate armed force.

63. i.e. other than medical personnel and chaplains.

64. Article 44.

65. The conundrum of the status of members of the regular forces who fail to distinguish themselves from the civilian population is dealt with in Rogers, "Armed Forces and Developments of the Law of War", *Military Law and Law of War Review*, (1982), p. 219.

66. Article 1.

67. Article 4, para. 2.

68. Of course, in combat in the temperate regions the uniform of the infantry soldier may not be immediately apparent. He may be wearing a steel helmet, respirator, NBC suit and webbing. His face and hands will be daubed with camouflage cream. Leaves and foliage will be stuck into his clothing and webbing to break up the outline. The new

very small infantry rifle might not be evident at first glance. However, it is highly unlikely that any self-respecting civilian would go about dressed like that! In polar regions and high mountains it may be difficult to distinguish between military personnel and civilians because of the nature of the protective clothing issued. In a nuclear environment, too, soldiers and civilians wearing NBC suits and gas masks might be virtually indistinguishable, apart from the fact that soldiers would probably also be carrying weapons and military equipment. It would of course, be possible to issue civilians with different coloured suits from soldiers. Of course, the Protocol makes a saving for the custom of wearing uniform in the regular armed forces, see Article 44, para. 7.

69. Since they are acting clandestinely, they may be treated as spies or saboteurs. See note 47 above.

70. See Kalshoven, "Reaffirmation and Development of International Humanitarian Law applicable in Armed Conflicts, etc." *Netherlands Year Book of International Laws* Vol. IX (1978) pp. 130-131.

71. Article 44, para. 4. This permits the person captured to be put on trial for being an illegal combatant and sentenced accordingly. What is meant by equivalent treatment is not clear, but it would behove the capturing State to treat the captured person in all other respects as if he were a PW.

72. Kalshoven has pointed out that this exception applies to situations, not to regular forces generally. See Kalshoven, *op.cit.*, p. 127.

73. The *Mohamed Ali* case, *op.cit.*, at note 47, would, no doubt, have been decided the same even had the Protocol applied to the situation unless, perhaps, the accused had been carrying their weapons openly when they planted the bag containing explosives in the building.

74. i.e. those covered by Article 1, para. 4, which by legal fiction, are treated as international armed conflicts. See Kalshoven, *op.cit.* p. 128 who says that at the Diplomatic Conference there was a consensus that the situations envisaged in the second sentence of para. 3 can only arise in occupied territory or in wars of national liberation. For an interesting discussion of two South African decisions

concerning the status of members of SWAPO and the ANC, see Murray, "The 1977 Geneva Protocols and Conflict in Southern Africa", 33 *International and Comparative Law Quarterly* (1984), p. 462.

75. For a discussion of the different views expressed at the Diplomatic Conference, see Kalshoven *op.cit.* pp. 128-129. The PLO representatives said "visible" means visible to the naked eye, while the Syrian delegate thought it meant that the combatant knew or ought to have known that he was visible to the enemy. That must, at the very least, include use of binoculars which are commonplace in all armies. It is of interest that upon ratification New Zealand declared that it "will interpret the words 'visible to the adversary' ... as including visible with the aid of any form of surveillance, electronic or otherwise, available to help keep a member of the Armed Forces of the adversary under observation". Note of the Swiss Ambassador to Her Majesty's Secretary of State for Foreign and Commonwealth Affairs, 16th March, 1988.

76. Hague Rules, Article 29; Protocol I, Article 46.

77. e.g. under Article 64 of the Fourth Geneva Convention of 1949.

78. Protocol I, Article 46, para. 1.

79. Protocol I, Article 75.

80. Hague Rules, Article 30.

81. Protocol I, Article 46, para. 2.

82. Protocol I, Article 46, para. 3.

83. Protocol I, Article 46, para. 4; Hague Rules, Article 31.

84. Article 47, para. 2.

85. Third Geneva Convention of 1949, Article 5.

86. The Gurkhas are not mercenaries because they serve in the British and Indian armed forces nor, for example, are Cuban soldiers sent to Angola as part of the Cuban armed forces. See Rowe, *Defence: the Legal Implications*,

Brasseys, 1987, p. 160. The provision is aimed essentially at soldiers of fortune, those who will serve any armed faction principally for private gain.

87. The Third Geneva Convention of 1949, Article 84; Protocol I, Article 44, para. 4.

88. Hague Rules, Article 30; Protocol I, Article 75, especially para. 4 as to the procedure.

THE VALUE OF THE 1977 GENEVA PROTOCOLS FOR THE PROTECTION OF CIVILIANS

*L. Doswald-Beck**

1. Introduction

Probably the most valuable contribution of the 1977 Protocols is the codification of the principle of distinction between civilians and combatants during the conduct of hostilities. This principle may seem fundamental, but a student of this branch of law, studying the subject from the time of the Second World War until the early 1970's, could legitimately ask himself whether the principle existed at all. Indeed, this doubt as to whether civilians were entitled to be spared in any way during hostilities, detracted, in the student's eyes, from the credibility of the law of armed conflict. Before the 1977 Protocols, arguments in favour of a rule prohibiting the deliberate aerial bombardment of the civilian population were perceived by many as somewhat flimsy. Their detractors argued as follows: the 1907 Hague Conventions were out of date and did not deal with attacks from the air; the 1923 Hague Rules were not adopted as a treaty by States, a fact suspicious in itself; State practice during the Second World War was disastrous for civilians; the Fourth Geneva Convention 1949, with its provisions for optional shelters for certain narrowly-defined members of the population, assumed a total war situation; nuclear weapons speak for themselves.

This picture was indeed bleak, and resolutions reaffirming the principle of distinction by the International Conference of the Red Cross in 1965 and the United Nations General Assembly in 1968 and 1976, did not cut much ice with the cynics.

It is this author's personal opinion that writers in this post-world-war period were too obsessed with that war,

* For footnotes see p. 164.

whereas State practice had begun to reaffirm the principle of distinction in international wars since that event. However, this State practice was certainly not consistent and doubts remained. There is no way one can overestimate the value of the Protocols in codifying the principle that civilians are not to be made the object of attack as such. This principle appears in both Protocols, including Protocol II which regulates internal armed conflict. As the only previous provision on internal armed conflict, namely, common Article 3 of the 1949 Geneva Conventions, did not directly regulate the conduct of hostilities, the inclusion of this principle in Protocol II is a major step forward. The principle of distinction does not mean that civilians are immune, but the Protocols realistically afford them as much protection as possible that is consistent with military necessities. We shall be studying this aspect in detail later on in the paper.

2. Historical context of the Protocols

A. The situation before the Second World War

It may at first sight seem unnecessary in this short paper to go back to this early period, but when one remembers that without Protocol I, the latest general codification that exists on the conduct of hostilities dates back to 1907, one appreciates that this incursion into history is not without value. An understanding of the military and legal system into which the Hague Conventions fit is necessary for an appreciation of their contribution and of their limitations for modern times.

Unlike the law of Geneva,(1) the law on the conduct of hostilities stems from the practice of States as it has developed over the centuries. The development of professional armies in the 18th and 19th centuries, brought with it the organisation of codes of discipline within these armies(2) as well as the belief that fighting wars was to be exclusively done by such professionals.(3) The actual method of fighting at this time, i.e. predominantly by armies facing each other in the field, had the effect of keeping much of the civilian population relatively uninvolved in direct hostilities. However, it would be fallacious to imagine that the civilian population was always unaffected. It was, in particular, considered perfectly acceptable to starve the civilian population, and this was done in two major ways: first, besieging a town or larger area was a common way of forcing the surrender of these areas. Secondly, the right of general devastation was recognised in situations of absolute military necessity.

Thus with regard to the right of siege, the Lieber Code[4] states that:

> "War is not carried on by arms alone. It is lawful to starve the hostile belligerent, armed or unarmed[5], so that it leads to the speedier subjection of the enemy .... When a commander of a besieged place expels the non-combatants, in order to lessen the number of those who consume his stock of provisions, it is lawful, though an extreme measure, to drive them back, so as to hasten on the surrender."[6]

With regard to devastation. Lieber prohibits the use of "wanton" devastation[7] which is translated in the Hague Regulations as a prohibition of such behaviour "unless such destruction or seizure be imperatively demanded by the necessities of war".[8]

We will consider in greater detail the customary right of siege and devastation when studying Article 54 of Protocol I 1977. The civilian population could also suffer great hardship as a result of requisitions of an invading army. In the Napoleonic wars, in particular, large armies lived off the land, often having a very adverse effect on the nutritional needs of the population of the invaded territory.[9]

As Lieber therefore stated:

> "The citizen or nature of a hostile country is thus an enemy, as one of the constituents of the hostile state or nation, and as such is subjected to the hardship of the war."[10]

He evidently saw no contradiction between this statement and the subsequent Article:

> "Nevertheless, as civilisation has advanced during the last centuries, so has likewise steadily advanced, especially in war on land, the distinction between the private individual belonging to a hostile country and the hostile country itself, with its men in arms. The principle has been more and more acknowledged that the unarmed citizen is to be spared in person, property, and honour as much as the exigencies of war will permit."[11]

He in effect explains this apparent contradiction immediately afterwards:

> "Private citizens are no longer murdered, enslaved, or carried off to distant parts, and the inoffensive individual is as little disturbed in his private relations as the commander of the hostile troops can afford to grant in the overruling demands of a vigorous war."(12)

The Lieber Code has been quoted at length here because it explains better than any other instrument the mentality behind the law on the conduct of hostilities as it developed during that period. In fact the key phrases in the two quotations just cited are:

> "as much as the exigencies of war will permit"

and

> "can afford to grant in the overruling demands of a vigorous war."

It meant, in effect, that the army was entitled to do what it considered to be necessary in order to bring about the subjection of the enemy but that wanton acts of violence and cruelty to civilians was prohibited. This approach underlined the professionalism of the soldier's task, and, being military in origin, the rules reflect military needs.

With regard to the direct effects of hostilities, these were, as mentioned before fairly slight as a result of the normal method of conducting hostilities. If, however, a city resisted occupation by the approaching army, that army could either decide to besiege that city in order to starve it into submission, or bombard it in order to breach the city walls and take possession of it. If a city, however, offered no resistance as was often the case after the defeat of its army in the field, the hostile army could simply take possession. Bombardment in such a case would be futile and would amount to wanton cruelty as well as a waste of military resources. It is this practice that is reflected in the Hague Regulations when it speaks of the prohibition of the attack or bombardment of towns, villages etc., which are "undefended".(13) However, when bombardments of population centres were necessary, the Hague Regulations provide that:

> "all necessary steps must be taken to spare, as far as possible, buildings dedicated to religion, art, science or charitable purposes, historic monuments, hospitals and places where the sick and

wounded are collected, provided that they are not being used at the time for military purposes."[14]

The same provision affirms the duty of the besieged to indicate the presence of these buildings by distinctive and visible signs, which should be notified to the enemy beforehand.

It is to be noted that civilians are not expressly mentioned in this Article, reflecting the practice that during the bombardment of a defended city a distinction between civilians and military objects could not be made as such. This Article reflected the extent of precautions that could be taken by a besieging army when attempting to breach the city walls and still give them a good chance of success. Concern for the civilian population, however, is indicated in two other Articles of the Hague Regulations, namely, the duty of the attacking army to warn of their forthcoming bombardment when this is possible,[15] and the prohibition of pillage[16] once the city has fallen. The other restriction on the army is of purely customary origin and reflected in the Lieber Code, namely, the rule quoted above[17] that "private citizens are no longer[18] murdered, enslaved or carried off to distant parts".

As Spaight pointed out in 1933, the right to bombard defended cities was:

"founded on the right to assault, take and occupy the city. It is, indeed, a heritage of an age when customs of war were more barbarous and perimeters of defence more restricted than now. Its origin goes back to the time when to defend a city after a summons to surrender involved the forfeiture of the lives of all its occupants upon its subsequent capture ... and when, moreover, cities were defended from their narrow circuit of walls...."[19]

This practice of murdering all the occupants of conquered defended cities dates back to medieval times, whereas customs since then had changed, as Lieber pointed out. As the reader will certainly have noticed, therefore, the Hague Regulations were not a complete codification of the practices of war at the time, but are to be read together with the Lieber Code and other historical accounts of military practice as it had developed by the beginning of this century. When the Hague Regulations are read together with the historical military context just described, it is clear that they made perfect sense for the time.

The arrival of aircraft, however, totally undermined these rules which were tied to the notion of advancing land-based armies through the field which could occupy without problem undefended cities, but which needed to bombard defended cities in order to occupy them. The appearance of balloons and early aircraft at first prompted States to try to restrict them so as not to upset the traditional practices of war. Thus the First Hague Conference in 1899 adopted a declaration[(20)] prohibiting for a term of five years "the launching of projectiles and explosives from balloons or by other new methods of a similar nature".

However, the temptation of aircraft was too great for States, and although the declaration of 1899 was renewed in 1907 "up to the close of the 3rd Hague Conference",[(21)] this second document was ratified by only few, and was unobserved in the First World War. Aircraft put within the reach of States, for the first time in military history, the possibility of attacking the enemy within his own territory, still occupied by him, and thus well behind enemy lines. Bombardments, therefore, no longer needed to be linked with the attempt to occupy a city. The notion of "defended" or "undefended" had no sense whatever for bombardments behind enemy lines, and this was immediately appreciated in State practice during the First World War.[(22)]

A broad distinction between civilian and military objects was retained in that war by the creation of the notion of the "military objective".[(23)] According to this principle any object of direct military importance could be attacked behind enemy lines, although the notion of "defended" or "undefended" still held good for cities about to be occupied. State practice also acknowledged, however, that an attacker could not be blamed if military objectives were located in such places that an attack upon them must involve incidental damage to innocent life or property. Such incidental damage, nevertheless, was not to be entirely disproportionate to the military results achieved.[(24)] Spaight argued that although a number of attacks in the First World War were alleged to be indiscriminate, most pilots carefully tried to limit themselves to the objectives chosen. The problem was more one of accuracy, as planes - chased by other planes or being attacked by anti-aircraft defences - had to travel at speed and at relatively high altitudes.

An attempt was made after the war to formally regulate the use of air power. States at the 1921-1922 Washington Conference on the Limitation of Armament appointed a Commission of Jurists for this purpose which adopted in 1923 the "Rules of Aerial Warfare". These were not adopted in legally binding form, but were stated by many to be an authoritative interpretation of the law.(25) These rules reaffirmed the notion that aerial bombardment is legitimate only when directed at a military objective, defined as: "an object of which the destruction or injury would constitute a distinct military advantage to the belligerent".(26) Subsequent provisions, however, place limitations on this principle firstly by giving a fairly narrow and exclusive definition of what is considered to be such a military objective,(27) and secondly by appearing to limit such bombardments to the neighbourhood of military operations.(28) These restrictions would have in fact rendered illegal a number of bombardments in the First World War which took place outside zones of military operations and which destroyed a number of commercial factories.(29) It may have been for this reason that these rules were not formally adopted, or perhaps because States were not at this time willing to limit this new means of warfare in a definitive legal instrument.

It is clear that there was a certain uneasiness about the fate of the civilian population in this inter-war period. In 1930, the ICRC had consulted a number of experts on the question whether it was possible to lay down precise rules of international law protecting the civilian population against bombardments or to render these rules more effective.(30) The response they received was hardly encouraging, as the experts underlined the difficulty of limiting the use in war of effective weapons.(31) The predominant concern, however, was the fear of the widespread use of gas against the civilian population, which thankfully did not materialise.

The actions of the Italian air force during the invasion of Ethiopia, and the German air force during the Spanish civil war demonstrated the danger of the inexistence of rules on air bombardment. In 1938, the British Prime Minister enunciated in the House of Commons three fundamental principles of international law applicable to air warfare, namely: the direct attack of the civilian population is unlawful; targets for air bombardments must be legitimate, identifiable military objectives; reasonable care must be taken in attacking military objectives to avoid bombardment of a civilian population in the neighbourhood. These principles were embodied in a resolution unanimously adopted by the League of Nations Assembly in the same year[32] (Germany was no longer a member at that time).

B. The Second World War and its legal effects

There is no need in this paper to go into details on the bombing raids of the Second World War. Suffice it to say that although the British and French governments stated at the beginning of the war that they would only bomb military objectives "in the narrowest sense of the word" only a year later this approach changed to one of extensive bombing of cities. This seemed to be at first a reaction to German indiscriminate bombing but it was later justified principally on the basis of the need to crush German war-making industry. Because of extensive defences in major cities, it was argued it was impossible to bomb with precision certain targets, and therefore in order to make sure that the targets were hit the whole area in which they were situated needed to be attacked. This so-called "target area bombardment" was satirized by Spaight during the war as follows:

> "One might almost say that it has been found necessary to reverse the process by which the Chinese arrived at the secret of roast pork. The cooking could be done, after all, only by the burning of the house down."[33]

It must also be pointed out, however, that a number of directives issued by the British War Cabinet included the "morale" of the population as a target.[34] Although much of the destruction was caused by target-area bombardment, one could seriously question whether it was really necessary to destroy an entire town in order to eliminate its industry. Spaight in 1947 argued in favour of target-area bombing as follows:

> "If the purpose had been to spread terror, to slaughter women and children, and to shatter the morale of the population at large, then the objectives selected would never have been the powerfully defended industrial centres which were in fact attacked. Other towns, hardly protected at all, would have been raided in preference. There is no shadow of a doubt what the objectives were. They were armament and accessory factories, U-boat factories and bases, aircraft factories and bases, steel works, oil and benzol plants,

ball-bearing plants, railways, canals, viaducts and road bridges of military importance."(35)

One could seriously question however whether this is consistent with a statement made just prior to the above-quoted one viz.:

"At the end of July 1943, Hamburg was swept by a tornado of fire and flame in a week of devastating raids. The result, according to an officially inspired statement, was "probably the most complete blotting out of a city that has ever happened."(36)

This bombing of Hamburg caused the death of approximately 50,000 people, and that of Dresden in February 1945, 135,000 people.

Despite Spaight's justification of all this, he nevertheless found the atom bombing of Hiroshima and Nagasaki to be beyond the pale:

"To the present writer it seems that to approve atom bombing would be to confess that all the denunciation of indiscriminate bombardment at The Hague and elsewhere was nothing but hypocrisy and insincerity. International law cannot trim its sails so quickly to the winds of expediency as that. It should hold to the view that, while target-area bombing comes close to the border line of permissibility, atom bombing definitely oversteps it."

With all the discussion surrounding nuclear weapons these days, one almost forgets that they were actually used in the Second World War. The horrified reaction of those that had just lived through the excesses of Nazism and elimination of cities by fire-bombing serves as a reminder that these were perceived as the final straw in that war. Indeed, the Second World War serves as a lesson of what can happen without the rule of law: behaviour in war can all too quickly deteriorate into a veritable orgy of the worst malignant and callous behaviour unfortunately known to mankind.

Legal writings for the two decades following the war were about as bleak and desolate as the ruined cities that that war had left. Events following the war only served to confirm this picture. The Nuremberg Tribunal conspicuously omitted indiscriminate bombing from its list of war crimes. Indeed in one case it appeared to condone the bombing in rejecting a German defence that its killing of civilians was no worse than the number killed by allied bombing:

> "... there ... is no parallelism between an act of legitimate warfare, namely the bombing of a city, with a concomitant loss of civilian life, and the premeditated killing of all members of certain categories of the civilian population in occupied territory ....
>
> as grave a military action as is an air bombardment, whether with the usual bombs or by atomic bombs, the only purpose of the bombing is to effect the surrender of the bombed nation ...."(37)

The four Geneva Conventions, concluded in 1949, did not attempt to regulate the conduct of hostilities and the Fourth Convention "Relative to the Protection of Civilian Persons in Time of War" is principally devoted to the treatment of persons once they are in the power of the enemy. However, it does contain one section entitled "General Protection of Populations Against Certain Consequences of War"(38) which has been interpreted by some as envisaging a "total war" situation. This is because although some articles prohibit the attack of medical installations and personnel, the only protection envisaged for civilian populations during hostilities is the herding of certain sections of the population into sanctuaries removed from the effects of war. This is to be achieved by the optional creation of "hospital and safety"(39) zones, or "neutralised"(40) zones in regions where fighting is taking place.

Although the creation of such sanctuaries is a realistic and useful possibility, these provisions all too easily led to an *a contrario* conclusion that civilians could expect no other protection.(41)

The massive build-up of nuclear weapons and NATO's proclaimed reliance on the use of them as its means of defence completed this gloomy picture.

Schwarzenberger writing in 1958, stated that:

> "The practice of belligerent States in the Second World War and the trends in the relevant post-1945 treaties suggest that the immunity of the civilian population from international attack is reaching vanishing point.
>
> ... legitimate target areas are no longer limited to military objectives, even if those are understood in a very liberal sense, but extend to centres of communications, large industrial and

> administrative establishments of any kind and to any area likely to become important for the conduct of the war. Thus, at present, the principle of the protection of the enemy civilian population appears to apply at the most in favour of a residue of persons who fulfil two conditions. They must not be connected with the war effort and be remote from important target areas."[42]

Schwarzenberger continued to express the same views in 1968.[43]

Stone, writing on air warfare in 1954, stated that this new weapon has raised many questions on which the law offered no guidance, but only an "ominous silence".

> "Despite the earnest professions of the Powers, the Hague Air Warfare Rules of 1923 ... remain even today unratified. Nor can it really be said that these Draft Rules ... have seriously influenced belligerent practice on any critical matter."[44]

Stone went so far as to state that the workforce of the military objectives under attack should be considered as "quasi-combatants" who could be attacked even in their homes. "True civilians" are best removed to other places. He further admonished as "merely illusory" and "pure verbalism" the statement that morale is not an object of attack as it would not make any difference in reality.[45]

Lauterpacht, as editor of Oppenheim in 1952, acknowledged the difficulty in defining a "military objective" in modern war and also the technical difficulty of confining the effects to the intended object of attack. He conceded that the principle of immunity of non-combatants does not mean absolute immunity, and that sections of the civilian population "closely identified with military objectives proper" may be legitimately exposed to air attack.[46]

On target-area bombardment, he stated that the practice of the Second World War:

> "reduced to the vanishing point the protection of the civilian population from aerial bombardment ... It is a moot point whether the general recourse to strategic target-bombing had the result of endowing it with a measure of legality and of abolishing ... the principles underlying the Hague Rules of 1923."[47]

However, in spite of this, Lauterpacht argued in favour of the continued existence of the rule against the intentional targeting of civilians and stated that it should be possible to conduct aerial bombardment whilst ensuring compliance with the basic rules of warfare as understood before the Second World War.[48]

These texts have ben quoted at length as they were considered the principal authorities on the subject until at least the mid-1970's.

As the 1958 version of the *British Manual of Military Law on Land* was revised by Lauterpacht, it is not surprising that the general principle that non-combatants must not be made the object of direct attack is repeated.[49] However, the section actually dealing with bombardment, which declares unlawful the direct bombardment of non-military objectives, expressly excludes from its ambit bombardment by aircraft.[59]

The *U.S. Military Manual of 1958*[51] states that:

> "There is no prohibition of general application against bombardment from the air of combatant troops,[53] defended places,[52] or other legitimate military objectives."

The *U.S. Department of Army Pamphlet of 1962*[54] poses in this respect more questions than it answers. It recognises that the criterion of whether a city is defended or undefended is unsuitable for aerial bombardment, and then goes on to question whether attacks can be aimed at the civilians' will to resist or whether one can aim at a legitimate target a weapon that is so large and inaccurate that it will kill a lot more than the legitimate target. The manual does not provide a conclusive answer to these questions.

These U.S. and U.K. military manuals are presently in the process of being rewritten in order to take into account changes in treaty and customary law, but they were looked at as authoritative evidence of the *opinio juris* of these States until at least the early 1970's.

In 1956 the ICRC had prepared a document entitled "Draft Rules for the Limitation of the Dangers Incurred by the Civilian Population in Time of War". These rules provided that military operations were to be confined to the destruction of military resources, and that incidental civilian injury was not to be disproportionate. They also forbade area bombardment and weapons with "uncontrollable effects". The latter provision, as it included the spread of radioactive agents in its definition, included atomic weapons, and it was for this reason, it seems, that the Draft Rules did not achieve support from governments.[55]

C. State practice after the Second World War

Although academic writings concentrated on the events of the Second World War and the ominous nuclear build-up, the actual pattern of armed conflicts was taking a new course. In one respect, there was an improvement on the Second World War in that there was a move back to target selection in city bombings, with virtually no repetition of the extensive area bombardment destroying entire cities or major sections of them. Nuclear weapons have not been used since Nagasaki. However, although civilians casualties were said to be 50% of the total in the Second World War they are now said to represent about 90% of the total. This appalling statistic is not the result of extensive bombing practices in modern international conflicts but rather the predominance these days of internal conflicts together with an increased importance of guerilla warfare. Both these phenomena existed, of course, before, but since the Second World War, traditional international conflicts have been the exception, and major powers have preferred to extend their influence through interventions in varying degrees in internal conflicts. Both these conflicts, and those of national liberation in colonial wars, have involved fighting forces of a dissimilar nature. The sophisticated forces with superior fire-power, in their frustration at not being able to identify and localise the enemy, have tended to use that fire-power in a relatively blind way, hoping thus to sometimes hit home. The guerillas opposing such forces know that their only chance of success lies in their invisibility, including their melting in with the civilian population. The Vietnam war was, of course, the epitome of such a scenario. The legal problems posed by these developments are two- fold: first, internal conflicts are not subject to the full protection of international humanitarian law; Article 3 common to the Geneva Conventions of 1949 does not address itself directly to the actual conduct of hostilities. Secondly, guerilla warfare seriously threatens the possibility of identifying the civilian population and distinguishing them from combatants. Not only is there the phenomenon of worker by day, guerilla by night, so that the same individuals play a dual role, but there is also the problem of how to define certain roles. Guerillas largely depend on the civilian population for shelter and supplies and the entire question of "quasi-combatants" could arise with regard to such civilians.

The problem of guerilla warfare has been most carefully examined by Michel Veuthey in his work "Guerilla et Droit Humanitaire". Having looked at the characteristics of guerilla warfare, he states:

> "Ces caracteristiques de la lutte ont souvent fait penser que la distinction entre civils et militaires .... n'existait plus dans la guerilla et ont pu donner pretexte a la non-application des lois et coutumes de la guerre pertinentes."[56]

The problem of internal wars is exacerbated by the personal nature of these wars. The struggle is less one of the acquisition of territory as that of the allegiance of the people. Externally the government does not want the rebels to be seen to have any form of recognition, which they erroneously believe is the result of the formal application of humanitarian law. Internally the people are more clearly seen as personal enemies if their allegiance is with the other party. The actual logistics of internal conflicts also means that all the population is closely involved with events.

D. The resurrection of the protection of civilians in the law on the conduct of hostilities

The turning point in humanitarian law can be said to have begun in 1965, with the adoption in that year of a resolution by the International Conference of the Red Cross, to the effect that lauching attacks against the civilian population as such is prohibited and that civilians are to be spared as much as possible.[57]

Of particular importance is the fact that the United Nations began to take an interest in this field.[58] In 1968, the United Nations International Conference on Human Rights held in Teheran passed a resolution stating the need for "additional humanitarian international conventions ... to ensure the better protection of civilians".[59] In that same year, the

United Nations General Assembly unanimously passed a resolution stating that "it is prohibited to launch attacks against the civilian population as such" and that a "distinction must be made at all times between persons taking part in hostilities and members of the civilian population to the effect that the latter be spared as much as possible".[60] In 1970, the General Assembly passed another resolution to similar effect.[61] By 1971, the process of the creation of the Protocols was well under way with the first Conference of Government experts leading to further meetings and finally the Diplomatic Conference of 1974-1977.

In the meantime, academic opinion also began to awaken from its total pessimism, and recognised that, in international conflicts at least, the notion of the distinction between civilians and combatants had begun to reappear. The most notable work in this respect is a report by Denise Bindschedler-Robert written for a Conference on the subject organised in 1970 by the Carnegie Endowment for International Peace.[62] In her report, she argued in favour of the continuing existence of the principle of distinction citing in particular, the fact that the distinction had been asserted by both sides in the Korean War, the Vietnam War and the Nigerian-Biafran War. She admitted, however, that the need extensively to argue the problem indicated that the principle was "fairly fragile".[63] Her report also examined the difficulties of defining military objectives and the civilian population and indicated various methods of approaching this task. Other authors at this time who argued in favour of the principle of distinction included Sydney Bailey[64] and Frits Kalshoven.[65] The latter, in particular, attacked the notion of "quasi-combatants", either in city attacks or in guerilla warfare. Once one starts on this road, he argued, the rule of distinction becomes eliminated. Concerted attacks on civilians, he affirmed, are in any event ineffective for military purposes. Taking into account recent trends he concluded:

> "There is some hope left that it will prove possible effectively to restore the principle of distinction between the belligerents and the civilian population."[66]

As far as State *opinio juris* is concerned, the United States Department of Defense indicated in 1972 its opinion on the law relating to the protection of civilians during hostilities.[67] After approving United Nations General Assembly Resolution 2444, 1968, as declaratory of existing customary international law, the Department stated as follows:

> " ... it is recognised by all States that they may not lawfully use their weapons against civilian population or civilians as such, but there is no rule of international law that restrains them from using weapons against enemy armed forces or military targets. The correct rule of international law which has applied in the past and continued to apply to the conduct of our military operations in Southeast Asia is that "the loss of life and property must not be out of proportion to the military advantage to be gained".

On the eve of the Diplomatic Conference that was to create the Additional Protocols, we can conclude that there existed at that time a certain consensus of State opinion in favour of the principle of distinction(68), i.e. that the civilian population should not be made the object of attack and that civilians are to be spared as much as possible. Academic opinion had also begun to recognise this change, albeit somewhat cautiously.(69) The general opinions of this period (1968-1973) were in effect very similar to those of the 1930's on the eve of the Second World War. Without the Protocols, customary law of this time was necessarily as fragile as that of the 1930's, perhaps worse, because of mounting civilian casualties and memories of the Second World War which had certainly not died. Here the parallel hopefully ends, for the creation of these treaties, after very long and serious negotiations, has crystallised the principle of distinction in a way that can only be done by a treaty.

3. The principal provisions on the protection of civilians in the Protocols

A. General

One of the most significant aspects of the preparation of the Protocols is that the Conference was attended by virtually all States in existence at that time, including the major military powers, as well as a number of liberation movements who participated as observers. They are thus the first major treaties on humanitarian law that were directly contributed to by new States. This is important in that such States can identify with the result, whereas they have all too often reasonably complained that international law has been principally created by western powers.

The Protocols also represent the only recent codification (the last being in 1907) of the entire question of the conduct of hostilities. The negotiators of the Conference faced the realities of modern conflict squarely in the face. Unlike the balloon declarations of 1899 and 1907, and the Hague Rules of 1923, negotiators did not conclude a treaty that looks pleasant on paper, but which will not be applied in practice. Those which expect to find civilians virtually immune from hostilities within its provisions will therefore be disappointed. Experience has shown only too well that attempts to limit military effectiveness are not only useless, but also dangerous because States feel free from unreasonable constraints and therefore free to follow their own counsel. In this sense, the customary law of Lieber's time was easy: actual means of combat were limited in their effect and restrictions forbade useless suffering. The law was the normative result of actual military practices. These days the means of combat can destroy the world thousands of times over. Aviation and guerilla warfare, in particular, make it no longer so obvious as to what is purely useless suffering. Military practice is to some extent a guide of today's law but not totally, as it has resulted in losses that have been recognised as excessive. The Protocols therefore attempt to limit the use of military capabilities whilst preserving a combatant's ability to win within these rules, which is essential for the Protocols' survival. These two concerns are not inherently contradictory as they might at first seem. Military effectiveness involves economy of force and thus the need to concentrate on the real military strength of the opponent. Targeting of civilians is not only inhumane, but also wasteful, and far from destroying their will to resist, it usually strengthens it.

Finally it might be mentioned that the Protocols do not address the use of nuclear weapons. States excluded them from its ambit in order to retain the deterrent effect of such weapons. This does not in itself justify the use of such weapons, their legality or otherwise being governed by the rules of customary law. The Protocols are in no way jeopardised by this omission for they deal with the reality of today's conflicts which in practice do not use nuclear weapons.

B. Protocol I

Part IV of Protocol I containing thirty-one articles, is devoted to the protection of the civilian population. Nineteen of these are concerned with protection against the direct effect of hostilities. The most important of these, as it contains the general principle, is to be found in Article 48 at the beginning of Part IV:

> "In order to ensure respect for and protection of the civilian population and civilian objects, the Parties to the conflict shall at all times distinguish between the civilian population and combatants and between civilian objects and military objectives and accordingly shall direct their operations only against military objectives."

This paper does not permit a full explanation of all the relevant articles, but the major areas now regulated in this Protocol will be assessed.

(a) Bombardment

The principal provisions regulating bombardment are Articles 51-53, 56-57 and 59-60.

Article 51(2) states that the "civilian population as such as well as individual civilians, shall not be made the object of attack". This prohibition applies to all means of such attack, i.e. both aerial, artillery and missile bombardment as well as infantry attack. The rest of Article 51 in effect provides detail as to how to give effect to this provision as well as to the general principle in Article 48. Article 57 is to be read together with Article 51, as it provides for the precautions that the commander must take in order to fulfil his duties under Article 51.

However, before going into further detail, some definitional provisions are necessary. The most important of these are the definitions of military objectives and of the civilian population.

Military objectives are defined in Article 52(2) as:

> "those objects which by their nature, location, purpose or use make an effective contribution to military action and whose total or partial destruction, capture or neutralisation, in the circumstances ruling at the time, offers a definite military advantage".

This definition avoids the pitfalls of the 1923 Hague Rules by refraining from giving a list of actual objects. As such, it provides the military commander with sufficient discretion to assess the need to target certain objects or places. A definition more restrictive than this would certainly not have been accepted by military experts, and the definition as it stands reflects the fact that the Protocol was significantly contributed to by such military personnel. What this definition clearly excludes, however, is the bombardment of targets which might vaguely further the attackers' war effort. Civilian "morale" is plainly excluded[70] as well as commercial activity of no great importance for the opponents' defence. Article 52(3) is also aimed at preventing the destruction of all unidentified buildings on the assumption that they might be being used in a hostile way. Overtly civilian objects are to be considerd as such unless there is reason to believe otherwise.

The second important definition is that of "civilian" and the "civilian population". Article 50(1) gives a negative definition, by stating that civilians are all those persons who are not members of the armed forces, within the meaning of Article 4 of the Third Geneva Convention 1949 and Article 43 of the Protocol. Paragraph (2) states that the civilian population comprises all persons who are civilians.

The value of this definition is enormous, as it puts to rest all arguments in favour of "quasi-combatants" such as advocated by Stone. The total rejection of the notion of "quasi-combatants" is reinforced by Article 51(3) which states that:

> "Civilians shall enjoy the protection afforded by this Section, unless and for such time as they take a direct[71] part in hostilities."

Thus working in munitions factories, or otherwise supplying or supporting the war effort does not justify the targeting of these civilians in their homes. This provision was essential to avoid the massive attack of urban areas under this pretext.

Returning to the operational provisions of Article 51, these are basically aimed at the protection of the civilian population through the prohibition of "indiscriminate attacks". The purposeful targeting of civilians as such being, it will be remembered, forbidden by Articles 48 and 51(2). Indiscriminate attacks are defined as those which are not directed at a specific military objective, and the use of means of combat which cannot be directed at a specific military objective. This would exclude weapons such as the Nazi V-1 and V-2 rockets, which are, in any event, outmoded.

Target-area bombardment is forbidden by paragraph 5 of Article 51. This provision aims at regulating bombardment in populated areas. It means, in effect, that if in such an area there are a number of different military objectives that are capable of being hit separately then it is forbidden to treat the entire area in which they are situated as one large objective. A further refinement to this is provided in the second part of paragraph 5. This contains in effect the proportionality principle already postulated in the First World War and repeated in state practice prior to the conclusion of Protocol I. It recognises that in attacks on military objectives, civilian casualties are frequently unavoidable, but requires the commander to consider beforehand the extent of casualties to be expected from the bombardment. He then has to make an assessment of the value of the bombardment compared with the likely civilian loss, and if the latter is excessive in this context, then it cannot be continued. Such an assessment is inevitably subjective to some extent, and certainly depends entirely on the tactical situation at the time. It is impossible to state that a factory is worth x civilians and such a ludicrous interpretation is not meant. If, for example, the destruction of a bridge has a crucial importance for the success of a particular campaign, higher casualties will be tolerable to achieve this than, for example, the destruction of a munitions factory of secondary importance.

It should also be noted that the principle of proportionality is being interpreted by some States as applying to the effects of a particular attack as a whole, rather than solely in relation to the incidental damage around one object. Thus the United Kingdom on signing the Protocol, and Netherlands and Italy on ratification, stated that:

> "in relation to paragraph 5(b) of Article 51 and paragraph 2(a)(iii) of Article 57, ... the military advantage anticipated from the attack is intended to refer to the advantage anticipated from the attack as a whole and not only from isolated or particular parts of the attack."

This approach should be acceptable if seen within the context of a given tactical operation: such an operation may necessitate, for example, the destruction of six military objectives, one of which, being particularly difficult to get at, might involve far greater casualties than the other five. The attack of that one objective on its own might be of no great use, but within the context of the operation as a whole, absolutely essential. The yardstick, in this example, would be the number of casualties overall in relation to the value of the operation as a whole.

It should at this point be stressed that Articles 51 and 57 can only require a State Party to try its best to limit damage and to apply the provisions in good faith. This self-evident fact is recognised by the use of words "feasible" and "may be expected" in Article 57 paragraph (2) which outlines the precautions to be taken by the commander before launching an attack. This decision can only be based on the facts he has before him after he has in good faith collected as much intelligence as possible in the circumstances.

Further, it would be fallacious to imagine incidental damage as only constituting a circle of damage around the destroyed military objective. Although the accuracy of weapons has improved over the years, targeting whether from the air or from the surface, still remains a major problem. Hays Parks noted this problem as follows:

> "Despite the development of sophisticated computer systems, many variables influence the accuracy equation. With conventional ... munitions, one combat-experienced pilot has noted that bombing remains an inherently inaccurate process ... Aiming errors, boresight errors, system computational errors all act to degrade the system. Unknown winds at altitudes below the release point and the 'combat degradation' factor add more errors to the process. In short, it is impossible to hit a small target except by sheer luck ...".[72]

The pilot is frequently also acting under the stress of anti-aircraft defences, preventing him from making as careful an aim as possible. Damage which may seem the result of totally indiscriminate action may well therefore be due to the causes just described.

The result of all this is that the poor civilian is certainly not immune from aerial bombardment, far from it. These provisions of the Protocol have, however, limited the damage that has to be expected by preventing the deliberate targeting of civilians or a callous indifference to their casualties when planning military operations. As such it is a great achievement, and the fact that military needs are fully taken into account only serves to reinforce the applicability of those rules.

It might also be mentioned that the provisions just described apply to all military operations that are aimed at inflicting damage to the enemy. Article 49 makes it clear that the term "attack" is meant not only for forward offensive actions, but also for defensive operations. Thus the laying of a mine-field would be subject to the same principles, as well as other attacks not amounting to "bombardments" as such.[(73)]

As far as ground attacks are concerned which are aimed at the immediate occupation of the attacked place, the same rules apply. As such this is an improvement on traditional customary law which did not specify the distinction between civilian and military objects whilst bombarding such defended areas. The Protocol also reaffirms the notion of the undefended place in Article 59 and the uselessness and thus illegality of attacking it. This Article is however conceived for modern times, defining the meaning of an undefended place, as cities are no longer made "open" for occupation by the mere opening of the city gates!

(b) Works and installations containing dangerous forces

Article 56 of the Protocol prohibits the attack of dams, dykes and nuclear electrical generating stations, "if such an attack may cause the release of dangerous forces and consequent severe losses among the civilian population".

This provision is, in its effect, a specific application of the proportionality principle. The prohibition is subject to two conditions, namely, that the type of attack envisaged may cause the release of such forces, and that these forces will result in severe losses among the civilian population. Thus an attack which could not cause either of these two results is not prohibited. However, as these objects are particularly dangerous, an attacker would have to be very sure of not causing these results before launching an attack. An exception to the probibition is made for cases of where these objects are used in "regular, significant and direct support" of military operations and if an attack is the only way to end such support. However, even in such a case, the general rule of proportionality in Article 51 is still applicable.

This author is of the opinion that military considerations are amply taken care of in this Article, and criticims are often based on a misunderstanding of its provisions.[74] It would be unfortunate if such misunderstanding results in hasty reservations to this Article, as damage from bombed nuclear power plants, in particular, is to be measured in terms of decades, and the widespread targeting of such plants barely bears thinking of. The results of such a scenario i.e. widespread radiation sickness and cancers are bound to be disproportionate to the military tactical value that the plants might have had during the war.

(c) Starvation of civilians

Article 54 of Protocol I definitely breaks new ground. The starvation of civilians in certain circumstances was as has already been seen,[75] an accepted method of combat in customary law, provided that such starvation was achieved in accordance with customary practice. These were essentially, siege and general devastation.

The purpose of a siege was to induce a defended place to surrender by preventing any supplies from entering the place, or anyone from leaving the place and thus easing the shortages inside. A similar result was achieved from the sea by the use of a "blockade".[76]

Article 54, paragraph 1, declares that:

"Starvation of civilians as method of warfare is prohibited."

The effect of this is not to outlaw siege and blockade as such, but they may not be carried out in such a way as to starve the civilians within the besieged area. This author is unimpressed with arguments to the effect that siege and blockade are not affected because their purpose is surrender and not starvation.[77] The purpose of all warlike acts is the surrender of the enemy. Humanitarian law merely imposes limitations on the methods of achieving such surrender.

In order to conduct a successful siege without starving civilians, the only available method is to allow relief shipments through as provided for in Article 70 of the Protocol. That Article guarantees that such supplies go to civilians only by various safeguards including their being supervised by the Protecting Power, or its substitute.

General devastation, namely the destruction of property on a wide scale, including crops, was allowed in customary law if essential for the preservation of the force. Hall, for example, would have allowed the invader to cut the dykes of Holland to save himself[(78)] (now forbidden under Article 56 of the Protocol). Spaight added that devastations have also been used to deprive the enemy's forces of supplies and shelter. They were, however, only justified as an extreme measure of military necessity, and this was confirmed in Article 23(g) of the Hague Regulations and in the Nuremberg trials.[(79)]

It might also be noted that the *British Manual of Military Law*[(80)] states that although water in wells, pumps, reservoirs, rivers etc. may not be poisoned there is no rule preventing their being dried up or diverted.

Article 54 discards all these old customs, and tackles the problem from the point of view of the survival of the civilian population on the one hand, and military necessity on the other. This article forbids the destruction or otherwise rendering useless objects indispensable for the survival of the civilian population, giving a list of examples of such objects. Destruction is allowed, however, of objects used solely for the members of the armed forces, or for their direct support, provided that in the latter case, the civilian population is not left destitute.

Action similar to general devastation is only allowed by a party to a conflict on its own national territory, if imperatively necessary for its national defence.

(d) Guerilla warfare

The most important provision of the Protocol, as far as the protection of civilians in a guerilla war context is concerned, is the definition of civilians in Article 50. As we have already seen,[(81)] the major problem was the notion of "quasi-combatants" being applied to persons indirectly supporting the guerillas, in particular, by feeding and sheltering them. Article 50 firmly excludes this notion by defining civilians as those who do not belong to the armed forces as such. Of especial importance for guerilla warfare is paragraph 3 of Article 50 which states that the "presence within the civilian population of individuals who do not come within the definition of civilians does not deprive the population of its civilian character". Thus a general attack on a village e.g. in which guerillas are known to shelter is not justifiable and a genuine attempt must be made to distinguish between civilians and guerillas. If certain persons in a village are peasants by day and guerillas by night, they should be preferably attacked whilst engaging in their belligerent activities. Although it is not forbidden to attack or capture by day persons known to be members of guerilla groups it is clearly forbidden under the Protocol to attack the entire village in order hopefully to include the guerillas amongst the casualties.

As far as guerilla behaviour is concerned, Articles 43 and 44 of the Protocol (on combatant and prisoner-of-war status) are conceived to encourage the guerilla to comply with humanitarian law. These Articles recognise the factual existence of guerillas, and detractors of Protocol I are not going to make guerillas disappear by refusing to legally recognise them.[82] Their principal allegation is that Article 44(3) puts civilians at greater risk because it would allow prisoner-of-war status to guerillas who do not wear uniforms but only carry their arms openly. However, it must be remembered that this is the exception to the rule and only allowed where it would be suicidal to wear uniform, namely, in enemy-controlled areas. Guerillas in practice do not wear uniform in such situations and therefore the Protocol does not encourage behaviour which is not at present already widespread. On the other hand, by allowing prisoner-of-war status to such guerillas if they abide by the law of war, guerillas themselves should be encouraged to aim their attacks only at military objectives and spare civilians. It goes without saying, however, that the hopes of this new approach can only succeed if guerilla groups have sufficient knowledge of humanitarian law to make them workable.

(e) Reprisals

The Protocol goes a long way towards the prohibition of reprisals against protected objects and persons. Those which concern us here, in particular, are the prohibitions of reprisals against the civilian population and civilians (Article 51(6)); against objects indispensable to the survival of the civilian population (Article 54(4)); and against works and installations containing dangerous forces (Article 56(4)).

The prohibition of reprisals has led to bitter criticism by critics of the Protocol, who say that reprisals are the only effective law-enforcement mechanism during armed conflict.[83] Certain delegations also expressed misgivings to this effect during the Diplomatic Conference negotiating the Protocol.[84] It should be remembered, however, that for every reprisal threat which has prevented a violation, there are hundreds of violations of the law masquerading as reprisals. Not only does the resort to reprisals tend to degenerate into forbidden counter-reprisals but they also provide an excuse for outright violations. Thus, far from being a law-enforcement mechanism, they have tended to be a law-avoidance mechanism. It has tended to be civilians who have borne the brunt of this. Reprisals following the bombing of cities are particularly likely to degenerate as they depend on a subjective assessment of the illegality of the opponent's actions.[85] As we have seen, civilian damage frequently results from inaccuracy and other errors and the proportionality equation is not evident for the receiver of the damage, as he does not know the tactical plans of the opponent.

Reservations to these provisions should therefore be avoided or at least very carefully and restrictively formulated, particularly as they are reciprocal in effect.

(f) Other provisions protecting civilians

Space prevents a full assessment of all remaining provisions benefitting the civilian population but the following are particularly worthy of note.

Article 55 provides that care should be taken to protect the natural environment against widespread, long-term and severe damage. Damage during warfare is unfortunately inevitable, and this Article is not meant to cover the type of damage caused through normal conventional warfare but through methods that would result in damage over a large area lasting for decades.

Article 58 of the Protocol urges Parties to avoid placing military objectives within or near densely populated areas. The deliberate placing of civilians during a conflict in such a way as to shield military objectives is forbidden in Article 51(7), and therefore Article 58 addresses itself to longer-term planning. It recognises, however, that it is not always possible to clearly separate civilian and military installations.

Finally, Articles 72-79 provide an important extension of protection to persons in the power of the enemy, by including those not covered by Geneva Convention IV 1949. Particularly important is Article 75 which provides basic human rights-type guarantees to all civilians.

C. Protocol II

Although the Lieber Code was written for a civil war, international law did not traditionally regulate internal conflicts. The first modest attempt appeared in Article 3 of the Geneva Conventions of 1949,(86) and Protocol II of 1977 was not adopted without difficulty.(87) The ICRC's draft Protocol II was very similar to that of Protocol I, but the final document is a drastically reduced version of the original one. The only benefit of this is that Protocol II is simpler and quicker to read than Protocol I.

As far as the conduct of hostilities is concerned, Protocol II includes the fundamental provisions found in Protocol I. Article 13, in particular, states that the civilian population as well as individual civilians shall not be the object of attack, and that they shall enjoy this protection "unless and for such time as they take a <u>direct</u>(88) part in hostilities". Although the detailed definition of a civilian is not included in this Protocol, nor the detailed provisions relating to bombardments, it is clear that this provision is meant to avoid the characterisation of large parts of the civilian population as "quasi-combatants".

Article 14 provides for the protection of objects indispensable to the survival of the civilian population in a similar way to Protocol I but without its detail, and the same is true for Article 15 which prohibits attacks against dams, dykes and nuclear power stations.

What these Articles conspicuously lack is the careful assessment of military needs in relation to these basic prohibitions in favour of the civilian population. As, however military needs will not thereby disappear in fact, it is to be hoped that further guidance will be taken from the provisions of Protocol I. Protocol II also provides for humane treatment of persons in the power of the enemy, including civilians, thereby going into greater detail than common Article 3.

Despite the high threshold for the applicability of Protocol II, it is to be hoped that it will have an effect on the conduct of these wars. This is particularly important as a large number of internal wars involve international elements without being characterised as international as such. The existence, however, of the prohibition, in black and white, on the targeting of civilians during hostilities in these wars is of immense importance.

4. Conclusion

The 1977 Additional Protocols have liberated the law of armed conflict from rules stemming from old outdated practices, and have addressed the regulation of the conduct of hostilities from the basic point of view of the balance between military and humanitarian needs. They are modern instruments catering for the realities of today. This is particularly true for Protocol I which regulates hostilities in some detail. As such, these instruments are bound to have an effect beyond the behaviour of only those who have ratified.(89) The mere fact of having a modern set of rules, largely reflecting recent customary law, written in black and white, is likely to affect the development of future customary law. This is because they provide a concrete reference for behaviour. To complete this process, however, it is very important that the major military powers ratify both Protocols. It would be tragic if non-ratification based on overcaution or misunderstanding of certain articles were to undermine the achievement of these instruments. The maximum protection of civilians that is realistically possible within modern war is provided for the first time in treaty form and it can only be hoped that this achievement remains.

FOOTNOTES

* The views expressed are personal and do not necessarily reflect those of the International Committee of the Red Cross.

1. The law regulating the protection of victims as developed within the Geneva Conventions.

2. The so-called "Articles of War", later developing into "Military Manuals". For a general description of the development of the law on the conduct of hostilities in relation to the protection of civilians, see W. Solf, "Protection of civilians against the effects of hostilities under customary international law and under Protocol I", 1 *The American University Journal of International Law and Policy*, 1986, p. 117.

3. Hence the use of uniform to clearly distinguish such professionals.

4. *Instructions for the Government of Armies of the United States in the Field*, 1863. Prepared by Francis Lieber at the time of the American Civil War.

5. Emphasis added.

6. Articles 17 and 18.

7. Article 16.

8. Article 23(g) Regulations Respecting the Laws and Customs of War on Land, Annex to the 1907 Hague Convention Respecting the Laws and Customs of War on Land.

9. See in particular G. Best, *Humanity in Warfare*, 1980, pp. 89-96.

10. Article 21.

11. Article 22.

12. Article 23.

13. Article 25. These are sometimes referred to as "open" cities i.e. open for immediate occupation.

14. Article 27.

15. Article 26.

16. Article 28.

17. Text to note 12.

18. Emphasis added.

19. J.M. Spaight, *Air Power and War Rights*, 2nd ed., 1933, p. 240.

20. Declaration (IV, 1) of 29th July 1899 to Prohibit, for the Term of Five Years, the Launching of Projectiles and Explosives from Balloons, and Other New Methods of Similar Nature.

21. Which never took place.

22. However, legal tribunals deciding on war criminality after that war still spoke of the notion of "defended" or "undefended" during the aerial bombardment of cities. See, for example, the cases of *Coenca Bros. v. Germany* (1927) and *Kyriadolou v. Germany* (1930) where the Greco-German Mixed Arbitral Tribunal held that the prohibition of attacking undefended cities continued to apply to attacks from the air.

23. In so doing, States borrowed from a notion that already existed to some extent in relation to naval bombardment, albeit very imperfectly. By the nineteenth century it was recognised that defended enemy coastal towns could be bombarded, whether such forces were acting in co-operation with a besieging army or not. However, it remained a controversial question whether undefended coastal towns could be bombarded, the problem being that such undefended towns could not be occupied by the naval forces. The 1907 Hague Convention IX Concerning Bombardment by Naval Forces in Time of War attempts a kind of compromise solution: it provides that in all bombardments, all necessary measures should be taken as far as possible to spare certain buildings dedicated to charity etc., whereas in bombardments against undefended towns, only certain defined military objects could be attacked. Bombardment was also allowed to force the town to comply with requisitions, if necessary.
This treaty retains, therefore, the rather illogical distinction between defended and undefended towns, even when occupation is not possible. It gives insufficient protection to "defended" towns (like in The Hague Regulations), but creates an embryonic notion of a military objective for "undefended" towns.

24. J.M. Spaight, *op.cit. supra* note 19, p. 197.

25. See, e.g. L. Oppenheim, *International Law* vol. II, 7th ed. p. 519.

26. Article 24(1).

27. Article 24(2): "Such bombardment is legitimate only when directed exclusively at the following objectives: military forces; military works; military establishments or depots; factories constituting important and well-known centres engaged in the manufacture of arms, ammunition or distinctively military supplies; lines of communication or transportation used for military purposes.

28. Article 24(3)(4).

29. Spaight lists a number of such attacks as including, e.g. factories producing iron, electric works, gas works, motor works, oil and petroleum depots or refineries, steel works, warehouses and waterworks; *op.cit. supra* note 19, at pp. 223-225.

30. "La protection des populations civiles contre les bombardments: Consultations juridiques", ICRC, 1930.

31. See, in particular, the replies of Mr. W. Royse (USA) and Lt.Gen. MacDonogh (UK).

32. League of Nations Paper A.69, 1938, IX, 28th September 1938, Protection of Civilian Populations against Air Bombardment.

33. J.M. Spaight, *Air Power and War Rights* 3rd ed., 1947 p. 271.

34. See D. Johnson, *Rights in Air Space*, 1965, pp. 48-49.

35. J.M. Spaight, *op.cit. supra* note 33, at pp. 279-280.

36. *Ibid*, p. 278.

37. *U.S. v. Ohlendorf*, IV Trials of War Crimes before the Nuremberg Military Tribunals, 1948, pp. 446-467.

38. Part II.

39. Article 14.

40. Article 15.

41. See, for example, D. Johnson, *op.cit. supra* note 34, pp. 55-56, and Schwarzenberger, *The Legality of Nuclear Weapons*, 1958, p. 21.

42. G. Schwarzenberger, *op.cit. supra*, note 41, at pp. 19 and 21-22.

43. *International Law Vol. II Armed Conflicts*, 1968, pp. 157-159.

44. J. Stone, *Legal controls of international conflict*, 1954, p. 609.

45. *Ibid.* pp. 630-631.

46. L. Oppenheim, *International Law*, vol. II, 7th ed., p. 525.

47. *Ibid.* p. 529. See also D. Johnson, *op.cit. supra* note 34, in which the author stated in 1965 that international law permits "strategic" bombing, but forbids "terror-bombing" (p. 57).

48. *Ibid.*, p. 530.

49. *Manual of Military Law*, Part III: The Law of War on Land, 1958, para. 86, note 2(b).

50. *Ibid.* paras. 283 and 288.

51. FM 27-10, 1956.

52. Emphasis added.

53. Para. 42.

54. *International Law*, vol. II, 1962. DA PAM 27-161-2.

55. The Draft Rules were presented to the XIXth International Conference of the Red Cross, New Delhi 1957. They were approved in principle at the time, but governments did not agree to take any further action.

56. M. Veuthey, *Guerilla et Droit Humanitaire*, 2nd ed., 1983, p. 271. For a resume of the principal characteristics of guerilla warfare, see *ibid*, pp. 368-370.

57. Resolution XXVIII of the 20th International Conference of the Red Cross, October 1965.

58. Until that time, the United Nations took no interest in humanitarian law, on the basis that it is contradictory with the prohibition of the use of force in the Charter. Practice showed, however, that the need for the regulation of conflicts in progress was still essential.

59. Resolution XXIII adopted by the International Conference on Human Rights, Teheran, 12th May 1968.

60. United Nations General Assembly resolution 2444 (XXIII) adopted 19th December 1968.

61. United Nations General Assembly resolution 2675 (XXV) adopted 9th December 1970.

62. D. Bindschedler-Robert, "A reconsideration of the Laws of Armed Conflicts", 1970, Conferences on Contemporary Problems of International Law I, Carnegie Endowment for International Peace.

63. *Ibid*. p. 20.

64. S. Bailey, *Prohibitions and Restraints in War*, 1972, especially pp. 77-79.

65. F. Kalshoven, *The Law of Warfare*, 1973.

66. *Ibid*. p. 41.

67. Letter from the General Counsel of the Department of Defence to Senator Edward Kennedy, Chairman of the Subcommittee on Refugees of the Committee of the Judiciary, 1973, *AJIL*, pp. 122-125.

68. See in particular W. Hays Parks, "Conventional Aerial Bombing the Law of War", *Proceedings Naval War Review*, 1983, p. 98, where he describes the application of the principle of distinction and proportionality in the Vietnam War.

69. Some authors do not see a change in customary law between the Second World War and the adoption of the Protocols e.g. H. Meyrowitz, "Le bombardement strategique d'apres le Protocole additionnel I aux Conventions de Geneve", 41 *Zeitschrfit fur auslandisches offentliches Recht und Volkerrecht*, 1981, p. 1. Da Saussure, writing in 1979, thought that the rules prohibiting area bombardment in Protocol I were inconsistent with customary law and, in his opinion, air operational necessity. H. de Saussure, 4 *Annals of Air and Space Law*, 1979, p. 459.

70. Further, the second sentence of Article 52(2) states that: "Acts or threats of violence the primary purpose of which is to spread terror among the civilian population are prohibited".

71. Emphasis added.

72. *Op.cit. supra* note 68, at p. 112. This Article is a very good description of the operational problems connected with aerial bombing, within the context of the law of war.

73. It might also be mentioned that the duty to warn of an attack when this is possible is also applicable to all types of attack, including defensive ones such as laying minefields. The possibility of warning and how this could be done must be guided by common sense which will inevitably include the safety of the attacker. Such warnings have, however, taken place and are therefore not unrealistic.

74. See, e.g. G. Roberts, "The New Rules for Waging War: the Case against Ratification of Additional Protocol I", 26 *Virginia Journal of International Law* 6, 1985, p. 709 at pp. 155-159.

75. *Supra.*, pp. 159-160.

76. It might also be mentioned that the traditional right in naval warfare of capturing enemy goods caused shortages, and "conditional contraband" i.e. food for enemy soldiers, could be similarly captured. Although Protocol I does not affect naval warfare as such, practices directly affecting civilians on land are included (Article 49).

77. E.g. H. Meyrowitz, "Le Protocole Additionnel I aux Conventions de Geneve de 1949 et le droit de guerre

maritime", 89 *Revue Generale de Droit International Public*, 1985, p. 245 at p. 271, and C. Mudge, "Starvation as a means of warfare", 4 *The International Lawyer*, 1970, p. 228.

78. Quoted in J.M. Spaight, *op.cit. supra* note 19, p. 242.

79. *The trials of Jodl; Wilhelm von Leeb and others; Wilhelm List and others* (quoted in Oppenheim, *op.cit. supra* note 45, at pp. 415-416). The latter two were not convicted for unjustified devastation, as they were carried out during the retreat of the army in arduous conditions and may thus have been necessary. Spaight cited Sheridan's and Sherman's devastations of Virginia, Georgia and the Carolinas in 1864-1865 and Kitchener's devastation of the Boer Republics in 1901-1902 (*op.cit. supra* note 19, at p. 242).

80. *Supra* note 49.

81. *Supra* pp. 175-176.

82. See, in particular, G. Roberts, *op.cit. supra* note 74, and D. Feith, "Law in the service of terror - The strange case of the Additional Protocol", *The National Interest*, No. 1, Fall 1985, p. 36.
For excellent replies to these allegations, see G. Aldrich, "Progressive Development of the Law of War: A reply to criticisms of the 1977 Geneva Protocol I", 26 *Virginia Journal of International Law*, 1986, p. 693; W. Solf, "A response to Douglas J. Feith's 'Law in the service of terror - The strange case of the Additional Protocol' ", 20 *Akron Law Review*, 1986, p. 261; H.-P. Gasser, "An appeal for ratification by the United States", 81 *A.J.I.L.*, 1987, p. 912.

83. E.g. G. Roberts, *op.cit. supra* note 74, at pp. 139-146.

84. E.g. Canada and France recorded in H. Levie, *Protection of War Victims*, 1980, pp. 134 and 163 respectively. These delegations argued that one cannot stand by and watch one's cities being bombed without being able to respond in kind.

85. Initial attacks on civilians on land and at sea in the Second World War were justified as reprisals, as well as, for example, the series of city bombardments in the Iran/Iraq

war in the spring of 1983 and 1985 and the winter of 1986-1987.

86. For a description of the effects and shortcomings of Article 3 of the 1949 Geneva Conventions, see J. Bond, "Internal Conflicts and Article 3 of the Geneva Conventions", 48 *Denver Law Journal*, 1971.

87. For a comprehensive account of the development of Protocol II, see D. Forsythe, "Legal management of internal war: The 1977 Protocol on non-international armed conflicts", 72 *American Journal of International Law*, 1978, p. 272.

88. Emphasis added.

89. See, for example, B. Carnahan, " 'Linebacker II' and Protocol I: The convergence of law and professionalism", 31 *American University Law Review*, 1981-1982, p. 861, where the author argues that the U.S. bombings of Hanoi in December 1972 were in conformity with the rules of Protocol I.

PART III

HUMANITARIAN ASSISTANCE

CIVIL DEFENCE AND INTERNATIONAL LAW[(1)]*

Adam Roberts

The status of civil defence in international law can easily appear arcane. Civil defence - that is, measures to protect the civilian poulation from the effects of war and disasters - may be thought to have problems enough to cope with in the nuclear age without needing to be the subject of disputations as to what international law does or does not say about it.

However, the provisions of international law with respect to civil defence are worth exploring for several reasons. One consideration of a not entirely technical character, is that for the first time the subject has been addressed systematically in a treaty: in Part IV, Section I, Chapter VI, of the 1977 Geneva Protocol I. As its title makes clear, the whole of this laws of war agreement relates to 'the protection of victims of international armed conflicts', and is thus in one way or another germane to civil defence. Up to now, what the Protocol says directly on civil defence has naturally attracted less attention than what it says on other subjects, such as combatant status. Yet the Protocol could have a bearing on the manner in which humanitarian tasks are carried out in armed conflicts, on the treatment by belligerents of those engaged in such tasks, and also on centrally important military matters, obviously relevant to civil defence, such as targeting.

A further reason for this exploration is that with civil defence, as with a number of other subjects, examining it through the prism of international law may contribute something to an under standing of the subject itself. International law, whether customary or in treaty form is the product of a great deal of experience, of extensive diplomatic exchanges, and of very different national view points. In short, looking at civil defence in an international law perspective may be one way of getting beyond the elements of parochialism, and of preoccupation with purely topical issues, which have characterised many discussions of the subject.

* For footnotes see p. 200.

Yet another reason for considering the international legal aspects of civil defence is that in creasingly - whether in time of peace or war-civil defence activities themselves may have an international dimension. Certain dangers - including fall-out from nuclear accidents and nuclear weapons explosions - are not confined to a single country. They may require complex international systems of monitoring and notification. Moreover, certain civil defence activities may require an element of international assistance. The need for some practical rules to cope with such problems is apparent.

The Chernobyl nuclear reactor fire in April 1986 showed only too clearly the importance of being able to cope with nuclear disasters which fall short of full-scale nuclear war. This disaster led very promptly to the drafting, under the auspices of the International Atomic Energy Agency, of two conventions, which were opened for signature on 26th September 1986: first, the Convention on Early Notification of a Nuclear Accident; and second, the Convention on Assistance in the Case of a Nuclear Accident or Radiological Emergency.[2] This was a tribute, albeit belated, to the importance of having at least some international legal framework for protecting populations from certain dangers.

This paper addresses the following questions:

1. What is civil defence?

2. What provisions relating to civil defence are there in the laws of war?

3. Is there an international legal obligation on States to provide civil defence preparations?

4. Is there an international legal obligation on States to keep possible military targets separate from densely populated areas?

5. During a conflict can special designations of cities or zones offer possibilities of protecting the civilian population.?

6. Is there an international legal obligation on States not to obstruct civil defence and relief activities in a conflict?

There has been relatively little written about legal aspects of civil defence. True, the subject of the status of civil defence in domestic law has received some attention, especially in the UK just before and during the Second World War.[3] But the international law aspects of civil defence attracted almost no attention then.[4] They have only recently begun to attract attention - in the form, exclusively, of short commentaries on the relevant provisions of the 1977 Geneva Protocol I.[5] One reason for the relative dearth of attention to the international law aspects of civil defence may be that for the most part (though by no means always) civil defence activities do not involve direct contact with the armed forces of the adversary: so they have not called out for international regulation to anything like the same extent as, say, treatment of prisoners of war. However the idea that civil defence can be left entirely to municipal law and to the varying policies of different governments has been challenged since at least 1949 and is certainly now outdated.

1. What is Civil Defence?

Civil defence is conceived of, and organised, very differently in different countries. In some countries it has been viewed as being largely, if not entirely about the question of protecting populations from the effects of large-scale nuclear war. Perhaps because of the grimness of this question and the possible failure of deterrence which it seems to imply, it has been a controversial subject and almost a taboo one. It has attracted very little serious academic attention.[6]

(a) The UK Preoccupation with Armed Hostilities

In Britain, the main legal basis of civil defence, the Civil Defence Act 1948, contains in Section 9 a definition of civil defence which relates exclusively to armed hostilities, and not at all to peacetime emergencies:

> Civil defence ... includes any measures not amounting to actual combat for affording defence against any form of hostile attack by a foreign power or for depriving any form of hostile attack by a foreign power of the whole or part of its effect ...

The Civil Defence Act 1948 makes provision in Section 8 for civil defence regulations of which there have been a large number over the years.[7] They echo the 1948 Act in being concerned above all with the question of hostile attack. Within this framework, since 1983 the extensive guidance issued by the Home Office to local authorities has identified three particular cirucmstances which civil defence planning must encompass: periods of international tensions, conventional attack, and nuclear attack.

This British preoccupation with civil defence as being concerned solely with hostile attack has contributed to its peacetime decline. In the post-war period it has not been well funded or supported. Indeed, it still seems to reflect the aim spelt out in the 1957 defence white paper: "In 1957-58 the main task will be to keep the existing local organisation in being, so as to provide a basis on which realistic planning can continue."[8] In 1968 the Government placed civil defence on a care and maintenance basis, and the Civil Defence Corps was disbanded. It remains the case today that there is no specific body of civil defence personnel. Civil defence is a co-ordinating concept and a series of preparations and plans rather than a specific force, and comes under the Emergency Planning Division of the Fire and Emergency Planning Department of the Home Office.

The problem that UK civil defence preparations are not geared to situations other than hostile attack was addressed in the Civil Protection in Peacetime Act passed in June 1986.[9] It specifically enabled local authorities to use their civil defence resources in peacetime to deal with emergencies and disasters unconnected with any form of hostile attack by a foreign power. Civil Protection is not a specific organisation as such. Rather it is "a useful way to describe the co-ordinated efforts of a number of people and organisations who are making plans and training to cope with effects of major emergencies, in peacetime or wartime".[10] Civil protection comes under the same division of the Home Office as civil defence.

As far as accidents involving nuclear weapons are concerned, it is not self-evident that counter measures would be organised by the Home Office through its civil defence and civil protection frameworks. There have been indications that the Ministry of Defence Nuclear Accident Response Organisation (NARO) would be in charge, jointly with the police. If an accident involved US nuclear weapons, then US contingency plans might be activated: however, there are said to be 'special arrangements' allowing the UK to maintain its sovereign rights during such emergencies.[11] All this underlines the confusingly complex and multi faceted character of UK preparations for emergencies.

Serious public discussion of civil defence has been the exception rather than the rule in the UK in the post-1945 period. When civil defence has been the subject of extensive political debate, it has been so only briefly and at times of heightened national concern about the international situation - as in the early 1960's and in 1980. Such discussions as there have been have focused on one single and fundamental policy question: whether or not there should be civil defence preparations to protect populations against major nuclear attack.[12] Questions as to whether such protection is worth pursuing at all in the nuclear age have been frequently raised and are serious. They are especially difficult because an attacker (assuming his aim is to cause maximum civilian damage) would quite possibly be able to increase the scale of an attack so as to match - or outmatch - any civil defence preparations.[13] The sheer chaos following any nuclear attack on the UK has been stressed in many expert reports.[14] Some have viewed civil defence as only useful against less than total nuclear attack.[15] There have been questions raised as to whether, within a nuclear weapons state, preparations for civil defence might not appear provocative to an adversary. A further theme in some writings has been extreme scepticism about UK civil defence preparations not only because of their inadequacy in face of massive nuclear attack, but also because they can be seen as a potentially sinister means of extinguishing public dissent and creating an authoritarian state.[16]

(b) A possible broader view

While these public debates in Britain about civil defence have undoubtedly been important, they have often neglected several legal and practical dimensions of the question. In most, if not all, of the countries where they exist, civil defence forces have numerous functions quite distinct from protection against deliberate and massive nuclear attack: they have actual or potential functions in dealing with other forms of hostile activity, including conventional war and limited nuclear attacks. They also have major peacetime functions, which could include dealing with the consequences of earthquakes, floods, nuclear weapons or reactor accidents, and fall-out from a distant nuclear war.

It is thus well to be clear at the start that the term 'civil defence' can refer not just to a particular organisation and its members, nor just to the particular task of protection against the effects of war in general or nuclear war in particular. Rather it can mean 'the performance of some or all' of a wide range of 'humanitarian tasks intended to protect the civilian population against the dangers, and to help it recover from the immediate effects, of hostilities or disasters and also to provide the conditions necessary for its survival'. These words, taken from Article 61 of the 1977 Geneva Protocol I (which is quoted in full further on), convey an unambiguously broad view of the character and functions of civil defence. This broad definition accepted for the purposes of this paper, is not necessarily the only correct definition of civil defence. Nor is 'civil defence' the only possible term to cover the performance of a range of tasks that often go under quite different names such as home defence, civil protection, and population protection.(17)

2. Provisions on Civil Defence in the Laws of War

Civil defence is not the main subject matter of any major multilateral treaties between States. However, the subject has been addressed in various ways as one subsidiary aspect of a number of law of war agreements. Civil defence thus falls within a body of law which has often proved difficult to implement once the bullets start to fly. Many questions can legitimately be raised about the legal status, scope of application, content and practical efficacy of particular laws of war agreements.(18) It is foolish to be sanguine about the possibilities of limiting by formal agreements the cruelty and destructiveness of war. However it is also true that such agreements have provided an important standard by which to assess the actions of belligerents and they have contributed to the protection of countless war victims, starting with those wounded or sick on the battlefield. For all their faults, laws of war agreements cannot be entirely neglected.

Ever since they began to be codified in the form of multilateral conventions in the second half of the nineteenth century, the laws of war have always had as one central interest the protection of victims of war. Indeed, this aspect of the laws of war, at least as it relates to the protection of some groups such as prisoners of war, has arguably been more successful than the attempt to regulate the methods and means of combat. It is perhaps surprising, therefore, that early agreements said relatively little about the protection of civilians from the effects of hostilities.

The words 'respected and protected' occur frequently in the laws of war including in provisions which relate to civil defence. They have a particular meaning in this context. The word 'protect' may sometimes (as in the 1977 Geneva Protocol I, Article 61, mentioned above) have the common colloquial meaning of taking physical measures, such as building shelters, to war off certain dangers. However, when particular individuals, activities, things or places are described in the laws of war as 'respected and protected', what is usually meant is something different: that they must not knowingly be made the target of an attack; and must be given some assistance or at least not prevented from discharging their proper functions.(19) The idea of 'protection' in this sense has changed over time: in the 1864 Geneva Convention on wounded and sick combatants it was expressed largely in terms of neutrality, but subsequent agreements, starting with the 1906 Geneva Convention, have put less emphasis on this. Subsequent agreements have also put more emphasis on the role of outside bodies in assisting protection in its various forms.

(a) Nineteenth Century Agreements

Most of the early treaties on the laws of war put much emphasis on certain basic principles which are relevant to civil defence but they are short on detail, especially as regards the means of protecting civilians.

The 1864 Geneva Convention for the Amelioration of the Condition of the Wounded in Armies in the Field specifies that personnel and institutions caring for the wounded should be treated as neutral, be respected and remain free: however, according to its specific terms it refers only to the care of wounded and sick combatants, not to that of the population as a whole.

The 1868 St. Petersburg Declaration on explosive projectiles declares in a preambular paragraph 'that the progress of civilisation should have the effect of alleviating as much as possible the calamities of war' - a sentiment echoed in numerous subsequent accords.

(b) 1907 Hague Convention IV

Both the 1899 Hague Convention II on land warfare, and the closely similar 1907 Hague Convention IV, contain many statements germane to civil defence. It is most useful to refer to the second of these agreements because that is the one to which more states are formal parties and it is also the one which was explicitly viewed by the International Military Tribunal at Nuremberg in 1946 as declaratory of customary international law.

The 1907 Hague Convention IV on land warfare says in the preamble that its wording was 'inspired by the desire to diminish the evils of war as far as military requirements permit ...' The Regulations annexed to the Convention elaborate on this. Article 21 states that the sick and wounded are to be cared for in accord with the Geneva Convention.[20] It is forbidden to declare that no quarter will be given, to employ arms calculated to cause unnecessary suffering, or to wantonly destroy people or property (Article 23). Thus, although there is no specific reference in the Hague Convention and Regulations either to civil defence forces or to all the types of activities they undertake, it might be inferred that such activities ought to be protected. In the absence of any specific rule, however, it is not absolutely clear whether civil defence personnel are entitled to the considerable degree of protection afforded to those treating sick and wounded combatants. One further provision of the 1907 Hague Regulations, namely Article 25, has some bearing on the question of the protection of civilians from air attack:

> The attack or bombardment, by whatever means, of towns, villages, dwellings or buildings which are undefended is prohibited.

'Undefended' here has a very specific meaning: open for occupation by the adversary. The concept of undefended places is broadly similar to 'open cities', and also 'non-defended localities'. These are discussed further below.

(c) The Four 1949 Geneva Conventions

The four 1949 Geneva Conventions, to which virtually all States in the world are parties,[21] do make reference to those kinds of protection activities and services which we associate with the term 'civil defence'. However, what these conventions say on this subject is for the most part curiously indirect, dealing for example with the application of civil defence to particular groups such as prisoners of war and internees. Thus the 1949 Geneva Convention III (the Prisoners of War Convention), Article 23, paragraph 2, says:

> Prisoners of war shall have shelters against air bombardment and other hazards of war, to the same extent as the local civilian population. With the exception of those engaged in the protection of their quarters against the aforesaid hazards, they may enter such shelters as soon as possible after the giving of the alarm. Any other protective measure taken in favour of the population shall also apply to them.

The 1949 Geneva Convention IV (the Civilians Convention) is a little more explicit. Articles 13-26 (i.e. Part II of the Convention) deal with the general protection of populations against certain consequences of war. Article 14 provides for the establishment of 'hospital and safety zones and localities'. The purpose of such zones is 'to protect from the effects of war, wounded, sick and aged persons, children under fifteen, expectant mothers and mothers of children under seven'. Article 15 deals with the closely analogous concept of 'neutralised zones', which are intended to shelter from the effects of war '(a) wounded and sick combatants or non-combatants; (b) civilian persons who take no part in hostilities, and who, while they reside in the zones, perform no work of a military character.' Neutralised zones require a written agreement by the belligerent powers.[22]

Articles 18-19 of the Civilians Convention deal with the important issue of the designation, marking and protection of civilian hospitals, which 'may in no circumstances be the object of attack'. Other articles deal with such important matters as the protection of medical personnel, the probihition of attacks on medical aircraft, and relief consignments for children.

Civil defence activities are addressed directly in Article 63, but only in the very special circumstances of foreign military occupation. Article 63 falls within the section of the

Civilians Convention dealing with occupied territories. The opening words of this article make it only too clear that the permission it gives to pursue various kinds of humanitarian activities is far from absolute. Article 63 says in full:

> Subject to temporary and exceptional measures imposed for urgent reasons of security by the Occupying Power:.
>
> (a) recognised National Red Cross (Red Crescent, Red Lion and Sun) Societies shall be able to pursue their activities in accordance with Red Cross principles, as defined by the International Red Cross Conferences. Other relief societies shall be permitted to continue their humanitarian activities under similar conditions;
>
> (b) the Occupying Power may not require any changes in the personnel or structure of these societies, which would prejudice the aforesaid activities.
>
> The same principles shall apply to the activities and personnel of special organisations of a non-military character, which already exist or which may be established, for the purpose of ensuring the living conditions of the civilian population by the maintenance of the essential public utility services, by the distribution of relief and by the organisation of rescues.

On internees, the 1949 Geneva Convention IV spells out, in Article 88, that internees in places exposed to air raids and other hazards of war are to have protection such as shelters. This article applies both to aliens in the territory of one of the belligerent powers and to inhabitants of occupied territory who are interned by the occupying power. (The terms of Article 88 are virtually identical to the paragraph quoted above from the 1949 Geneva Convention III, Article 23, paragraph 2, and are therefore not quoted here.) Finally the 1949 Geneva Convention IV, Article 95, paragraph 3, refers to the right of the Detaining Power to require internees 'to undertake duties connected with the protection of internees against aerial bombardment or other war risks'.

In summary, these provisions of the 1949 Geneva Conventions III and IV only make civil defence measures mandatory in respect of prisoners of war and civilian internees. Moreover, only in respect of occupied territory is the principle explicitly enunciated that organisations carrying out the types of functions associated with civil defence should not be interfered with. While there appears to be an expectation that States will protect their own civilian population, there is no specific reference to any wider obligation on States to provide civil defence services - presumably because that was seen at the time as a matter between States and their own citizens, and therefore one in which international law need not get involved. Further, there is no specific reference to any protection measures against nuclear weapons or their effects. Overall, the protection accorded to civil defence in the 1949 Geneva Conventions is much less absolute than the protection accorded to, say, civilian hospitals.

(d) The 1954 Hague Cultural Property Convention

The 1954 Hague Cultural Property Convention makes extensive provision in Articles 8-10 for sheltering works of art etc. in refuges, for the public identification of such refuges and for their immunity from attack in war. Although there is an element of the permissive in some of these provisions, the whole convention is based on a presumption that States will do what they can to protect cultural property. Some seventy-five States are parties to the Convention. However, neither the United Kingdom nor the USA are parties: although they signed it in 1954 they have not yet ratified.

(e) The 1977 Geneva Protocol I

The 1977 Geneva Protocol I is the only major laws of war treaty to refer at all systematically to civil defence. The Protocol as a whole deals with very many different aspects of international armed conflicts and is additional to the 1949 Geneva Convention.

The Protocol has, up to now, far fewer parties than the 1949 Geneva Conventions.(23) Among the many states which have signed but not ratified are Canada, the UK, the USA and the USSR.

The principal obstacle to more extensive ratification of the Protocol has been the position adopted by the USA. It signed the Protocol in 1977, subject to two understandings, but it has not ratified. This has reinforced hesitations about ratification among the USA's allies and adversaries. As outlined by President Reagan, the US position is based first and foremost on the view that the Protocol would 'give recognition and protection to terrorist groups'; and also on a view of the

Joint Chiefs of Staff that 'a number of the provisions of the Protocol are militarily unacceptable'.[24] These views have been vigorously challenged; but the significant point here is that the US objections appear not to be based on the Protocol's provisions regarding civil defence.

The position of the UK in respect of the Protocol is similar. It signed in 1977 but has not yet ratified. When signing, the UK said in its understanding (i) that "the new rules introduced by the Protocol are not intended to have any effect on and do not regulate or prohibit the use of nuclear weapons', but there has never been any suggestion that this is or the similar US declaration relates to the provisions directly on civil defence.[25] Other UK understandings at the same time included two relating to Article 58 which is partly about civil defence, and is discussed further below. So far as is known, the reasons for non-ratification by the UK are not in any way connected to the provisions on civil defence.

Even though the UK and the USA are not at present formally bound by this agreement in the sense of being a party to it, they may well be willing to carry out a part of the agreement about which they have not expressed any reservation, especially to the extent that it can be viewed as a codification of existing customary law, as an elaboration of already existing provisions in the four 1949 Geneva Conventions, or in other agreements, or as inherently worthwhile.[26]

The 1977 Geneva Protocol I contains many provisions with a bearing on civil defence. These provisions were the product of some twenty years of diplomatic effort since at least the time of the International Red Cross Conference in New Delhi in 1957.[27] The actual negotiations leading to agreement on this subject in the 1977 Geneva Protocol I were clearly very difficult.[28] The most conspicuous of the Protocol's provisions on civil defence comprise Part IV, Section I, Chapter VI (Articles 61-67).

However, there are also in Protocol I many other Articles with a bearing on the subject some of which break new ground while others restate well-known principles. Thus Article 48 largely reaffirms existing rules:

> In order to ensure respect for and protection of the civilian population and civilian objects, the Parties to the conflict shall at

> all times distinguish between the civilian population and combatants and between civilian objects and military objectives and accordingly shall direct their operations only against military objectives.[29]

Other key provisions in the 1977 Geneva Protocol I which have a bearing on civil defence include the requirement that belligerents limit their attacks to military objectives (Articles 51, 52 and 57), and the emphasis on the protection of objects indispensable to the survival of the civilian population (Article 54).

A crucially important Article in Protocol I, so far as civil defence is concerned, is Article 58. The article as a whole requires certain precautions to be taken against the effects of attacks. In so doing, it establishes the basic principles for the detailed provisions on civil defence which follow. It says in full:

> The Parties to the conflict shall, to the maximum extent feasible:
>
> (a) without prejudice to Article 49 of the Fourth Convention, endeavour to remove the civilian population, individual civilians and civilian objects under their control from the vicinity of military objectives;
>
> (b) avoid locating military objectives within or near densely populated areas:
>
> (c) take the other necessary precautions to protect the civilian population, individual civilians and civilian objects under their control against the dangers resulting from military operations.

The wording of this article strongly suggests that there is an obligation on a State to protect its own population as well as that in occupied or enemy territory.[30] That there is such an obligation is perhaps indicated by the fact that Switzerland, upon signature of the 1977 Geneva Protocol I, considered it necessary to make a formal declaration in respect of Article 58: 'Bearing in mind that this article contains the words "to the maximum extent feasible", paragraphs (a) and (b) will be applied under reservation of the requirements of the defence of the national territory.' This was reaffirmed as a formal reservation, with almost identical wording, when Switzerland ratified the Protocol on 17th February 1982.

In somewhat similar vein, the UK, at signature, declared in its understanding (b) that in Articles 41, 57 and 58 'the word "feasible" means that which is practicable or practically possible, taking into account all circumstances at the time including those relevant to the success of military operations'. The UK understanding (d) also encompassed Article 58, but, like its understanding (b), this referred more to the conduct of military operations than to the obligation to protect one's own population.(31)

Articles 59 and 60 of the 1977 Protocol I deal respectively with 'non-defended localities' and 'demilitarised zones'. The former may be declared unilaterally by the appropriate authorities of a Party to the conflict: the latter have to be the subject of agreement between adversaries.

On the basis of some of the provisions mentioned above, especially Article 58, the 1977 Geneva Protocol I goes on in Articles 61-67 (i.e. Part IV, Section I, Chapter IV) to deal explicitly with civil defence. Also Articles 68-71 (i.e. Part IV Section II) deal with the subject (which may be closely related in particular conflicts) of relief in favour of the civilian population.

'Civil defence', its organisations, personnel and material are defined for the first time in international law in Article 61 of the 1977 Geneva Protocol I:

Article 61 - Definitions and scope

For the purposes of this Protocol:

(a) 'civil defence' means the performance of some or all of the undermentioned humanitarian tasks intended to protect the civilian population against the dangers, and to help it to recover from the immediate effects, of hostilities or disasters and also to provide the conditions necessary for its survival. These tasks are:.

(i) warning;

(ii) evacuation;

(iii) management of shelters;

(iv) management of blackout measures;

(v) rescue;

(vi) medical services, including first aid, and religious assistance;

(vii) fire-fighting;

(viii) detection and marking of danger areas;

(ix) decontamination and similar protective measures;

(x) provision of emergency accommodation and supplies;

(xi) emergency assistance in the restoration and maintenance of order in distressed areas;

(xii) emergency repair of indispensable public utilities;

(xiii) emergency disposal of the dead;

(xiv) assistance in the preservation of objects essential for survival;

(xv) complementary activities necessary to carry out any of the tasks mentioned above, including, but not limited to, planning and organisation;

(b) 'civil defence organisations' means those establishments and other units which are organised or authorised by the competent authorities of a Party to the conflict to perform any of the tasks mentioned under sub-paragraph (a), and which are assigned and devoted exclusively to such tasks;

(c) 'personnel' of civil defence organisations means those persons assigned by a Party to the conflict exclusively to the performance of the tasks mentioned under sub-paragraph (a), including personnel assigned by the competent authority of that Party exclusively to the administration of these organisations;

(d) 'materiel' of civil defence organisations means equipment, supplies and transports used by these organisations for the performance of the tasks mentioned under sub paragraph (a).

These definitions provide the legal basis for the protection of civil defence. They are, it should be noted, essentially functional in character: the important criterion is the type of tasks performed by an individual or unit rather than the particular name or organisational set-up.[32] However, the following articles show rather clearly that the new protection established by this chapter of the Protocol is not of any and every civil defence activity but relates to such activities when they are clearly distinct from participation in hostilities.

Article 62 introduces the term 'civilian civil defence organisations', which is discussed further below; and it specifies that their personnel 'shall be respected and protected' and 'shall be entitled to perform their civil defence tasks except in case of imperative military necessity'. Civilians who, even if they are not members of such organisations, perform civil defence tasks under their control are similarly protected.

Article 63 deals with a special problem, namely civil defence in occupied territories. Its detailed terms reflect the special considerations which apply to such territories of which two may be mentioned here: the concern that the inhabitants should continue to be protected from the dangers of hostilities and disasters even when their own government has been supplanted by a foreign military occupation; and the parallel concern that the occupying power should not in any way use civil defence in a manner prejudicial to the interests of the inhabitants.

Article 64 deals with another special problem, namely the status of outside civil defence organisations (e.g. from states which are not parties to the conflict) and also international co-ordinating organisations when they perform civil defence tasks in the territory of a party to the conflict, or indeed in occupied territory. The work of such organisations is subject to the same protection and conditions as any other civilian civil defence organisation.

Article 65 specifies that the protection to which civilian civil defence is entitled may cease if it is used to commit acts harmful to the enemy. This article is but one expression of a concern that civil defence might get entangled with, or be used as a cover for, military operations. It reflects the basic rule, spelt out in Article 48, of maintaining a clear distinction between the civilian population and combatants. Article 65 goes into some detail in its second, third and fourth paragraphs about how certain acts, the carrying of certain light weapons, and the organisation of civilian civil defence along military lines, should not deprive civilian civil defence of protection. Inevitably, some areas of uncertainty remain: for example, there is likely to be scope for dispute as to whether certain particular actions are protected, such as repairing a bridge which is vital both for the civilian population of a country and also for its military operations. Such areas of uncertainty are familiar to students of the laws of war and are absolutely inevitable. Article 65 paragraph 1, tries to get round this problem by the device sometimes difficult to observe in practice - of requiring a warning: 'Protection may, however, cease only after a warning has been given setting, when ever appropriate, a reasonable time-limit, and after such warning has remained unheeded.'

Article 66 requires all aspects of civil defence to be clearly identifiable through the use of distinctive signs and signals: it establishes, for the first time, an international distinctive sign for civil defence, in the shape of a blue triangle on an orange ground.

Article 67 deals with the status of military personnel who may be assigned to civil defence organisations: this was a very sensitive question in the negotiations, as military participation in civil defence could clearly affect its civilian character, and could hence have a bearing on its entitlement to protection from attack by an adversary. Yet the fact is that the character and functions of civil defence vary greatly from country to country, and its civilian or exclusively humanitarian character is not always clear: hence the need for this Article. It tackles the problem by specifying that military personnel assigned to civil defence units shall be protected and respected provided that they meet certain conditions. These conditions, briefly summarised, are that they are permanently assigned and exclusively devoted to the performance of civil defence tasks; that they do not perform any other military duties during the conflict and do not participate directly in hostilities; that they are clearly distinguishable from the other members of the armed forces, for example by displaying the international distinctive sign for civil defence; that they are equipped only with light individual weapons to maintain order or for self-defence; and that they perform their civil defence tasks only within their national territory.

These conditions as spelt out in Article 67 are clearly controversial.[33] Two of the problems which they pose merit discussion here. The first is that there would seem on the face of it to be a contradiction between these conditions and what is said about combatant status in Article 43(2) of the Protocol:

> Members of the armed forces of a party to a conflict (other than medical personnel and chaplains covered by Article 33 of the Third Convention) are combatants, that is to say, they have the right to participate directly in hostilities.

So it would seem that under Article 43 military personnel assigned to civil defence are combatants, but under Article 67 they do not have the right to participate directly in hostilities. There are various ways in which this apparent contradiction can be explained, but it may not be of enormous practical importance anyway. The provisions of Article 67 makes it clear beyond doubt that such personnel should be respected and protected. Moreover, whether viewed as combatants or not, they are still entitled to prisoner-of-war status if captured.[34]

A second problem which is thrown into sharp relief by the terms of Article 67 is this: what is the status of civil defence activities conducted on an *ad hoc* and temporary basis by military units or personnel? If such activities do not meet the strict conditions laid down in Article 67, are they protected? The answer would appear to be that they are not protected under the Protocol's Chapter VI, which deals with civil defence. Nevertheless, to the extent that such activities, however they may be organised, are clearly directed to civil purposes, they could possibly benefit from the general protection of the civilian population, civilian objects etc. which permeates the entire Protocol.(35)

As for the separate but related subject of relief in favour of the civilian population, the 1977 Geneva Protocol I adds to the already substantial provisions of the 1949 Geneva Convention IV. Article 69 places an obligation on the occupying power to provide for basic needs in occupied territories. Article 70 says that if the civilian population within a belligerent state is not adequately provided with supplies, then humanitarian and impartial relief actions shall be undertaken, and facilitated by the parties to the conflict. Clearly in the aftermath of any use of nuclear weapons in war such relief from outside, including from abroad, would be desperately needed, and would be entitled to protection.

In summary, the 1977 Geneva Protocol I is explicit, where previous treaties are much less direct, in defining civil defence and other measures to protect and provide relief for the civilian population; and in specifying that such measures are entitled in certain circumstances to protection from attack and interference. All in all, the terms of this Protocol, and especially Article 58, militate in favour of such policies as: (a) limited evacuation of civilians from areas near military objectives; (b) avoiding locating military objectives in or near cities; and (c) taking other measures to protect the civilian population from the effects of military operations.

3. An Obligation on States to Provide Civil Defence?

Can one say that there is actually an international legal requirement that individual States provide civil defence preparations for their own citizens? And, if there is such a requirement, does it cover preparations against the effects of nuclear war? To a large extent, these questions are about the relations between a State and its own citizens - an area in which international law does not always rush to get involved.

In the 1949 Geneva Conventions there seems to have been an expectation that there will be shelters for the local civilian population against the hazards of war. But this is not expressed in terms of a formal legal requirement; and one would have to press a rather fragile argument by analogy (that if prisoners of war and civilian internees are entitled to shelters, then so must ordinary civilians be) in order to attempt to establish that such a definite requirement existed in the 1949 Conventions.

The 1977 Geneva Protocol I, Article 58(c), requires the parties to take the 'necessary precautions to protect the civilian population'. This is the clearest legal obligation on States to provide civil defence. This obligation, like the rest of the Protocol, applies first and foremost in wartime, but there is no doubt that it has also to be translated into measures to be taken in peacetime.[36]

Some questions inevitably arise about the nature of this obligation to provide civil defence. For one thing, Article 58 is qualified by the words 'to the maximum extent feasible' which call for comment. Clearly civil defence cannot be expected to do the impossible and protect people from every imaginable scale and pattern of nuclear attack. So whether Article 58 necessarily calls for those specific precautions (e.g. shelters) most commonly associated with the term civil defence may possibly be debatable.

Further, if the obligation exists, who is to hold a State to it? This kind of obligation on States is first and foremost an obligation on their governments, which must interpret and apply the international legal provisions by which they are bound. It may be that failure to provide civil defence could be viewed as a cause for complaint by another State - for example a neighbouring State fearing an influx of refugees. Whether it could be viewed as a breach of human rights or a failure to observe the minimum international standard must be more debatable.

To the extent that there is an international legal obligation on States to provide civil defence, that might constitute an argument which would be used by a government against a local authority if it were to embark on a very extreme course of refusing to provide any civil defence preparations at all against any kind of danger, nuclear or otherwise.

4. Separation of Military Targets from Populated Areas

Is there an international legal obligation on States to keep possible military targets separate from densely populated areas? This is just one of a host of quite general laws-of-war questions which is germane to civil defence: it bears on the likelihood of cities being subject to attack; on the chances of civil defence facing threats sufficiently limited that it can be useful; and also on the possibilities (or otherwise) of keeping civil defence separate from military defence.

The question has many distinct aspects, which cannot all be explored here. It affects not only the conduct of military operations (e.g. targeting so as to avoid civilians) but also the organisation of society (e.g. so siting possible military targets and human habitations that an attack on the former would not put civilians at risk).

In the laws of war - and indeed in more general considerations of war and security - the entire issue of the distinction between legitimate military targets on the one hand, and civilian objects, places and people on the other, has a long and tangled history.

Defining a 'military objective' is far harder than might at first appear. In the 1907 Hague Convention IX on naval bombardment, Article 2, there is a list of military objectives, but it can hardly be viewed as exhaustive. In the 1954 Hague Cultural Property Convention, Article 8(1)(a), refuges for such property are supposed to be 'situated at an adequate distance from any large industrial centre or from any important military objective constituting a vulnerable point such as for example, an aerodrome, broadcasting station, establishment engaged upon work of national defence, a port or railway station of relative importance or a main line of communication'. The 1977 Geneva Protocol I, Article 52(2), offers a somewhat abstract definition of military objectives. The difficulty, even in theory, of defining what is military and what is civilian, and then of keeping them at a distance from each other is obviously immense.

In practice, rules against attacks on non-military targets have often proved fragile in twentieth-century warfare. This is partly because of the sheer difficulty of clearly identifying military targets and confining an attack to them; partly because war is a political activity, in which belligerents have political objectives and may think they can gain results by attacks on civilian targets; partly because weaker powers sometimes resort to the desperate measure of attacking what are seen as easy, vulnerable or rewarding targets; and partly because, through a process of escalation, an isolated, limited or accidental attack on a civilian target can lead to a general breakdown of international legal restraints.

Nuclear weapons add a new dimension to this problem. The theory of nuclear deterrence is often seen as dependent, to a greater or lesser extent, on holding out the prospect of destroying an adversary's society - and is thus inevitably in tension with laws of war ideas about restraint and discrimination. This may have been one consideration underlying the UK and US declarations that the new rules in the 1977 Geneva Protocol I do not regulate or prohibit the use of nuclear weapons.

Yet however difficult and fragile the distinction between the military and the civilian may be, especially in crowded modern industrial states, it is at the heart of most of our ideas about what is or is not a legitimate target. Moreover common prudence suggests that there is some merit in keeping likely military targets as far away as possible from centres of civilian population. The terms of the 1977 Geneva Protocol I, Article 58(a) and (b) strongly suggest that, at least as far as conventional war is concerned, there is an obligation on governments to keep the civilian population away from military objectives and vice versa - if only 'to the maximum extent feasible'.

In the UK, as in many countries, keeping civilians apart from military objectives can never be easy to achieve. For example, neither the Ministry of Defence nor Heathrow Airport, both potential military targets in a war could be moved away from London without negating their normal peacetime purposes. In all small and crowded countries a separation of military objectives from the civilian population presents special difficulties. However, more might be achieved in this direction, and this points to the need for a thorough reconsideration of all likely military targets in and around towns and cities with a view to their possible relocation to more remote places. The extent to which this can be achieved without causing massive inconvenience and inefficiency, or making military targets more vulnerable to attack, must be doubtful.

In a hypothetical future war with the USSR, any serious violation by the UK or its allies of rules restricting attacks to military targets could clearly lead to comparable attacks by Soviet forces on similar western targets. Against this background, the notable British emphasis on achieving deterrence by maintaining a capacity for nuclear strikes against Soviet cities, including Moscow, raises problems.(37) Any initiation of such strikes would clearly pose special risks for the inhabitants of British cities. This capacity might theoretically be justified as providing a basis for a reprisal in case UK cities are attacked, and nothing more. However the implication of most official statements is that this capacity has a broader strategic purpose, to deter a wide range of attacks.(38)

The fact that there is a NATO policy of possible first use of nuclear weapons means that there is an apparent absence of restriction on other matters as well as on targeting. Overall, successive UK governments have been notably reluctant to make clear statements about the applicability of laws of war restraints to the use of nuclear weapons.(39) US policy on nuclear targeting appears to allow greater scope for discrimination between civilian and military targets. In general, the US has accepted the idea that basic principles of the laws of war do apply also to the use of nuclear weapons.(40) Moreover, successive annual reports of the US Secretary of Defense to Congress have stated that 'under no circumstances could nuclear weapons be used for the purpose of destroying populations'.(41) These positions suggesting the possibility of using nuclear weapons in a less than all-out manner, no doubt reflect the fact that a superpower with a large nuclear arsenal can afford to be more discriminating than a smaller power with a nuclear deterrent of last resort. A superpower may also be in a better position to think in terms of counter-force rather than counter-value strategies - that is, attacking the adversary's military installations etc. rather than cities and civilian targets. However, counter-force strategies present notorious problems, not least because they can encourage arms races and can fuel fears of pre-emptive strikes. Whether they are a contribution to stability may be doubted.

5. Specially Designated Cities and Zones

The idea of particular areas being given a special designation of some kind, and being protected from attack, has arisen frequently both in laws of war agreements, and in military operations. This idea is simply a formal and precise extension of the idea of keeping military targets and civilian populations distinct. It is germane to civil defence for the same reasons.

Many different forms of protected zones can be found in international agreements. The 1907 Hague Regulations, Article 25, refer to 'undefended' towns, villages dwellings or buildings - meaning that they are open for occupation by the adversary, but should not be attacked or bombarded. The 1949 Geneva Convention IV, Article 14, refers to 'hospital and safety zones and localities'; and in Article 15 to 'neutralised zones'. The 1977 Geneva Protocol I, Article 59, refers to 'non-defended localities' which can be declared unilaterally and are open for occupation by the adversary; and Article 60 to 'demilitarised zones', which can only be declared by agreement, and are not open for occupation.

These legal concepts have some similarities to the idea of 'open cities', of which there was a good deal of experience in the Second World War.[42] In recent years there has been some discussion in West Germany as to whether the 'open cities' idea could have relevance to West German security problems in the context of a possible East-West war. The main objection appears to be that a network of 'open cities' could in the event provide a chequerboard for enemy advance.

Overall, there is bound to be some scepticism as to whether the concept of specially designated cities and zones can make a major contribution to reducing the costs of a future war. The record of past efforts in this direction is not altogether encouraging.[43] There can be many motives for a State to attack such a zone: fear that, despite protestations to the contrary, it is being used for military purposes of one kind or another; desire to retaliate against a perceived violation by the adversary; desire to induce the adversary to retaliate in kind, so reducing his direct threat to hard-pressed military forces; and a belief that attacking such a 'soft' target will hasten the end of the war. That these motives may at times be mistaken does not necessarily make them less potent.

If special designations of one kind or another could be effectively established (whether unilaterally or by agreement between adversaries), then additional possibilities of protecting the population might emerge, even in the event of a war in which some nuclear weapons were used. Even within such areas, civil defence might well be needed, both to protect against the effects of war such as radioactive fallout, and to cope with possible direct violations of the protected status. Such zones, too, could be useful as centres to which victims of warfare outside them could be taken. Their overall effect, in some limited conflicts at least, might be to assist the performance of civil defence functions.

6. An Obligation not to Obstruct Civil Defence?

Is there an international legal obligation on States not to obstruct civil defence and relief activities in a conflict? The question has obviously to be answered in the affirmative, but many difficult problems remain.

The net effect of all the provisions of the 1949 Geneva Conventions is that there is an obligation on the parties not to obstruct *bona fide* civil defence activities. However, this obligation is reinforced and given much more precision in the 1977 Geneva Protocol I.

In the chaotic context of a war, and especially one in which nuclear weapons were used, the exact practical effect of this obligation would be far from clear. The most important practical effect often relates to the provision of assistance, including from abroad, during or immediately after a war. There is an obligation on the parties not to obstruct such assistance, both in civil defence specifically and in relief actions more generally, at any rate as long as an armed conflict or occupation continues and the assistance meets the various conditions laid down in the Protocol.

7. Conclusions

This paper has only touched on very limited aspects of the subject. It has not addressed the question of civil defence in internal conflicts - a matter on which the 1977 Geneva

Protocol II (on non-international armed conficts) is largely silent.[44] It has said nothing about the complex question of the position of civil defence in human rights law.[45] It has only touched tangentially on some of the many complex policy issues involved in civil defence. In short, this paper is nothing more than an initial foray into a subject which, for perfectly understandable reasons, has been long neglected.

Any provisional evaluation of the laws of war provisions in respect of civil defence must begin with a note of scepticism. If civil defence activities are, as their very name implies, civilian in character anyway, then why should they need special protection? Is not the protection of civil defence activities in war likely to be no better, and no worse, than the protection of civilians generally? Is there not a risk of creating needless categories and distinctions, all on the admirable but insecure foundation of a belief that belligerents will be willing to confine their attacks to targets which are military in character?

Against this, a defence of the laws of war provisions on civil defence runs as follows: civil defence activities can only too easily be interpreted as quasi-military in character, because they can involve uniformed groups of people acting in areas where combat has been taking place, attempting to reverse certain effects of the adversary's military action, and in some cases acting under the direction and control of the military authorities. Granted all these elements of ambiguity, there is a need for some ground rules on the basis of which the civilian *bona fides* of civil defence activities can be established, and proper means of identification worked out: exactly the things the 1977 Geneva Protocol I seeks to do.

The laws of war provisions on civil defence are significant not just because they do the obvious, and seek to protect civil defence. They are also significant because they appear to create an obligation on governments to provide civil defence - not just for special categories of person in whom there is an international interest, such as prisoners of war and inhabitants of occupied territory but also more generally. The exact nature of this obligation, and what it means in actual practice, may be interpreted differently by different governments: but its existence in some form, at least for parties to the 1977 Geneva Protocol I, is not in doubt.

Perhaps the most important implication of the laws of war provisions on civil defence is to strengthen the legitimacy of civil defence activities in peacetime as well as in wartime. Against the background of the 1977 Geneva Protocol I it would be hard to sustain a claim that civil defence activities constitute preparations for aggressive war, or indicate that a State is belligerent in intent.

Finally, the laws-of-war provisions on civil defence, and especially Article 61 of 1977 Geneva Protocol I, may contribute to a change in the ideas about civil defence that are held in many States. These provisions may strengthen ideas to the effect that civil defence is something distinct from the main body of the armed forces; is essentially civilian in character; is concerned with a very wide range of military threats, and not just the apocalyptic possibility of total nuclear war; and also has a significiant role in peacetime disasters - whether familiar ones such as flood and earthquake, or modern ones such as Chernobyl 1986.[46]

FOOTNOTES

1. This paper is a substantially revised version of one originally prepared for the Greater London Area War Risk Study in December 1985. I am grateful to Hans-Peter Gasser, Legal Adviser to the Directorate, International Committee of the Red Cross, for his comments on an earlier draft; to members of the Discussion Group on the Laws of Armed Conflict of the British Institute of International and Comparative Law for their suggestions after a version of the paper was presented at a meeting on 14th December 1987; and to Air Commodore George Innes, Chief Emergency Planning Officer of the London Fire and Civil Defence Authority, for enlightenment on the organisational basis of civil defence in the UK.

2. The provisions of these two 1986 IAEA Conventions are usefully summarised in *American Journal of International Law*, vol. 81, no. 3, July 1987, pp. 646-53. For details of numerous other agreements in related fields, see *Nuclear Law Bulletin*, founded in 1968 and published in two issues per annum by the Nuclear Energy Agency of the Organisation for Economic Co-operation and Develop-

ment, Paris. On 31st March 1988 the UK and the USSR initialled an agreement on nuclear safety, including the disclosure of nuclear accidents. See also Philippe Sands (ed.), *Chernobyl: Law and Communication*, Grotius Publications, Cambridge, 1988.

3. See for example Donald Hamilton, *The Civil Defence Act 1939 as it Affects Employers and Property Owners*, Jordan, London, 1939; T.S. Simey and Mary L. Williams, *The Civil Defence Acts 1937 and 1939*, Knight, London, 1939; R. Wynne Frazier, *The Law of Civil Defence*, Solicitors' Law Stationery Society, London, 1940; and Leslie Maddock, *Maddock's Civil Defence Acts and Orders 1939-1941*, Eyre and Spottiswoode, London, 1941. None of these works makes any reference to international law.

4. The exception that proves the rule was J.B.S. Haldane, *A.R.P.*, Gollancz, London, 1938. Haldane's advocacy of air-raid precautions included a brief discussion (pp. 58-61) of international law, but this was only to note regretfully the absence of specific prohibitions of bombing. He concluded: 'International law no longer exists in any serious sense ...'.

5. Two English-language works of this type are Erik Schultz, *Civil Defence in International Law*, Danish National Civil Defence and Emergency Planning Directorate, Copenhagen, September 1977; and Dr. Bosko Jakovljevic, *New International Status of Civil Defence: as an Instrument for Strengthening the Protection of Human Rights*, Martinus Nijhoff, The Hague, 1982. Both these short works (89 and 142 pages respectively) are essentially text and brief commentary on 1977 Geneva Protocol I, Articles 61-67.

6. For a recent exception, referring to much of such writing as there has been on civil defence in the nuclear age, see the useful comparative study of civil defence planning, Lawrence J. Vale, *The Limits of Civil Defence in the USA, Switzerland, Britain and the Soviet Union: the Evolution of Policies since 1945*, Macmillan, London, 1987.

7. The text of the Civil Defence Act 1948 is in *Halsbury's Statutes of England*, 3rd edn., vol. 38, Butterworths,

London, 1972, pp. 505-514. The texts of regulations issued between 1949 and 1983 in accord with the Act are in *Halsbury's Statutory Instruments*, vol. 4, Butterworths, London, 1986, pp. 133-161.

8. *Defence: Outline of Future Policy*, Cmnd. 124, HMSO, April 1957, p. 3.

9. Civil Protection in Peacetime Act 1986, *The Law Reports: Statutes 1986*, Part 2, p. 299. This was the outcome of a private Member's Bill moved by Sir Nicholas Bonsor MP several months before the Chernobyl disaster gave the subject topicality. On the thinking behind this Act see particularly the debate on the second reading on 21st February 1986, *House of Commons: Official Report*, sixth series, vol. 92, cols. 587-627.

10. *Civil Protection*, booklet prepared by the Central Office of Information for the Home Office, HMSO, 1986, p. 24.

11. Mark Urban, 'Police Chief Contradicts US Weapons Disaster Plan', *The Independent*, London, 2nd April 1988.

12. The preoccupation with nuclear war as the main problem which civil defence has to address was very evident in the UK, at least up to 1983. For example, a House of Lords debate on Home and Civil Defence on 5th March 1980 (*House of Lords Official Report*, vol. 406, no. 92, pp. 260-388) dealt almost entirely with the utility of civil defence in relation to nuclear attack rather than other possible threats. In May 1980 the government published its booklet on the subject, *Protect and Survive*, which described what people should do 'if nuclear weapons are used on a large scale'. This inspired E.P. Thompson's riposte, *Protest and Survive*, published first as a pamphlet and then as part of E.P. Thompson and Dan Smith (eds.), *Protest and Survive*, Penguin Books, Harmondsworth, 1980: this, like the government booklet it denounced, was preoccupied with the single issue of nuclear attack as the raison d'etre of civil defence.

13. Professor Lawrence Freedman has expressed this view succinctly: 'For practically all offence-defence duels the cost-exchange ratios dramatically favour the offence' - Royal United Services Institute for Defence Studies (ed.), *Nuclear Attack: Civil Defence*, Brassey's, Oxford, 1982,

p. 50. In the same volume, p. 169, Peter Evans said that the British government neither had plans to evacuate people from big cities, nor did it intend to set aside money for the general provision of shelters. For an official UK account of the scientific considerations relating to civil defence against nuclear attack, see the Home Office booklet, *Nuclear Weapons*, HMSO, London, 1975.

14. See for example the British Medical Association's report, *Selection of Casualties for Treatment after a Nuclear Attack*, Professional Division Reports, London, May 1988.

15. One serious study of civil defence which puts some emphasis on its value 'in relation to a war scare, non-nuclear attacks, and even in the unlikely event of a small nuclear attack', but not in relation to a major nuclear attack, is Robin Clarke (rapporteur), *London under Attack: the Report of the Greater London Area War Risk Study Commission*, Blackwell, Oxford, 1986. See especially the conclusions at p. 303.

16. The two most notable books taking this critical view of UK civil defence preparations are Peter Laurie, *Beneath the City Streets*, Allen Lane The Penguin Press, London, 1970; and Duncan Campbell, *War Plan UK*, Burnett Books, London, 1982.

17. I have in the past favoured changing to the term 'population protection' on several grounds, not least that it clearly distinguishes civil defence from the quite distinct concept of 'civilian defence' i.e. a policy of defence based on civil (non-violent) resistance against invasion etc. However, the terms 'civil protection' and 'civil defence' have secured wide acceptance: especially the latter, not least in the 1977 Geneva Protocol I. Thus a change in nomenclature to 'population protection' would now be hard to achieve.

18. The full texts of the various treaties etc. on the laws of war are to be found in Dietrich Schindler and Jiri Toman (eds.), *The Laws of Armed Conflicts: A Collection of Conventions, Resolutions and Other Documents*, 3rd edn., Martinus Nijhoff, Dordrecht, 1988. Also in Adam Roberts and Richard Guelff (eds.), *DocuAents of the Laws of War*, 2nd rev. edn., Clarendon Press, Oxford, forthcoming 1989.

19. On 'respected and protected' see Michael Bothe, Karl Josef Partsch and Waldemar A. Solf, *New Rules for Victims of Armed Conflicts: Commentary on the Two 1977 Protocols Additional to the Geneva Conventions of 1949*, Martinus Nijhoff, The Hague, 1982, pp. 108, 118 and 401; also Yves Sandoz, Christophe Swinarski and Bruno Zimmermann (eds.) *Commentary of the Additional Protocols of 8 June 1977 to the Geneva Conventions of 12 August 1949*, Nijhoff, Geneva, 1987, pp. 146-147, 166-167, and 739.

20. This is a reference to the 1906 Geneva Convention on wounded and sick combatants, a successor to the 1864 Geneva Convention.

21. There were 165 States parties to the four 1949 Geneva Conventions as at 1st July 1988. Figures supplied by the Swiss Federal Department for Foreign Affairs, July-September 1988.

22. On localities and zones under special protection, see also 1977 Geneva Protocol I, Articles 59-60, mentioned further below.

23. There were 76 States parties to the 1977 Geneva Protocol I as at 1st July 1988. Figures supplied by the Swiss Federal Department for Foreign Affairs, July-September 1988.

24. President Reagan's Letter of Transmittal to the Senate, 29th January 1987. See also the reply, entitled 'An Appeal for Ratification by the United States' by Hans-Peter Gasser, Legal Adviser to the Directorate, International Committee of the Red Cross. Both texts appear in *American Journal of International Law*, vol. 81, no. 4, October 1987, pp. 910-925.

25. The first US understanding at signature of the 1977 Geneva Protocol I was almost identical. For texts of the reservations etc. by various states at signature and/or ratification of the Protocol, see Roberts and Guelff (eds.), *Documents on the Laws of War*, pp. 461 ff.

26. There is some evidence to support the proposition that the UK may be willing to observe part or all of the provisions on civil defence in the 1977 Geneva Protocol I, regardless of ratification. For example, the Ministry of Defence has recognised the use of the international distinctive sign of

civil defence as prescribed in Article 66: see Annex D of *The Law of Armed Conflict*, a short booklet issued by the Ministry of Defence in revised form in 1981 summarising the main provisions of the laws of war.

27. On the background to the civil defence provisions in the 1977 Geneva Protocol, see Schultz, *Civil Defence in International Law*, pp. 3-6; Jakovljevic, *New International Status of Civil Defence*, pp. 7-12 and 77-81; and Sandoz et al (eds.) *Commentary on the Additional Protocols*, pp. 587, 589 and 713-716.

28. The Protocol's provisions on civil defence were only adopted 'after long and arduous negotiations', according to an official Swiss government message regarding the Protocols which was issued on 18th February, 1981.

29. For commentary on this article, pointing out the extent to which it reaffirms existing law, see Bothe, Partsch and Solf, *New Rules for Victims of Armed Conflicts*, pp. 280 286; and Sandoz et al (eds.) *Commentary on the Additional Protocols*, pp. 598-599.

30. On the significance of Article 58, and the implications of the word 'feasible' in characterising the obligation contained therein, see Bothe, Partsch and Solf, *New Rules for Victims of Armed Conflicts*, pp. 370-375; and Sandoz et al (eds.) *Commentary on the Additional Protocols*, pp. 692-695. As these sources indicate, the concern of States with densely populated territories that it would be difficult to locate military objectives away from heavily populated areas was fully voiced at the Diplomatic Conference which negotiated the text of the 1977 Geneva Protocols.

31. UK understanding (d) at signature of the 1977 Geneva Protocol I was as follows: 'In relation to Articles 51 to 58 inclusive, that military commanders and others responsible for planning, deciding upon or executing attacks necessarily have to reach decisions on the basis of their assessment of the information from all sources which is available to them at the relevant time.'

32. On the functional character of the Article 61 definitions, see Bothe, Partsch and Solf, *New Rules for Victims of Armed Conflicts*, pp. 391 and 397; and Sandoz et al (eds.) *Commentary on the Additional Protocols*, p. 719.

33. Schultz, *Civil Defence in International Law*, pp. 32-35; Jakovljevic, *New International Status of Civil Defence*, pp. 60-63 Both are critical of the rather complex provisions of Article 67. See also Sandoz *et al* (eds.) *Commentary on the Additional Protocols*, p. 797.

34. 1977 Geneva Protocol I, Articles 44(1) and 67(2). See also Sandoz *et al* (eds.) *Commentary of the Additional Protocols*, p. 800.

35. Note in particular the possible relevance in such a situation of Articles 1(2) and 51-58.

36. These conclusions about the implications of Article 58(c) are reinforced by a reading of Sandoz *et al* (eds.) *Commentary of the Additional Protocols*, pp. 692, 694-695 and 723-724.

37. On the British emphasis on attacking Soviet cities, particularly Moscow, in a future war see especially P.M.S. Blackett, *Studies of War*, Hill and Wang, New York, 1962, pp. 87-88; Andrew J. Pierre, *Nuclear Politics*, Oxford University Press London 1972 p. 295; Lawrence Freedman, *British and Nuclear Weapons*, Macmillan, London, 1980, pp. 46, 54, 60-61; and various reports of the House of Commons Defence Committee, including *Strategic Nuclear Weapons Policy*, Fourth Report of the Defence Committee, H.C. No. 36 of 1980-81, pp. viii, 83-88, 107-107 and 315. The official defence of the 'Moscow criterion' is that the Soviet Union should be 'unable to get sanctuary for Moscow and surrounding areas'. (pp. 87 and 107.)

38. Note the emphasis on a capacity for nuclear strikes against 'key aspects of Soviet state power' in *Statement on the Defence Estimates 1987:1*, HMSO, Cm.101-I, London 1987, p. 41.

39. In this connection, note the careful wording of the UK understanding (i) at signature of the 1977 Geneva Protocol I, cited on p. 218 above. This does not deny that there may be some existing rules which regulate or prohibit use of nuclear weapons. See also the 1958 *UK Military Manual*, para. 107.

40. On 10th December 1968 the US Delegation to the UN General Assembly issued a statement on nuclear weapons

and international law which included the following: 'There are indeed principles of law relative to the use of weapons in warfare, and these principles apply as well to the use of nuclear and similar weapons.'

41. United States, Secretary of Defense, *Annual Report to the Congress: Fiscal Year 1984*, Washington DC, 1st February, 1983, p. 55. See also the FY 1985 edition, p. 29, where the importance of limiting the level of destruction is stressed; and the FY 1987 edition, pp. 74-75, where these themes are strongly reiterated.

42. See W.R. Born, *Die Offene Stadt*, Gottingen, 1982. Cases of open cities during the Second World War discussed include: Warsaw in 1939; Brussels, Paris, Reims and Rotterdam in 1940; Rome in 1943; Bologna in 1944; and Constance in 1945.

43. See for example Donald Cameron Watt, 'Restraints on War in the Air Before 1945', in Michael Howard (ed.), *Restraints on War: Studies in the Limitation of Armed Conflict*, Oxford University Press, 1979, pp. 57-77.

44. On the dropping of civil defence provisions in the 1977 Geneva Protocol II, see Jakovljevic, *New International Status of Civil Defence*, pp. 64-65.

45. The idea that civil defence is 'endeavouring to protect and assure the advancement of certain human rights' is advanced by Jakovljevic on p. 24. This view has some force, but civil defence could in extreme circumstances involve taking some very harsh decisions, putting the community above the individual, or the government before the citizens. The 1977 Geneva Protocol I, Article 63, recognises this possibility, so far as occupied territories are concerned, when it prohibits various acts which might be prejudicial to the civilian population.

46. The artificial separation of civil defence and disaster relief is reflected in the fact that no reference to civil defence is to be found in Peter Macalister-Smith, *International Humanitarian Assistance: Disaster Relief Actions in International Law and Organization*, Martinus Nijhoff, Dordrecht, 1985, nor in the Sands book on Chernobyl mentioned in n.2 above.

DEVELOPMENT OF THE LAW GOVERNING RELIEF OPERATIONS

*Michael A. Meyer**

The two 1977 Protocols additional to the 1949 Geneva Conventions provide increased protection for civilians during international and non-international armed conflicts. The establishment of provisions pertaining to relief operations is one important way in which this enhanced protection is achieved. These articles on relief law are significant not only from humanitarian and practical operational viewpoints. They also illustrate the need to achieve a realistic balance between the interests of the State or military forces and those of humanity. Such a balance has been inherent in the Law of War since its inception.[(1)]

1. International Armed Conflicts

Additional Protocol I of 1977 covers international armed conflicts. Such conflicts are defined in Article 1 of the Protocol and include not only those situations falling within Article 2 common to the four Geneva Conventions of 1949 (such as undeclared wars and belligerent occupation), but also struggles against colonial domination, alien occupation and racist regimes, within the meaning of the United Nations Charter (sometimes called wars of national liberation).

A. Existing Law

Before the adoption of the Fourth Geneva Convention of 1949, there were no widely accepted treaty rules on the provision of relief to the civilian population. This is in contrast to the treaty provisions concerning relief for prisoners of war, which date from the 1899 and 1907 Hague Regulations (Articles 15 and 16

* For footnotes see p. 223.

in each). This discrepancy resulted from the traditional notion that civilians are outside hostilities, military operations being confined to the armed forces. On this basis it was felt that there was no need to have many treaty provisions protecting the civilian population during wartime.

In practice relief actions in favour of the civilian victims of armed conflict were undertaken without any specific legal basis or on the basis of *ad hoc* agreements. A few illustrations: The Red Cross provided assistance to civilian populations during both World Wars and between the wars, for example, during the Sino-Japanese conflict; the Commission for Relief in Belgium was active during the First World War, and the United Nations Relief and Rehabilitation Administration (UNRRA) undertook relief operations during and after the Second World War.

After the First World War, International Conferences of the Red Cross approved a draft convention for the protection of civilians, and recommended that agreements should be reached by combatants to allow certain relief goods to pass through blockades when they are intended for certain categories of civilian persons. Unfortunately the start of the Second World War prevented the conclusion of a civilians convention.

Prior to 1949, certain customary international legal principles existed which may be said to have had some relation to relief in favour of civilians. As examples: There was a requirement in warfare to distinguish between combatants which are legitimate targets and non-combatants (including civilians) which are not, and between military objectives and civilian objects. It was accepted that belligerents are not permitted to cause unnecessary suffering and that loss of civilian life should be kept to a minimum. Yet starvation of civilians was a permissible method of warfare in certain circumstances, and was usually associated with blockade and siege.

The Fourth Geneva Convention of 1949 was adopted in the aftermath of the Second World War and in many respects, reflects that experience. It concerns the protection of civilian persons in time of war and it contains a number of articles on relief during international armed conflicts.

Article 23, applicable to the whole of the populations of the countries in conflict (Article 13), only covers the transit of specified relief consignments. This provision is, perhaps, particularly relevant to situations of siege or blockade and its terms are rather restrictive. For example, the obligation to allow free passage of the limited named consignments may be superseded if the High Contracting Party concerned is satisfied that there is a serious reason to fear that a definite advantage may accrue to the enemy from the provision of such relief. There is also no reference to personnel accompanying relief consignments.

Other articles refer to relief to persons protected by the Fourth Convention, in the main those civilians in the hands of a Party to the conflict or an Occupying Power of which they are not nationals (Articles 4, 3O and 142); to aliens in the territory of a Party to the conflict (Articles 38 and 39); and in greater detail, to the population of occupied territory (Articles 55, 56 and 59-63) and to internees (Articles 108-111). Generally these provisions, which balance security requirements and humanitarian needs, are satisfactory. However no mention is made of the provision of relief to the population in non-occupied territory.

In the light of the experience of armed conflicts since the Second World War, such as the Nigeria-Biafra conflict 1967-70, the International Conference of the Red Cross and the United Nations General Assembly passed several resolutions on relief to the civilian population. These include Resolution XXVI of the XXIst International Conference entitled "Declaration of Principles for International Humanitarian Relief to the Civilian Population in Disaster Situations" (Istanbul, 1969), and Resolution 2675 (XXV) of the UN General Assembly, entitled "Basic Principles for the Protection of Civilian Populations in Armed Conflicts" (9th December 1970).

Such resolutions influenced the relief provisions of Protocol I, which remedy a number of the deficiencies of the Fourth Geneva Convention.

B. Protocol I

(a) Field of Application

The articles of Protocol I on relief in favour of the civilian population comprise Section II of Part IV on the Civilian population. Their field of application is carefully defined. Article 68 stipulates that the provisions of Section II apply to the civilian population as defined in the Protocol (i.e. in Article 50). It further states that these provisions are supplementary to the relevant articles in the Fourth Geneva Convention, many of which were cited in paragraph 1A of this paper. The significance of this last point is that these new provisions on relief do not detract from the protection provided by the existing law, but rather develop or amend it when appropriate. Examples of each will be discussed in later sections of this paper.

Article 68 makes express reference to certain provisions of the Fourth Convention, including Article 23. It might be argued that such express reference implies that when interpreting the new provisions on relief, the text of Article 23 is only altered to the extent that it is supplemented, and that the conditions it prescribes remain unaltered. It is submitted that such an interpretation would be mistaken for two reasons. First, it would be incompatible with the rules on transit of relief consignments set out in Article 70 of Protocol I. Second, when in other articles of the Protocol the pre-existing law is to be preserved, the formula "without prejudice to" is used (e.g. see Article 53 on the protection of cultural objects and of places of worship).

(b) Essential Supplies and Occupied Territories

Article 69, paragraph one, expands the range of supplies deemed to be essential for the civilian population in occupied territory. Under Article 55 of the Fourth Convention, the Occupying Power has the duty to ensure "to the fullest extent of the means available to it", an adequate supply of food and medical supplies. This obligation has been expanded in Article 69(1) to include the provision "of clothing, bedding, means of shelter, other supplies essential to the survival of the civilian population of the occupied territory and objects necessary for religious worship". The reference to "other supplies essential to the survival of the civilian population" (etc.) indicates that the list of supplies enumerated is not exhaustive. For the purposes of interpretation, it would seem logical that whether or not certain supplies are essential will depend on local conditions.

The qualification has also been added that these basic items must be provided "without any adverse distinction", that is, recipients must not be discriminated against on the basis of their political views, religion or other factors irrelevant to their requirement, on medical or humanitarian grounds, for these essential supplies. How ever relevant distinctions may be made, for example, to give extra blankets to old people or extra food to nursing mothers.[2]

The second paragraph of Article 65 begins by reaffirming that relief actions for the benefit of the civilian population of occupied territory are governed by specified articles of the Fourth Geneva Convention, including those for internees. It goes on to add two new elements to this regime of the Fourth Convention: Article 71 of Protocol I, which concerns personnel participating in relief actions, applies to these relief actions in occupied territory, and such operations "shall be implemented without delay". Thus an Occupying Power which is unable to ensure the provision of essential supplies for the civilian population, and the Powers which must permit free passage of relief consignments over their territory, have a duty to act diligently and in particular, to avoid delays caused by procedural matters.[3]

(c) Relief Operations in Non-Occupied Territories

Article 70 governs relief actions in favour of the civilian population "of any territory under the control of a Party to the conflict, other than occupied territory". This provision then will apply to relief operations undertaken in a State's own territory. Article 70 addresses not only the Party to the conflict receiving relief but also the adverse Party and each High Contracting Party to the Protocol concerned with the facilitation of such relief actions. It is important to note that because a Liberation Movement may adhere to Protocol I under Article 96(3), references to "Party to the conflict", "adverse Party" or "High Contracting Party" may include such an entity. Thus Article 70 also covers territory under the control of such a movement.

i. Duties and character of relief operations

The first paragraph of Article 70 states that if the civilian population in the non-occupied territory is not adequately provided with the essential supplies referred to in Article 69 (described in paragraph 2B above), "relief actions which are humanitarian and impartial in character and conducted without any adverse distinction shall be undertaken, subject to the agreement of the Parties concerned in such relief actions". Several elements here are worth noting.

First, the expanded range of supplies which must be provided to the civilian population in occupied territories must also be provided to the civilian population in non-occupied territory. Thus the whole civilian population benefits from the enlarged definition of essential goods in Article 69.

Second, the Party to the conflict has an obligation to permit relief actions to be undertaken if the civilian population in its territory is not adequately provided with the essential supplies. Further, a High Contracting Party in a position to do so has a duty to make every reasonable effort to contribute to such relief actions, to undertake such actions where appropriate and to allow and facilitate relief operations which private organizations of its country, such as the National Red Cross Society, are prepared to undertake.(4) In addition a High Contracting Party (including the opposing or adverse Party to the conflict) which is a potential transit State must allow and facilitate the passage of relief consignments, equipment and personnel through its territory or through a blockade. This latter obligation is elaborated in the second paragraph of Article 70. As explained below, important qualifications exist to these implied duties on potential receiving, donor and transit States.

Third, the character and conduct of these relief actions are carefully defined. They must be humanitarian (that is, directed solely at bringing relief to the civilian population lacking essential supplies and in particular, not political); they must also be impartial (that is, the relief actions must not favour one side and they must help people solely according to their needs), and the relief actions must be conducted without any adverse distinction (that is, as explained earlier, potential beneficiaries must not be discriminated against on the basis of factors irrelevant to their position as human beings in distress, such as their political opinions or religion). The condition of impartiality does not mean that a relief action cannot be undertaken for the benefit of only one Party to the conflict or for the benefit of a specific sector of the population, such as children. It only means that a relief action must not give undue advantage to one side.

Fourth, the relief actions are subject to the agreement of the Parties concerned, such as the sending, receiving and transit States. For the purposes of interpretation a Party is only concerned if the relief initiates from, passes through or is received in territory controlled by it, although because Article 70(2) refers expressly to the transit of relief, the ICRC Commentary says that in this instance, the sending and receiving Powers are the Parties concerned.[(5)] In any event the requirement of consent is an essential recognition of the sovereignty of the States or other Parties involved. It does not signify that a State whose civilian population is in need has an unfettered discretion to refuse the required relief action or that the other Parties concerned can decline to co-operate without valid reason. Such an interpretation would nullify the earlier requirement that relief actions "shall be undertaken". The qualification takes account of practical and formal realities, recognising that the Parties concerned must have a measure of control over the relief action and that for compelling, normally exceptional reasons their co-operation may be refused. This is a realistic balance of the sovereign and humanitarian interests.

ii. Offer of assistance

Article 70(1) goes on to say that offers of relief as previously defined "shall not be regarded as interference in the armed conflict or as unfriendly acts". This is an important principle, raising the issue of relief to the civilian population to the level of general international, or supra-national, concern. In the past, States may have been reluctant to offer humanitarian assistance for fear of being accused of interfering in the internal affairs of another State, or of favouring one Party to a conflict over another. Also, potential recipient States may have regarded offers of assistance as injurious to their national pride, reflecting on their inability to handle their own affairs. The position is now clarified. Certainly an offer of relief which is needed and a relief action which is humanitarian and impartial, should not be considered as illegal interventions. Although Article 70(1) would seem to refer to offers by States, such offers may also be made by intergovernmental or non-governmental organizations and it is submitted that the same principles would apply to them.

It is worth noting that offers of relief made by the International Committee of the Red Cross (ICRC) under its customary international law right of initiative and as an impartial humanitarian organization under provisions of the 1949 Geneva Conventions, were never to be regarded as interfering or unfriendly acts.

iii. Priority distribution

Article 70(1) ends by stating that in the distribution of relief consignments, priority shall be given to those persons, such as children, expectant mothers maternity cases and nursing mothers, who under the Fourth Geneva Convention or Protocol I are to be accorded privileged treatment or special protection. This positive discrimination is sensible and is provided for in Article 23 of the Fourth Convention and elsewhere.

iv. Transit

The second paragraph of Article 70 concerns the transit of relief. The Parties to the conflict and each High Contracting Party to the Protocol "shall allow and facilitate rapid and unimpeded passage of all relief consignments, equipment and personnel provided in accordance with [Articles 68-71 of the Protocol], even if such assistance is destined for the civilian population of the adverse Party".

The obligations on the various Parties concerned to allow and to facilitate relief, even if destined for the civilian population of the opposing side, could not be more clear. However, in fulfilling these duties of passage, the Parties to the conflict and each High Contracting Party to the Protocol have, under paragraph three of Article 70, certain powers of control commensurate with the requirements of sovereignty. They "shall have the right to prescribe technical arrangements, including search, under which such passage is permitted". They "may make such permission conditional on the distribution of the assistance being made under the local supervision of a Protecting Power". Finally, they "shall, in no way whatsoever divert relief consignments from the purpose for which they are intended nor delay their forwarding, except in cases of urgent necessity in the interest of the civilian population concerned".

Compared with the restrictive conditions on transit prescribed under Article 23 of the Fourth Geneva Convention, those enumerated under Article 70(3) are more objective, while at the same time, safeguarding the interests of the transit State. As a matter of interpretation, Article 70(3) supplants the serious limitations contained in the second paragraph of Article 23 of the Fourth Convention.

It represents an advance in the law governing relief operations.

v. Distribution and international co-ordination

Article 70(4) says that the Parties to the conflict will protect relief consignments and facilitate their rapid distribution. These obligations refer primarily to the receiving State.

The final paragraph of Article 70 says that the Parties to the conflict and each High Contracting Party concerned shall encourage and facilitate effective international co-ordination of the relief actions referred to in the first paragraph, namely, those of a specified character and conduct undertaken in the territory of a Party to the conflict other than occupied territory. Article 70(5) does not specify a particular system for achieving effective international co-ordination, thus allowing for *ad hoc* solutions. In practice the International Committee of the Red Cross or an United Nations agency, such as the Disaster Relief Co-ordinator (UNDR0), could assume a co-ordinating role.

(d) Relief personnel

Article 71 is the first provision in general International Humanitarian Law to cover the personnel participating in relief actions. It applies to both occupied and non-occupied territories. In the Fourth Geneva Convention no reference was made to the existence of such personnel, although they may be a very important component of a relief operation. Under existing law, the status of relief personnel was normally governed by the rules applicable to civilians of States which are not Parties to the conflict and where appropriate, to neutral medical personnel.

The first paragraph of Article 71 says that where necessary, relief personnel may form part of the assistance provided in any relief action, in particular for the transportation and distribution of relief consignments. However it also stipulates that "the participation of such personnel shall be subject to the approval of the Party in whose territory they will carry out their duties". This is another illustration of the necessary balance between the sovereign and humanitarian interests. A refusal of approval for the participation of one or more relief workers must not be arbitrary or unjustified.

Paragraph two of Article 71 gives these officially recognised relief personnel a special protected status under International Humanitarian Law (the Law of War). It states that such personnel must be "respected and protected". This is the same formula used for other protected personnel, such as medical personnel. Put simply, it means that relief personnel must not be attacked and as circumstances require they must be actively assisted. Relief personnel have been killed and their work unnecessarily hindered in previous armed conflicts so this innovative provision is of significant practical benefit, both to the personnel themselves and to the civilian population they are intending to help.

Article 71(3) places the specific duty on each Party to the conflict in receipt of relief consignments, "to the fullest extent practicable", to assist the recognised relief personnel in carrying out their relief mission. Only in the case of imperative military necessity may the activities of these relief personnel be limited or their movements temporarily restricted.

The fourth and concluding paragraph of Article 71 provides for the necessary control of the activities of relief personnel. This is the natural corollary to their special protection. Under no circumstances may they exceed the terms of their mission under Protocol I. "In particular they shall take account of the security requirements of the Party in whose territory they are carrying out their duties. The mission of any of the personnel who do not respect these conditions may be terminated."

Some relief personnel may have functions, and meet other requirements, which enable them to qualify for special protection as medical or civil defence personnel under the Protocol. In such instances, these latter provisions would prevail as being *lex specialis.*[6]

(e) Additional Articles

In addition to the four articles in Protocol I specifically devoted to relief in favour of the civilian population, three other articles of the Protocol are worth noting in relation to the development of relief law. These are: Article 17 concerning the role of the civilian population and of aid societies; Article 81 on the activities of the Red Cross and other humanitarian organizations, and perhaps especially, Article 54 which prohibits starvation of civilians as a method of warfare.

2. Non-International Armed Conflicts

Protocol II of 1977 covers certain non-international armed conflicts. It is applicable in high intensity non-international armed conflicts as defined in Article 1(1). This Protocol does not apply to internal disturbances and tensions (Article 1(2)). In these latter circumstances relief operations will be governed by Human Rights Law, international customary law, *ad hoc* relief agreements and the relevant national laws of the territory concerned.

A. Existing Law

Before the adoption of the Geneva Conventions of 1949 there were no treaty rules applicable to non-international armed conflicts. However relief operations for the civilian victims of such conflicts did take place, most notably by the ICRC, on an *ad hoc* basis. Red Cross action during the Spanish Civil War is only one example of such an operation. A resolution passed by the International Conference of the Red Cross in 1938 envisaged the application by the Parties to a civil war of the essential principles of the then existing Geneva Conventions.

Article 3, common to the four 1949 Geneva Conventions, is the first treaty provision to apply to a non-international armed conflict. This so-called Common Article 3 applies to a broader range of non-international armed conflicts than Protocol II, although when the conditions for the application of Protocol II are met, that 1977 agreement develops and supplements the brief rules contained in Common Article 3.

Common Article 3 does not refer to relief actions. However it does provide a general duty of humane treatment for persons taking no active part in the hostilities, such as the civilian population, and stipulates that the wounded and sick must be collected and cared for. These obligations apply not only to the High Contracting Party to the Geneva Conventions of 1949, but also to each Party to the non-international armed conflict, including the insurgents.

Common Article 3 also permits an impartial humanitarian body, such as the ICRC, to offer its services to the Parties to the conflict. This could include an offer of a relief action. More generally, the ICRC's customary international legal right of initiative will enable it to offer its humanitarian services in armed conflicts of varying kinds and in situations of internal strife.

B. Protocol II

Protocol II contains only one provision, Article 18, on relief actions. It is more limited than the relief provisions in Protocol I relating to international armed conflicts.

The first paragraph of Article 18 provides for humanitarian assistance by relief societies and the civilian population located within the territory of the High Contracting Party (i.e. a State) to the Protocol. These local relief societies, such as the National Red Cross Society or a humanitarian organization set up by the insurgents, may offer their services for the performance of their traditional functions in relation to the victims of the armed conflict. The offer of such assistance may of course be rejected, but only for valid reasons, and does not detract from the right of initiative of the ICRC under Common Article 3. The traditional functions of relief societies may include medical assistance, food aid and the tracing of missing persons. Further under Article 18(1), the civilian population may, even on its own initiative, offer to collect and care for the wounded, sick and ship-wrecked. Again, such an offer may only be refused for legitimate reasons, particularly since under Common Article 3 and Article 7 of Protocol II, the Parties to the conflict have an obligation to collect and care for the wounded and sick.

Paragraph two of Article 18 resembles Article 70(1) of Protocol I, and reflects on the criteria for relief operations under international law. It states as follows:

> "If the civilian population is suffering undue hardship owing to a lack of the supplies essential for its survival, such as foodstuffs and medical supplies, relief actions for the civilian population which are of an exclusively humanitarian and impartial nature and which are conducted without any adverse distinction shall be undertaken subject to the consent of the High Contracting Party concerned."

In contrast to paragraph one of Article 18, paragraph two provides for the possibility of international relief actions, while safeguarding the security of the State concerned. There is an obligation to accept relief if necessary, and this obligation may be said to apply not only to the established government but also to the rebel authority controlling part of the territory of a High Contracting Party. The requirement of consent of the High Contracting Party affirms the notion of national sovereignty, although such consent can only be refused for legitimate reasons and it does not need to be express. The term "High Contracting Party" refers to the established government. However in some cases, the authority concerned from an operational viewpoint will be the insurgents, the government in power not having to grant transit to the relief. The established government should not object to humanitarian relief actions fulfilling the required conditions of impartiality and non-discrimination being undertaken in territory not under its control.

Article 14 of Protocol II prohibits starvation of civilians as a method of combat.

Taken together, the effect of these provisions of Protocol II will be to help to ensure that tragedies such as those which occurred during the Nigeria-Biafra conflict 1967-70 do not recur.

3. Conclusion

The 1977 Geneva Protocols represent a significant advance in the law governing relief operations.

From a general view, the Parties to the Protocols - which in the case of Protocol I may include a national liberation movement - have an obligation to accept relief actions if the civilian population under their control is inadequately provided with supplies essential to their survival.

Such relief actions must be exclusively humanitarian and impartial and conducted without any adverse distinction, and they are subject to the consent of the Parties concerned, which cannot be arbitrarily withheld. An impartial offer of humanitarian relief is not to be regarded as interference in the conflict.

Starvation as a method of warfare is prohibited. Parties to the Protocol in a position to do so are required to undertake, if necessary, relief actions in favour of the civilian population of another Party, or to contribute to them or to facilitate them. These are the principles governing relief operations in armed conflicts under international law and reflect the balance between the interest of State sovereignty or security and the interest of humanity.

Under Protocol I, provision is now made for relief actions in the territory of a Party to an international armed conflict other than in occupied territory, which was already provided for. The range of supplies considered essential to the survival of the civilian population has been expanded, and applies both to occupied and to non-occupied territories. The participation of relief personnel has been recognised and a protected status granted to enable them to perform their humanitarian function. The Parties concerned are required to grant Red Cross and other humanitarian organizations the facilities to carry out their activities, provided they meet certain requirements.

Provision is also made under Protocol II, for humanitarian relief actions in certain non-international armed conflicts, under the conditions of impartiality, non-discrimination and consent mentioned previously.

The articles on relief in both Protocols not only are a good example of the realistic balance between military necessity and humanitarian considerations. They may also be said to reflect the growth of the idea of an international community interest underlying International Human Rights Law, International Humanitarian Law and the concept of International Solidarity.

The 1977 Protocols provide more opportunities for officially authorised humanitarian organizations to provide assistance so long as they fulfil specified conditions. In armed conflicts facilitation of relief activities normally depends upon a willingness to accept a measure of control. The relief provisions in the Protocols put humanitarian organizations in a better negotiating position, making it more difficult for a receiving, transit or donor State or other competent authority to justify obstacles to relief actions.

FOOTNOTES

* The views expressed are personal and do not necessarily reflect those of the British Red Cross.

1. An overview of the entire field of relief law is given in P. Macalister-Smith, *International Humanitarian Assistance* (1985). A very useful and concise explanation of the legal aspects of relief operations, in both peacetime and in armed conflict, can be found in M. Bothe, "Relief Actions", in Bernhardt (ed.) *Encyclopedia of Public International Law*, Instalment 4 (1982) pp. 173-78.

2. See ICRC Commentary (1987), p. 813, paragraph 2785.

3. *ibid*, p. 814, para. 2789.

4. M. Bothe *et al.*, *New Rules for Victims of Armed Conflicts*, p. 433.

5. ICRC Commentary, p. 820 para. 2807

6. Bothe *et al.*, *op.cit.* p. 439.

PART IV

USE OF WEAPONS

REPRISALS AND RECIPROCITY IN THE NEW LAW OF ARMED CONFLICT

C.J. Greenwood

1. Introduction

Reprisals in war have a bad name. The atrocities committed in the name of retaliation during the Second World War and the spiral of reprisals and counter-reprisals against civilians in the Gulf Conflict together with the inherently unattractive nature of a concept reminiscent of Old Testament notions of retribution have led most commentators to agree with Professor Cassese's description of reprisals as "a primitive instrument through which violence escalates into barbarity".[(1)*] Nor has this view been confined to writers. Most of the international conferences on the law of armed conflict since 1874 have revealed a widespread hostility towards reprisals and each treaty on the law of armed conflict since 1929 has seen the scope for taking lawful reprisals further reduced. Nowhere was this approach more in evidence than at the 1974-1977 Diplomatic Conference on the Development of Humanitarian Law and in the principal agreement which it produced (Geneva Protocol I, 1977). The purpose of this paper is to examine the development of the law relating to belligerent reprisals and to ask whether the hostility towards reprisals has now been taken too far.

This study will be confined to belligerent reprisals in the true sense of that term, i.e. measures taken in the context of an existing armed conflict by one of the parties to that conflict in response to unlawful conduct by an adversary - for example, the use of prohibited weapons by one party in retaliation for their earlier use by its rival. It is not intended to address the different question of whether an initial resort to force in circumstances which would normally entail a breach of Article 2(4) of the United Nations Charter may ever be justified as a reprisal.[(2)] Nor will the legality of economic countermeasures and other non-violent forms of retaliation be considered.

* For footnotes see p. 247.

It is also important to distinguish belligerent reprisals from certain other, closely related, concepts with which they are frequently confused. The essence of reprisals is that they are acts which would normally be unlawful but which are justified because they are taken in direct response to earlier unlawful acts by the party against which they are directed. If the response takes the form of acts which, though they may be extremely damaging, are not ordinarily contrary to the law of armed conflict, those measures are not reprisals. Thus, if a State retaliates for unlawful acts, such as the ill-treatment of prisoners, on the part of its adversary by stepping up the level of its attacks but employing only lawful weapons against legitimate targets no question of reprisals will arise. Reprisals must also be distinguished from cases where a rule is so framed that its violation by one party automatically releases other parties from their obligations. The effect of the reservations entered by many States to the Geneva Gas Protocol, 1925[(3)] is that in most cases that Protocol prohibits only the first use of gas in a conflict. If, therefore, a State which can rely on such a reservation employs poison gas against an enemy which has already used that weapon, it has no need to rely upon the doctrine of reprisals in order to justify its action, since the effect of the reservation is that its action is lawful anyway. An important consequence is that in such a case the restrictions which the law imposes upon reprisals (e.g. that they must be reasonably proportionate) will not apply.[(4)]

2. Development of the Law regarding Belligerent Reprisals prior to 1974

International law has sought to limit recourse to reprisals in two different ways. On the one hand, principles of customary international law have evolved which regulate reprisals by prescribing conditions any lawful recourse to reprisals must meet. On the other hand, a succession of treaties have imposed total prohibitions upon reprisals against certain targets. It will come as no surprise that at times there has been considerable tension between these two approaches of regulation and prohibition.

Regulation of Reprisals

There is widespread agreement that an act must satisfy four conditions if it is to be justified as a legitimate reprisal:

a. it must be a response to a prior violation of international law;

b. it must be reasonably proportionate;

c. it must be undertaken for the purpose of putting an end to the enemy's unlawful conduct and preventing future illegalities and not for mere revenge; and

d. since reprisals are a subsidiary means of redress, no other effective method of redress must be available.

These requirements apply to all types of reprisal. In the case of belligerent reprisals it has sometimes been contended that there is a further requirement that reprisals must not violate basic principles of humanity. Each of these requirements must now be examined in more detail.

A. The Requirement of a Prior Violation of International Law

It has never been doubted that reprisals may only be taken in response to a violation of international law by the party against which they are directed (or its ally). In the case of belligerent reprisals, however, a question arises about the nature of the prior violation which provides the justification for the reprisal. Belligerent reprisals consist of acts which, if they could not be justified as reprisals, would constitute violations of the law which regulates the conduct of war or armed conflict (the *ius in bello*). Must the acts to which such reprisals are a response be a violation of the same body of law, or is it enough that there has been a violation of the separate body of law (the *ius ad bellum*) which regulates resort to force? In other words, may a State which is the victim of aggression retaliate by employing methods of warfare which would normally be prohibited, notwithstanding that the aggressor's conduct of hostilities (as opposed to its initiation of them) has hitherto been entirely lawful?

Although there are some suggestions to the contrary emanating from the Second World War[5] it is suggested that to permit a State to respond to aggression by taking reprisals in the form of measures which would otherwise be contrary to the *ius in bello* would be incompatible with the principle that the *ius in bello* applies equally to all parties in a conflict regardless of the legality of their resort to force. That principle, which was upheld by the United States Military Tribunal in *United States v. List*[6] and in many other war crimes trials, was reaffirmed in the Preamble to Protocol I, 1977 and must be regarded as one of the fundamental principles of the law of armed conflict. As Sir Hersch Lauterpacht has remarked:

> ... it is impossible to visualise the conduct of hostilities in which one side would be bound by the rules of warfare without benefitting from them and the other side would benefit from them without being bound by them.[7]

If the victim of aggression was allowed to disregard some of the rules for the conduct of hostilities as a reprisal for the aggressor's unlawful initiation of those hostilities, the application of those rules in that conflict would become one-sided. Moreover, since in most modern conflicts each side accuses the other of aggression such an approach would encourage both parties to invoke the doctrine of reprisals as an excuse for disregarding the *ius in bello*. The better view is therefore that belligerent reprisals may lawfully be taken only in response to a prior violation of the law of armed conflict and not in retaliation for an unlawful resort to force.[8]

B. The Requirement of Proportionality

That reprisals are required to be reasonably proportionate is clearly established. What is not so clear is the yardstick by which proportionality is to be assessed. The most commonly held view is that reprisals must be reasonably proportionate to the prior conduct to which they are a response. However, Professors McDougal and Feliciano have maintained that the real test should be whether the reprisal is proportionate to the legitimate end to be achieved, i.e. that the reprisal will be regarded as meeting the criterion of proportionality so long as it does not exceed what is reasonably necessary to prevent repetition of the unlawful act or to ensure that a continuing violation is terminated.[9]

There is much force in the idea that proportionality should not be assessed simply by reference to the scale of the illegality which triggers the reprisal but should have a forward looking element. As will be seen, it is generally agreed that the purpose of reprisals should be to prevent future unlawful conduct and to secure redress rather than simply to exact retribution. It follows that reprisals will become unlawful if their scale exceeds what is reasonably necessary to achieve those purposes, or if they are continued after those purposes have been achieved, even if the reprisals are proportionate to the wrong to which they are a response. What cannot be accepted is that proportionality should be determined exclusively by reference to the aims to be achieved and, in particular, that "the quantum of permissible violence, so determined, may under certain circumstances conceivably be greater than that inflicted in the enemy's original unlawful act".[10] Such a conclusion is difficult to reconcile with the approach to proportionality taken in the war crimes trials and is likely to lead to an escalation of violence. Instead, the purpose for which reprisals may lawfully be undertaken should be seen as imposing an additional limitation: reprisals should exceed neither what is proportionate to the prior violation nor what is necessary if they are to achieve their aims.

Whatever yardstick is adopted, it is no easy task to determine whether the requirement of proportionality has been met. As Professor Kalshoven has remarked:

> .... proportionality in this context means the absence of obvious disportionality, as opposed to strict proportionality. In other words, belligerents are left with a certain freedom of appreciation.[11]

Even then, the criteria to be adopted in deciding whether a reprisal is proportionate may be difficult to determine. In the trial of *Kappler* (the 'Ardeatine Caves case')[12] an Italian court had to decide whether the massacre of 335 prisoners, most of whom were captured Italian soldiers, could be a lawful reprisal for a bomb attack by the Italian resistance which killed 33 German military policemen. The court found that the reprisal was disproportionate not only because of the adoption by the Germans of a 10:1 ratio in determining the number of victims to be shot but also because the Italian soldiers who were executed included five generals and eleven colonels whereas the Germans killed in the bomb attack were men of much lower rank. Where reprisals do not take the form of retaliation in kind - for example, when a State retaliates for the murder of prisoners of war by employing prohibited methods of warfare against enemy troops in the field or by bombing civilian targets - the assessment of proportionality may become almost impossible to achieve on anything other than a very crude scale.

C. The Purpose of Reprisals

Both the United Kingdom and United States *Manuals of Military Law* emphasise that the purpose of reprisals is the enforcement of the law of armed conflict and not mere retribution.[13] It has already been shown that this consideration may have a bearing on the proportionality requirement. It also means that reprisals must cease if the party against which they are directed discontinues its unlawful conduct in circumstances which make it probable that there will be no recurrence of such conduct.

D. The Requirement of Subsidiarity

The principle that reprisals, as a subsidiary means of redress, should only be used as a last resort is often expressed in terms of a requirement that all other methods of securing redress must be exhausted before recourse is had to reprisals. Although the principle finds expression, in that form, in the *Naulilaa* award[14], it appears that there was little authority for a requirement to exhaust other methods of redress prior to that case. Kalshoven admits that "on theoretical considerations the possibility cannot be excluded of situations where the fruitlessness of any other remedy but reprisals is apparent from the outset"[15] and that in such situations the requirement of subsidiarity will be satisfied even if recourse to reprisals is immediate. While the availabilty of other sanctions for violations of the law of armed conflict should not be underestimated, it is likely that there will be occasions when the possibility to which Professor Kalshoven refers will be more than theoretical.

E. Possible additional Requirements

It is sometimes suggested that there is a customary law requirement that reprisals must not infringe basic principles of humanity. However, there is little support for the existence of such a requirement in State practice or the jurisprudence of the war crimes tribunals. Most reprisal measures which might be thought to contravene principles of humanity are now the subject of express treaty prohibitions. One type of reprisal which is not expressly prohibited but which might be thought to violate a general principle of humanity would be the retaliatory use of weapons causing unnecessary suffering, although if the suffering inflicted is indeed 'unnecessary', the reprisal will not satisfy the third condition listed above, quite apart from any considerations of humanity. The principal significance today of the question whether a general requirement of humanity exists as an additional restriction upon recourse to reprisals lies in determining whether customary international law prohibits reprisals against the enemy's civilian population, independently of the provisions of Protocol I.(16)

Finally, military manuals sometimes require that the decision to order reprisals must be taken at a senior level.(17) Given the serious consequences which such a decision may entail, it is highly desirable that it be taken only by a senior officer or political body after mature consideration but such a requirement would seem to be more a matter of internal military discipline than of international law.

Prohibition of Reprisals against Specified Targets

The first major treaty to impose a total prohibition on a class of reprisals was the Geneva Prisoners of War Convention, 1929, Article 2 of which prohibited reprisals against prisoners of war. This development was carried further by the 1949 Geneva Conventions, each of which expressly prohibits reprisals against the persons and objects protected in that Convention.(18) The most important innovation in this respect was the introduction of a prohibition on reprisals against those civilians who qualified as protected persons under the Fourth Convention (principally civilian internees and the civilian population of occupied territory). This provision represented a substantial departure from the law relating to belligerent occupation as it had applied during the Second World War. Finally the Hague Convention on Cultural Property, 1954, prohibited reprisals against cultural property.(19)

The combined effect of these prohibitions was substantially to reduce the scope for taking lawful belligerent reprisals. The only potential objects of reprisals not protected by a specific treaty prohibition were members of the enemy's armed forces who had not yet surrendered or been incapacitated, enemy shipping and the enemy's civilian population and civilian objects in unoccupied enemy territory.

Moreover, the question whether customary international law prohibited reprisals against those civilians not already protected by the Civilians Convention remained highly controversial. Long before a specific prohibition on such reprisals was included in Protocol I, it was suggested by writers that customary international law prohibited reprisals against the civilian population.[20] In 1970 the United Nations General Assembly, in Resolution 2675, affirmed as one of the "basic principles for the protection of the civilian population in armed conflict" that "civilian populations, or individual members thereof, should not be the object of reprisals". Nevertheless there was no consensus amongst writers on this subject - even some of those who contended that customary international law required that reprisals must not infringe the basic principles of humanity differed over whether reprisals against the civilian population necessarily violated that requirement. Nor was much support for a ban on such reprisals to be found in the practice of States or the jurisprudence of international tribunals.[21]

Reprisals in Internal Conflicts

The regulation of reprisals in internal conflicts did not receive the attention given to reprisals in conflicts between States. Common Article 3 of the Geneva Conventions contained no express provision regarding reprisals in internal conflicts. The ICRC, however, has maintained that, since the acts listed in Article 3 were stated to be forbidden in all circumstances, recourse to such acts by way of reprisals was impliedly prohibited.[22] In addition, it seems probable that the principles of customary law regulating recourse to reprisals were applicable to any reprisals not covered by that implicit prohibition.

3. The 1977 Geneva Protocols and the Debates at the 1974-1977 Diplomatic Conference[23]

When the preparatory work for the Diplomatic Conference on the Development of Humanitarian Law began, therefore, three questions concerning reprisals presented themselves:

a. should the specific prohibitions on reprisals in international conflicts be extended so as to outlaw reprisals against a wider range of persons and objects?

b. should the existing rules of customary law regulating recourse to reprisals against those persons and objects which might lawfully be subjected to reprisals be codified and, perhaps, tightened? and

c. should the law regarding non-international conflicts contain express provisions concerning reprisals?

The third question was dealt with separately, in the context of Draft Protocol II, and will be considered later. The first two questions, concerning international conflicts which were to come within the scope of Draft Protocol I, aroused considerable controversy from the start.

Reprisals in International Armed Conflicts: Protocol I

From an early stage of the Conference it was clear that recourse to reprisals was to be further restricted and that the right of States to take reprisals against those civilians not protected by the 1949 Civilians Convention, if such a right still existed, was to be removed or, at least, drastically curtailed. There were considerable differences, however, over the extent to which the right of reprisal was to be curtailed, over whether to proceed by way of a general prohibition of reprisals against persons and objects protected by the Protocol or by means of a series of provisions banning reprisals against specific targets and over whether any attempt should be made to deal with the rules regulating such reprisals as would remain legitimate.

Although the ICRC had at one time contemplated including a general provision dealing with reprisals in Draft Protocol I, the opposition which this proposal aroused at the Conference of Government Experts led it to abandon this idea. Instead, the ICRC chose what may be described as a middle course. The draft which it submitted to the Diplomatic Conference contained several provisions which prohibited reprisals against specific targets, most noticeably the civilian population and individual civilians. There was no general prohibition on reprisals against protected persons and objects. Indeed, it was clear that the ICRC had not intended to exclude recourse to reprisals against some of the objects protected by the Draft Protocol. Nor did the ICRC attempt to codify or develop the rules regulating recourse to reprisals against those targets not covered by a specific prohibition.

The ICRC's approach was challenged by two groups of States with widely differing views on the whole subject of reprisals. The first group, of which Poland was the principal spokesman, maintained that reprisals had no place in the law of Geneva. They therefore proposed that Draft Protocol I be amended to include a blanket prohibition of reprisals against persons and objects protected by the 1949 Conventions or the Protocol. The Polish delegate who introduced this proposal argued that such a provision was preferable to a number of specific prohibitions of reprisals for two reasons. First, even after the ICRC draft had been amended so as to increase the number of specific prohibitions of reprisals, there remained some persons and objects which were protected by Draft Protocol I but in respect of which there was no express provision outlawing reprisals. Secondly, he maintained that the inclusion of a general provision would make clear that recourse to reprisals was abhorrent to the international community.

If Poland and those States which supported it considered that the ICRC draft did not go far enough in outlawing reprisals, another group of States maintained that it went too far. It was France which took the initiative in this group, putting forward a proposal which, while avoiding the use of the term "reprisals", in effect sought to preserve a right for a party to an armed conflict which was confronted with "serious, manifest and deliberate" breaches of the Protocol by an adversary to respond by taking measures which would otherwise be contrary to the Protocol. Such measures were to be a matter of last resort and were to comply with certain regulations set out in the text of the proposal, which largely restated the existing customary law principles regulating recourse to reprisals. These measures were to be taken only where the party taking them considered it "imperative to take action to compel the party violating its obligations to cease doing so". In no circumstances were the measures to involve action prohibited by the 1949 Conventions.

In the end, both the French and Polish proposals were withdrawn and the final text of Protocol I followed the ICRC's approach of curtailing the right of reprisal by means of specific prohibitions. Nevertheless, the final text was very much closer to the Polish than the French proposal, particularly in view of the fact that, against the recommendation of the ICRC, the Draft Protocol had been amended to prohibit reprisals against all civilian (i.e. non-military) objects. As finally adopted Protocol I prohibits reprisals against:

- the wounded, sick and shipwrecked and those medical and other personnel, buildings, vehicles and aircraft protected by Part I (Article 20);

- the civilian population and individual civilians (Article 51(6));

- civilian objects (Article 52(1));

- cultural objects and places of worship (Article 53(c));

- objects indispensable to the survival of the civilian population (Article 54(4));

- the natural environment (Article 55(2)); and

- works and installations containing dangerous forces (Article 56(4)).

A glance at this list will suffice to show that the effect of Protocol I is drastically to curtail the scope for taking lawful reprisals in those conflicts to which it applies. In land warfare[24], the Protocol appears to leave room for reprisals only against members of the enemy's armed forces still actively engaged in hostilities. In those areas where reprisals may still be taken the Protocol is silent about their regulation which remains subject to what one delegate described as "the fog of customary law".

Reprisals in Non-International Armed Conflicts: Protocol II

The Draft Protocol II submitted by the ICRC contained provisions expressly prohibiting reprisals against civilians and the civilian population and against the wounded, sick, shipwrecked and protected medical personnel and transport. These provisions drew criticism from some delegations which maintained that the whole concept of reprisals was confined to international conflicts and from other delegations which wanted to extend the prohibitions to cover civilian objects in line with the changes introduced into Draft Protocol I. When it became clear, however, that only a truncated version of Draft Protocol II stood any chance of being adopted, all the provisions regarding reprisals were abandoned. Protocol II, like Common Article 3, thus contains no express provision on reprisals. Article 4, however, extends the list in Common

Article 3 of acts which are prohibited "at any time and in any place whatsoever" and the ICRC has maintained that this wording impliedly prohibits any reprisals which take the form of any of the acts listed in Article 4(2). In addition, the ICRC Commentary on the Protocols suggests that the prohibition, in Article 4(2)(b), of collective punishment "is virtually equivalent to prohibiting 'reprisals' against protected persons".[25]

4. Evaluation of the Provisions on Reprisals in Protocol I

With the exception of Article 20 (which is no more than a logical extension of the provisions on reprisals in the First and Second Conventions), the provisions on reprisals in Protocol I represent a major change in the law designed principally to protect civilians. While there is no doubt that these provisions are in keeping with the fundamental principles of humanitarian law, they are open to criticism on several grounds.

Removal of a Sanction

Discussing the reprisals provisions in Protocol I, Professor Draper commented that the virtual removal of one of the oldest means of law enforcement places a heavy strain on the residual methods.[26] Opinions differ as to the efficacy, as well as the morality, of reprisals as a means of law enforcement. There can be no doubt that in many cases reprisals have done little to promote respect for the law and may well have made matters worse. Nevertheless, the threat of reprisals appears to have operated as a form of sanction, however imperfect, and in an area of international law which is more than usually lacking in enforcement machinery, the removal of even an imperfect sanction creates problems.

There were some attempts at the Diplomatic Conference to create new machinery for ensuring compliance with the laws of armed conflict and some delegations made clear that they regarded these provisions as essential if the sanction of reprisals was to be reduced almost to vanishing point. The main product of this search for alternatives to reprisals was Article 90 of Protocol I, which provides for the establishment of an International Fact-Finding Commission to enquire into allegations of grave breaches of the Conventions or the Protocol. The thinking behind this provision was that it would provide an alternative mode of redress for a State which might otherwise be tempted to have recourse to reprisals.

It is most unlikely, however, that the International Fact-Finding Commission will ever amount to an effective mechanism for the enforcement of the law. Its powers are strictly limited. It may enquire into allegations of grave breaches and "facilitate, through its good offices, the restoration of an attitude of respect for the Conventions and this Protocol" but it has no sanctions at its disposal other than the pressure which may be brought to bear by public disapproval of a State which ignores its findings. Even the creation of this almost toothless body was seen as an affront to State sovereignty by some delegations and was acceptable only because it was made strictly optional. In terms modelled upon the "optional clause" of the Statute of the International Court of Justice, Article 90 provides that the parties to the Protocol may make declarations recognising the competence of the Commission in respect of allegations made by another party accepting the same obligation. If one party to a conflict alleges that another party is guilty of grave breaches, the Commission may not institute an enquiry unless both States have made such declarations or both give their consent. Moreover, the Commission will not even come into existence until twenty parties to the Protocol have made declarations under Article 90. At the time of writing, only 11 of the 73 States which had become parties to Protocol I had made Article 90 declarations. In these circumstances, it is difficult not to agree with Professor Draper's conclusion that the International Commission is unlikely to be able to operate during an armed conflict.[27]

Mention should also be made of Article 89, which provides:

> In situations of serious violations of the Conventions or of this Protocol, the High Contracting Parties undertake to act, jointly or individually, in co-operation with the United Nations and in conformity with the United Nations Charter.

This provision is the result of a Syrian initiative and was originally linked to the Polish proposal for a general provision on reprisals. It adds little to the obligation of the parties, under Article 1(1), to ensure respect for the Protocol in all circumstances and the intentions behind it are far from clear. While it may perform a useful function in acting as a spur to the United Nations to interest itself in the observance of the law of armed conflict, Article 89 is at most a very minor addition to the machinery for enforcing the law of armed conflict.

Public Pressure to Respond to Violations of the Law

A rather different criticism of the reprisals provisions in Protocol I is that they seek to impose upon governments a moral stance which public opinion will not sustain. If, it is said, a State is confronted with large-scale violations of the Conventions and the Protocol such as massive attacks on its civilian population, it will be unable to resist public pressure for a response in kind. As one member of the United States delegation put it:

> In the event of massive and continuing violations of the Conventions and the Protocol, this series of prohibitions of reprisals may prove unworkable. Massive and continuing attacks directed against a nation's civilian population could not be absorbed without a response in kind. By denying the possibility of a response and not offering any workable substitute, the Protocol is unrealistic and, in that respect, cannot be expected to withstand the test of future armed conflict.[28]

While the likelihood of popular demands for revenge should not be allowed to become the factor which determines the development of the law of armed conflict, there is some force in this argument. The law risks losing all credibility if it provides no redress for a State which is the victim of breaches of the law on a grand scale and yet denies that State the right to respond in kind to those violations.

The Enlarged Scope of Protocol I

The most telling criticism of the reprisals provisions, however, lies in the scope of Protocol I. Part IV of the Protocol, which contains all but one of the reprisals provisions, is likely to impose greater limitations on the actual conduct of hostilities than any of the provisions of the 1949 Conventions. The prohibition of "indiscriminate attacks" (which are very widely defined) in Article 51, the narrow definition of military objectives in Article 52, the prohibition in Article 55 of methods and means of warfare likely to cause "widespread, long term and severe" damage to the natural environment and the special protection given by Article 56 to works and installations containing dangerous forces are all motivated by the same humanitarian concerns which lay behind the adoption in 1949 of provisions for the protection of the sick, wounded, prisoners of war and civilians in occupied territory. Their observance, however, will restrict the options open to any army engaged in hostilities and will, in many cases, require such an army to sustain greater casualties than it would otherwise do in order to minimise the loss of civilian life. Unlike the 1949 Conventions, most of the provisions of which are concerned with the humane treatment of persons already in the power of an adversary, Part IV of Protocol I deals with civilians who may well be located in the very objectives which an army wishes to capture and thus imposes restrictions which may make it markedly more difficult for a State to win a conflict in which it becomes engaged.

It follows that a State which disregards its obligations under Part IV of Protocol I may derive a considerable military advantage from doing so. For example, attacks on dams, dykes or nuclear electrical generating stations, which in most circumstances are prohibited by Article 56, may seriously damage the victim State's capacity to wage war. In such a case, the need to respond and to prevent future violations becomes more than simply a matter of law enforcement, it may be essential if the victim is to avoid defeat. Of course it can be argued that military necessity has been held not to be a justification for disregarding the laws of armed conflict, so that a State which is losing a conflict in which its adversary is fighting in accordance with the law is not permitted to violate the law in an attempt to redress the military imbalance. Where, however, the military imbalance arises from the adversary's violation of certain rules of the law of armed conflict, it is unreasonable to forbid the victim of those violations to respond in kind unless other means of redress are available.

At this point, any discussion of reprisals necessarily becomes involved with the subject of reciprocity. Reciprocity poses something of a dilemma for the law of armed conflict. On the one hand, Protocol I, like any treaty, will be applicable between any two States only if both have become party to it or have otherwise consented to apply it. If either of these States has become party subject to reservations, those reservations will apply on a reciprocal basis. In that sense, the reciprocal acceptance of obligations is the basis for the application of all the treaties on the law of armed conflict. On the other hand, the ICRC has always stressed that the continued application of those treaties is not dependent upon reciprocity, in the sense that a breach by one party does not relieve the other parties of their obligations towards it. The ICRC Commentary to the 1949 Conventions states that a treaty on humanitarian law does not constitute:

> ... an engagement concluded on a basis of reciprocity, binding each party to the contract only in so far as the other party observes its obligations. It is rather a series of unilateral engagements solemnly contracted before the world as represented by the other Contracting Parties.(29)

This approach, which may also be found in the Commentary on the Protocols, is enshrined in Article 60 of the Vienna Convention on the Law of Treaties. Article 60 expressly provides that the rights to terminate or suspend the operation of a treaty on account of a material breach by another party:

> ... do not apply to provisions relating to the protection of the human person contained in treaties of a humanitarian character, in particular to provisions prohibiting any form of reprisals against persons protected by such treaties.

Reciprocity is thus essential to create, but not to continue, an obligation of this kind derived from a treaty of a humanitarian character.

While this approach perhaps owes more to considerations of humanity than of logic, it can be defended in relation to the traditional law of Geneva. Many of the provisions of that law have a character similar to that of the human rights agreements and their observance or violation has relatively little impact upon the military balance between States. The law of The Hague is a different matter.(30) In that context, a State's promise to abstain from conduct which might be greatly to its advantage is more reasonably viewed as being conditional upon similar observance by its adversary. The problem with the provisions on the civilian population in Protocol I is that they contain elements of both Hague and Geneva law and to expect one party to a conflict to continue to abstain from conduct from which its adversary is gaining considerable military advantages is indeed a tall order. It is not suggested that the continued application of the provisions of Part IV should be dependent upon strict reciprocity so that a material breach by one party would entitle its adversary to disregard the provisions for the remainder of the conflict. However, to prohibit reprisals (a more limited form of response since only proportionate measures would be permitted) is to tip the balance between military and humanitarian considerations too far in the direction of the latter and thus to risk undermining the credibility of the law.

5. The Response of States to the Reprisals Provisions in Protocol I

Although a clear majority of the States which were represented at the Diplomatic Conference expressed their support for the reprisals provisions of Protocol I, disquiet about those provisions has lingered. There are some indications that the extent of the new prohibitions on reprisals was a factor in the United States decision not to ratify Protocol I for the time being.[31] Even supporters of United States ratification such as Ambassador Aldrich, who had been the Chairman of the United States delegation to the Diplomatic Conference, argued that the United States should ratify subject to reservations concerning some of the reprisals provisions.[32] At the time of writing no State had entered a reservation expressly dealing with reprisals but Italy had made a declaration on ratification in the following terms:

> Italy will react to serious and systematic violations by an enemy of the obligations imposed by Additional Protocol I and in particular its Articles 51 and 52 with all means admissible under international law in order to prevent any further violation.[33]

The meaning of this declaration is far from clear but it appears to be a warning that Italy will retaliate in some form if it is the victim of any violation of Articles 51 and 52.

Even some of those who were most critical of reprisals at the Diplomatic Conference appear to have been a little uneasy about the implications of the reprisals provisions. Professor Nahlik, who, as a member of the Polish delegation, had been responsible for the Polish proposal on reprisals, has written:

> But what if a State, in a given case, has absolutely no other means of response against a "manifest and deliberate" violation of law by the unscrupulous enemy than a recourse to similar action? Let the State then, in case of doubt, invoke the plea of unavoidable necessity or legitimate self-defence (possibly before some tribunal

> or commission) rather than let it invoke an express and, though perhaps well meant, double-edged clause of a treaty boasting of its "humanitarian" nature.[34]

Similarly a member of the Egyptian delegation said at the Conference that:

> Particular consideration should be given to the lot of victims of illegal reprisals ... [Egypt] recognised the interdependence of the clauses on reprisals and, in the event of violation by an adversary, would reconsider its position on them.[35]

Professor Nahlik's point appears to be that less damage will be done to the law if the State which finds retaliation imperative has recourse to extra-legal notions of necessity rather than relying upon a legal doctrine of reprisals. The Egyptian state statement suggests that, whereas it would be unlawful for a State to respond to a breach of, for example, Articles 51 or 52 by means of reprisals in kind, it might be justifiable for a State to respond to violations of those provisions where those violations are themselves characterised as reprisals.[36] Not surprisingly, this is a view repudiated by the ICRC. In reality, neither of the statements quoted is the expression of a legal position. They are rather indications that no rejection of reciprocity or prohibition of reprisals can conceal the fact that States will not allow an adversary to flout the relevant provisions of the Protocol and derive a significant military advantage from so doing without responding in kind.

Those States which consider that the reprisals provisions of Protocol I go too far and wish to preserve an option of retaliating against some of the persons or objects protected by those provisions while remaining within the law have two options open to them. They can either attempt to become parties to the Protocol subject to reservations or they can remain outside the system of Protocol I, as France has elected to do. The first course of action raises the question whether reservations to the reprisals provisions would be impermissible on the ground that such reservations would be contrary to the object and purpose of the treaty.[37] Although it was suggested by some delegations at the Diplomatic Conference that the reprisals provisions could not be the subject of reservations, the better view, as Professor Kalshoven has argued, is that reservations may be made. The object and purpose of Part IV of Protocol I is surely the protection of the civilian population. The prohibitions of reprisals were considered, by the majority of participants at the Diplomatic Conference, to be a means of achieving that purpose. It is open to argument, however, that preservation of a limited right to take reprisals might actually be a more effective means to that end.[38] It was in those terms that the French proposal was couched and for that reason that it was welcomed by Professor Draper, speaking for the United Kingdom delegation, as an attempt to improve the machinery for the enforcement of the law of armed conflict which would "make that law a living reality rather than a series of hopeful aspirations that had no effect in binding the parties at war".[39]

It is also necessary to consider whether the prohibitions on reprisals reflect existing customary international law or are innovations.

As has been shown the question whether international law prohibited reprisals against those civilians who were not protected by the Fourth Convention was hotly debated prior to 1974. Such a prohibition would be in keeping with the general principles of humanitarian law and has received a measure of support. Both the United Nations and the ICRC have called upon the parties to the Gulf Conflict not to subject the civilian population to reprisals.[40]

Nevertheless, the lack of consistent State practice in support of such a norm, the differences of opinion amongst writers and the fact that the nuclear strategy of all the nuclear powers and their allies has at some time been based upon plans to retaliate against the civilian population of a nuclear-armed adversary suggest that the prohibition of reprisals against the civilian population remains at present a matter of treaty law only.

The same is true *a fortiori*, of the prohibition of reprisals against civilian objects, which was a controversial innovation introduced at the Diplomatic Conference, and the provisions regarding the environment and works containing dangerous forces. The position is less clear with regard to reprisals against cultural objects and objects indispensable for the survival of the civilian population, although this writer doubts whether any of these provisions may yet be regarded as stating customary international law.[41]

6. Conclusions

The effect of the reprisals provisions in Protocol I is that in conflicts to which the Protocol applies the scope for lawful recourse to reprisals will be very small indeed. In cases where the Protocol does not apply, customary international law allows the parties to the conflict greater latitude in resorting to reprisals. The prohibitions of reprisals in Protocol I have not been accompanied by the provision of any alternative sanctions which are likely to be effective. Since the provisions on reprisals in the Protocol, unlike their counterparts in the 1949 Conventions, are concerned with activities which may have a significant effect upon the military balance between the belligerents, it is likely that they will come under considerable strain in any conflict in which one of the parties is prepared to violate its obligations under the Protocol. For that reason, the present writer, while hoping that more States will become parties to Protocol I, is in favour of reservations in respect of at least some of the reprisals provisions.

Nevertheless, it would be wrong to overlook some of the beneficial effects which Protocol I may have in relation to reprisals. Although it is unlikely that Articles 51-56 will be successful in preventing recourse to reprisals against the persons and objects to which they apply in cases where a State has been faced with massive and continuing violations of those same provisions by its adversary, they will probably have the effect of making States less ready to resort to such reprisals. Moreover, the reprisals provisions in Articles 51-56 almost certainly mean that reprisals against those targets will no longer be taken as a response to violations of other provisions of the law of armed conflict. Henceforth, reprisals against civilian targets are likely to be acceptable only when they are a response in kind (or almost in kind: for example, an attack on civilian objects as a response to a prior attack upon the civilian population of the State taking the reprisals). Protocol I has almost certainly eliminated reprisals against the civilian population as a general sanction for the enforcement of a wide range of rules. These developments are highly desirable. The mistake in Protocol I, it is suggested, was to try to go too far too fast. Looking at some of the reprisals provisions in the Protocol, one is reminded of Krafft's comment on the reprisals provision in the Civilians Convention: "It seems too good to be true. I even wonder if certain general principles contained in the Convention can be reconciled with the idea of war at all."(42)

FOOTNOTES

1. A. Cassese, *International Law in a Divided World*, (Oxford, 1986), p. 274.

2. On this question, see D.W. Bowett, 'Reprisals involving Recourse to Armed Force' 66 *AJIL* (1972), p. 1, and R. Barsotti, 'Armed Reprisals' in A. Cassese (ed): *The Current Legal Regulation of the Use of Force* (Dordrecht, 1986).

3. XCIV LNTS (1929) 65.

4. See F. Kalshoven, *Belligerent Reprisals* (Leyden, 1971), pp. 347-348.

5. See the discussion of the United Kingdom Orders in Council regarding economic warfare against the Axis Powers in Kalshoven, *op. cit.*, note 4, above, at p. 147 *et seq* and S.W.D. Rowson, 'Modern Blockade: Some Legal Aspects', 23 *BYIL* (1946), p. 346. See also the decision of the Netherlands Special Court of Cassation in *Rauter*, 16 *Ann. Digest* 526 (discussed by Kalshoven, *op. cit.* at pp. 242-255).

6. 15 *Ann. Digest* 632 at 637.

7. 'The Limits of the Operation of the Law of War', 30 *BYIL* (1953) p. 206 at 212. See also C. Greenwood, 'The Relationship between *ius ad bellum* and *ius in bello*' 9 Rev. Int. Studies (1983), p. 221.

8. See e.g. Kalshoven *op. cit.* at p. 157 and M. McDougal and F. Feliciano, *Law and Minimum World Public Order* (New Haven, 1961), p. 681.

9. *Op. cit.* at p. 682.

10. *Ibid.*

11. *Op. cit.* at pp. 341-342.

12. 15 *Ann. Digest* 471. See also the trials of *Von Mackensen and Maelzer*, 8 *War Crimes Reps.* 1 and *Kesselring*, 8 *War Crimes Reps.* 9, in which two British Military Courts tried senior German officers in respect of the same incident.

13. *British Manual of Military Law*, Part III (1958), pp. 184-185, and the United States Department of the Army Field Manual, *The Law of Land Warfare* (FM-27-10) (1956) at p. 177.

14. 2 RIAA (1928) p. 1013.

15. *Op. cit.* at p. 340.

16. See Kalshoven, *op. cit.* pp. 342-344.

17. See, e.g. the *United States Manual*, note 13 above, at p. 177.

18. First Convention, Articles 14 and 46 (wounded and sick on land and the medical personnel, buildings and equipment covered by the Convention), Second Convention, Articles 16 and 47 (wounded, sick and shipwrecked at sea and the medical personnel, ships and equipment covered by the Convention), Third Convention, Article 13 (prisoners of war) and Fourth Convention, Article 33 (civilians qualifying as protected persons).

19. Article 4(4).

20. See the discussion of the different views in Kalshoven, *op. cit.* pp. 112-114, 173-178 and 357-361.

21. See, e.g. the decision in *List*, note 6 above.

22. J.S. Pictet, *Commentary to the Fourth Convention* (Geneva, 1958), p. 39.

23. For a discussion of the debates at the Conference, see R. Bierzanek, 'Reprisals as a Means of Enforcing the Laws of Warfare' in A. Cassese (ed.) *The New Humanitarian Law of Armed Conflict* (Milan, 1979), p. 233, F. Kalshoven, 'The Belligerent Reprisals in the Light of the 1977 Geneva Protocols' in Jagellonean University and ICRC, *European Seminar on Humanitarian Law* (1979), p. 31, and S. Nahlik, 'Belligerent Reprisals as Seen in the Light of the Diplomatic Conference on Humanitarian Law' 42-2 *Law and Contemporary Problems* (1978), p. 36. For analysis of the reprisals provisions in Protocol I, see M. Bothe, K.-J. Partsch and W. Solf, *New Rules for Victims of Armed Conflicts* (The Hague, 1982), pp. 311-315, and ICRC,

Commentary on the Additional Protocols (Geneva 1987), pp. 982-987.

24. Article 49(3) provides that the provisions of Articles 51-67, which contain six of the seven prohibitions on reprisals, do not apply to naval or air warfare except in so far as such warfare affects the civilian population on land or involves attacks on objectives on land.

25. *Commentary*, note 23, above, at pp. 1372 and 1374.

26. 'The Implementation and Enforcement of the Geneva Conventions of 1949 and the Two Additional Protocols', 164 *RC* (1979-III), p. 1 at p. 35.

27. *Ibid.* at p. 45. A glance at the list of States which have so far made declarations under Article 90 (Sweden, Finland, Norway, Switzerland, Denmark, Austria, Italy, Belgium, Iceland, the Netherlands and New Zealand) reinforces this conclusion. It is difficult to envisage a conflict between any of these States.

28. CDDH/SR.58, para. 81.

29. Pictet, *op. cit.* note 22 above, at p. 15.

30. Nahlik, while firmly opposed to preserving any right of reprisal in the law of Geneva, accepts that such a right is a necessary feature of the law of The Hague (although he regards the provisions of Protocol I as lying wholly outside the scope of Hague Law); *loc. cit.* note 23, above, at pp. 65-66.

31. Reprisals are not mentioned in the President's message to the United States Senate, 26 *I.L.M.* 561 (1987), but see C.B. Roberts, 'The New Rules for Waging War: The Case against Ratification of Additional Protocol I', 26 *Virginia Jnl. Int. Law* (1985), p. 109 at 139 *et seq.*

32. 'Progressive Development of the Laws of War: A Reply to Criticisms of the 1977 Protocol I', 26 *Virginia Jnl. Int. Law* (1986), p. 693 at p. 710 *et seq.*

33. 26 *Int. Rev. of the Red Cross* (1986), p. 114.

34. *Loc. cit.* n. 23 above, at p. 65.

35. CDDH.SR. 42, para. 32.

36. ICRC *Commentary*, note 23 above, p. 987 at para. 3459.

37. See the stimulating discussion of this question by F. Hampson, 'Belligerent Reprisals and the 1977 Protocols to the Geneva Conventions of 1949', 37 *ICLQ* (1988) 818.

38. Kalshoven, *loc. cit.* note 23, above, at p. 41. See also Hampson, *loc. cit.*, note 37 above.

39. 9 CDDH Official Records 73.

40. ICRC Annual Report, 1983, p. 58.

41. This question is discussed at greater length in C.J. Greenwood, 'The Application of the Geneva Protocols of 1977 and their Impact on General International Law in Humanitarian Matters', in L. Condorelli (ed), *Proceedings of the Geneva Colloquium on the Protocols of 1977, Ten Years On* (forthcoming). See also A. Cassese, 'The Geneva Protocols of 1977 and Customary International Law', 3 *UCLA Pacific Basin Law Jnl.* (1984), p. 55 at 102-103.

42. 'The Present Position of the Red Cross Geneva Conventions', 37 *Tr. Grotius Soc.* (1951), p. 146. The remark is more apposite in relation to parts of Protocol I.

CONVENTIONAL WEAPONRY: THE LAW FROM ST. PETERSBURG TO LUCERNE AND BEYOND

F. Kalshoven

> "In bringing before you the subject of tonight's lecture, I do so with the painful feeling that it is a very dry subject - indeed, one which may be instructive, but cannot be made amusing; I can only, therefore, express my pleasure and surprise that the uninviting nature of my title should not have prevented more from attending this evening."*

These are not my words, but a quotation from the published records of an earlier meeting, comparable to the present one. They were, in fact, the opening phrases of a paper on "Explosive Bullets and Their Application to Military purposes", read by a Major G.V. Fosbery, V.C. H.M. Bengal Staff Corps, in a meeting of the Royal United Services Institution, held in London, under the chairmanship of Rear-Admiral Sir Frederick W.E. Nicolson, in the evening of Monday, the 20th January, 1868[(1)*]. If nothing else, this proves at least that on one earlier occasion a group of professional people met in this country to discuss an aspect of the use of conventional weapons.

The date of that previous occasion, January 1868, is of obvious significance. In the month of November of that year an International Military Commission assembled at St. Petersburg "in order to examine into the expediency of forbidding the use of certain projectiles in times of war between civilised nations". And that Commission "having by common agreement fixed the technical limits at which the necessities of war ought to yield to the requirements of humanity", drew up the text of a Declaration by which "the Contracting Parties engage(d) mutually to renounce, in case of war among themselves, the employment by their military or naval troops of any projectile of a weight below 400 grammes, which is either explosive or charged with fulminating or inflammable substances". This so

* For footnotes see p. 269.

called St. Petersburg Declaration was signed on 11th December, 1868 by the representatives of seventeen states, and thus became the first conventional undertaking to renounce the use in war of a specific category of weapon.

Major Fosbery's explosive bullets obviously fell within this category. It may therefore be of some interest to see how he dealt with the matter in January 1868; was he already then predicting a ban on their use? To be sure, he expressed some concern at "hear(ing) the use of rifle-shell in war condemned as cruel, cowardly, or useless"(2). For his part, however, he "trust(ed) that the rifle-shell may receive, at all events, thoughtful consideration, as a candidate for the office of peacemaker to begin with, and as having a tendency to shorten any war once commenced, where its use is properly persevered in".(3) More specifically, he attributed to the rifle-shell which he had himself perfected and tested in actual war-time conditions in India, a number of beneficial effects: it would "explode gunpowder enclosed in stout cases, such as artillery limber-boxes at extreme ranges, and when an ordinary bullet would in no ways affect it"(4); it was "a ready means of estimating distances ..., more especially amongst mountains"(5); and, last not least, it had a profound effect on enemy morale.(6)

But was it not then true that the explosive bullet was a cruel weapon? In order to deal with this argument Major Fosbery introduced a character who took this position and who, he said (and I quote)(7):

> "... takes to himself credit, and honestly enough, I doubt not, for humanity, and a kind regard for the comfort of his fellow-creatures, even when arrayed in arms against him. Yet he will take a scientific pride in the acknowledged weapons and usages of war, and use them with a good conscience to the best effects." ... "On land he disembowels (his enemy) with rockets, buries in his path the self-acting fougass; tears his body with the angular fragments of segment-shell; plies him with grape and canister, old iron, and broken bottles; undermines him; fills up his wells, and destroys his habitations and supplies, and makes him to die of hunger, of thirst, and exposure, or linger, it may be, for weeks, from the fearful wounds of the bayonet, the sabre, or the Snider-Enfield bullet, the latter, by the bye, almost equalling in their effects on the body any produced by rifle-shell, as may be seen by the fragments into which such a bullet divides when fired into water. All this, moreover, with the best possible intentions and most serene good faith. But let me ask you, is this really humanity? Are any of the deaths to which the

> greater number of the killed in war are put, strictly speaking, humane? or, if they are not, what is this humanity of which so much is made? Is it indeed a branch of that quality which leads us to clothe the naked and feed the hungry, only developed in another direction? or is it not rather a term of variable quantity, applied to homicidal cruelty, and so adjusted as to be always just one step behind the last military discovery of the day?"

For Major Fosbery, these were obviously rhetorical questions. To his mind, not humanity lay at the root of this argument of cruelty; not "the desire to spare the infantry and cavalry soldier ... one atom of suffering, not one pang in death (for the shell kills much more instantaneously and more mercifully than the bullet)": rather, the desire was to spare him

> "that unpleasant feeling which attaches to any species of death which men have not been accustomed to look into the face - that dread of the unknown - which makes a child fear to enter a dark passage without a light - which keeps country people from a haunted lane - the bravest sailor from a harbour known to contain torpedoes - or makes gallant troops shaky on ground which is supposed to be mined. That feeling which is - say what you will - at least akin to the sentiment which more than all the bloodshed in the world has lost its battles, and which it should be the object of every improvement in war material to produce, whether by its known or by its supposed effects - I mean fear."(8)

Thus, rifle-shell, far from deserving to be banned, ought to be accepted everywhere and so should further improvements in war material, so as to continue to inspire into the adversary that beneficial dread of meeting a death he had not been accustomed to look into the face. "No one" - Major Fosbery felt - "will face a rapid and well sustained infantry fire of shell, as all who have seen them much used, are agreed, at all events until accustomed to them; and this takes time. But if they will not face them, then life is saved rather than destroyed. In fact the old argument holds good for each fresh step in advance; the more terrible the recognised engines of destruction, the greater will be the prospect of maintaining peace; or should war break out the shorter of necessity will be its duration."

So much for the optimistic views of Major Fosbery; views which, needless to say, were not shared by all his contemporaries, witness the adoption in that same year of the Petersburg Declaration. Yet, it did not seem to me a waste of your time to deal at some length with Major Fosbery's ideas: January 1868 may be a long time ago, but this is a far cry from saying that no one would be thinking today along similar lines.

There is another interesting aspect to his lecture. You may have noticed that he referred at one place to bullets being fired into water. This goes to show that even in his days, experiments with rifle ammunition were being carried out as a matter of course and an awareness existed that projectiles of different design could have different effects. It is simply not true, as has sometimes been suggested, that this awareness arose only recently, as a consequence of the introduction of the modern rifle projectiles with a calibre below 7.62 mm.

1. The Drafting of the 1981 Weapons Convention

This brings us to present times. For, although many an interesting debate took place in the period following after the adoption of the St. Petersburg Declaration, and in particular in the course of the negotiations at the Hague Peace Conference of 1899 which preceded the adoption of the Declaration Concerning Expanding Bullets (the so-called dum-dum bullets), it is not my intention to pursue this historical line any further.[10] Rather, attention will be focused on the proceedings which ultimately resulted in the adoption, on 10th October 1980, of the United Nations Convention on Prohibitions or Restrictions on the Use of Certain Conventional Weapons which may be Deemed to be Excessively Injurious or to have Indiscriminate Effects.[11]

To be sure, the records of those proceedings could easily be made to fill more than one evening. Therefore, to quote an often dramatically misused expression: I shall be brief, and concentrate on some highlights, especially as far as the earlier history is concerned. Another preliminary remark is that my focus will be more on Geneva than on New York: more, in other words on the work of the International Committee of the Red Cross (or ICRC) than on that of the United Nations.[12]

The Role of the ICRC

The interest of the ICRC in the matter of weapons stemmed not so much from any particular desire to get itself involved in questions of weapons technology and armaments, as from its concern to see the civilian population protected from the dangers of indiscriminate warfare. Aerial bombardment and, since 1945, the "atomic bomb" were obvious objects of its concern; but as early as 1956, it mentioned "incendiary agents" along with chemical, bacteriological and radioactive ones as devices which either by their nature or in given circumstances could have uncontrollable effects. In 1967, in a Memorandum to all Governments on the protection of civilian populations against the dangers of indiscriminate warfare, it raised the question whether "such new weapons as napalm and high velocity rockets" should not be regarded as "weapons inflicting unnecessary suffering". And in 1969, it invited a meeting of experts to give their opinion *inter alia*, on the questions of napalm, "high speed barbed missiles" (i.e. flechettes) and "fragmentation bombs".

Here, of course, the influence of the information concerning the conduct of war in Vietnam becomes clearly discernible. It is of interest to note that the experts which the ICRC had brought together were hopelessly divided on the question of whether the use of napalm was permissible or not and whether a prohibition on its use would be desirable or feasible (the Report of the meeting is silent on the other two types of weapon). Equally interesting was the advice offered by a number of these experts, to the effect that the task of the Red Cross in this sphere was not so much to bring about the prohibition of specified weapons but, rather, constantly to remind all those concerned of the basic principles governing their use.

This piece of advice was, in effect, in conformity with feelings that were widespread in Red Cross circles at the time on the desirability (or, rather, undesirability) of Red Cross involvement in questions of weaponry. But the ICRC did not give in yet: in one of the volumes constituting the documentation which it submitted to the Conference of Government Experts, convened for May-June 1971, the question was raised whether weapons such as "fragmentation bombs", "certain ultra rapid 'darts'" (i.e. flechettes), certain new types of rifle ammunition, "mines filled with glass splinters or rusted nails" and indeed the entire range of so called "anti-personnel" weapons should not be made the subject of a critical examination.

Significantly, the volume containing these suggestions was the one devoted to guerrilla warfare - the Vietnam war, in other words. In another document, dealing with "Rules relative to behaviour of combatants", the ICRC merely suggested the reaffirmation of the basic principle, embodied already in Article 23(2) of the Hague Regulations of 1899/1907, prohibiting the employment of "arms, projectiles or material calculated to cause unnecessary suffering", and it did not make any proposals for more specific prohibitions or restrictions on use of particular weapons.

Some such proposals were submitted by participants at the Conference, both in the course of its first (1971) session and in the second session, held in 1972. With respect to these proposals, it may suffice to note that while in 1971 their main thrust had been the protection of the civilian population, in 1972 a wider goal was sought as far as incendiary weapons were concerned: while the 1971 proposal had been for a prohibition on "napalm bombs and other Ancendiary weapons ... for use in circumstances where they may affect the civilian population", the restrictive closing phrase did no longer figure in the proposal for 1972. This broadening of its scope at the same time reduced the number of its proponents: while the Dutch experts had supported the earlier version, they withdrew their support in 1972. Thus, it became even clearer than before that the experts, and the governments behind them, were sharply divided over the issue of restrictions on the use of incendiary weapons.

By this time, the ICRC had completely abandoned any idea of making its own suggestions regarding prohibitions or restrictions on the use of specified conventional weapons. For one thing, had it followed its heart, it would simply have proposed an outright ban on the use of an assortment of weapons, with incendiary weapons among them, that it had come to regard as unnecessarily cruel. But it realised only too well that this way of the heart was closed. This being so, it was reluctant to get itself entangled in discussions about the relative merits and demerits of this, that or the other weapon, with the political overtones such discussions would inevitably have. After all, the war in Vietnam was not over yet, and charges of unlawful conduct of the war continued to fill the air. At the same time, the ICRC was loath to see the subject go to the United Nations for fear tht it would there become totally politicised. The question was therefore what course to steer.

The role of Government Experts

In resolving this problem, it was helped by outside factors. At the first, 1971, session of the Conference of Government Experts, the suggestion had already been made that the Conference should take up the study of all weapons which were not at the time the subject of discussions in other fora, such as the United Nations or the then Conference of the Committee on Disarmament. Neither this nor the 1972 session did in fact embark on such a wide-ranging debate. But a number of non-aligned countries, with Sweden very prominent among them, continued to repeat their demands for such an expert study. They voiced these demands both within and outside the United Nations. One memorable occasion was the XXIInd International Conference of the Red Cross, held at Teheran in November 1973. Virtually simultaneously with the United Nations General Assembly, that Conference adopted a resolution (No. XIV) requesting the ICRC to convene a conference of government experts to study the question of conventional weapons that might be deemed to cause unnecessary suffering or have indiscriminate effects. The resolution was the outcome of negotiations between two key figures representing opposing tendencies: Mr. George Aldrich of the United States Department of State and Dr. Hans Blix of the Swedish Ministry for Foreign Affairs, with the present author acting as mediator.

The adoption of this resolution, with the support even of the United States which up to that moment had shown itself unwilling to take part in such an exercise, cleared the way for the convening of the meeting of governmental experts which the non-aligned had so insistently demanded. After further careful and at times difficult preparations, the ICRC duly convened the Conference of Government Experts on the Use of Certain Conventional Weapons at Lucerne for 24th September - 18th October, 1974. It will be noticed that the qualifying phrase of Resolution XIV, that the weapons to be studied "might be deemed to cause unnecessary suffering or have indiscriminate effects", did not figure in the title of the Conference. For one thing, this reflected the unwillingness of some governments to concede beforehand that part of their weaponry might perhaps be open to some criticism from a legal point of view. For another, the change was more than cosmetic in that for all practical purposes it cleared the way for a study of the entire range of conventional weapons.

2. The Lucerne Conference 1974

The Conference was favoured by a broad attendance: the list of participants included experts from some 50 countries, from several national liberation movements, from the United Nations and the World Health Organisation, and from some non-governmental organisations including SIPRI. Among the experts were officers with wartime experience, ballistics and technological experts, military and civilian surgeons and other medical doctors, lawyers of all kinds, and diplomats, some of whom had not had to travel any further than from Geneva (and whose expertise in the field of conventional weaponry was correspondingly limited). The Conference was chaired by Dr. Jean Pictet of the ICRC, and I had the privilege of serving as its main rapporteur. What I have to say about the Conference is based on its report as well as on information I collected in the latter capacity.[13]

The Conference had an ambitious agenda, with as its first item a discussion of legal criteria. This was followed by a study of incendiary weapons, small-calibre projectiles, blast and fragmentation weapons, delayed action and treacherous weapons, and future weapons. A debate on the follow-up to be given to the work of the Conference, and of course a discussion of the report would conclude the proceedings.

Notwithstanding this heavy workload, and despite its heterogeneous composition, the Conference did not break up into working groups; the entire recorded debate took place in plenary sessions. The only exception was an informal working group on the definition and classification of incendiary weapons. Its informal character did not prevent this working group from reporting back to the Conference on the outcome of its deliberations and its report was annexed to the Conference report.

The opening debate on legal criteria profited greatly by a paper on "legal criteria for the prohibition or restriction of use of categories of conventional weapons" by Colonel (as he then was) Sir David Hughes-Morgan.[14] It may be of interest to note some of the observations he made in that paper. By way of introduction, he drew a distinction between the older type of ban on "the use of a specific weapon or projectile, necessarily involving a description of the weapon or projectile concerned", and prohibitions "drafted with reference to the effects resulting from use" of weapons. With respect to the former type of specific ban he wrote, repeating a warning voiced earlier by Baxter,[15] that

> "the more specific the prohibition, the greater the possibility of lawful circumvention of the rule. A detailed prohibition on a specific weapon which is militarily effective may well challenge technologists to devise a weapon having the same effect but whose characteristics are not caught by the prohibition."

A prohibition drafted with reference to effects, on the other hand, "is not only valid as a prohibition in itself, but is likely to contain the criteria by which future prohibitions on specific weapons ought to be judged". The first such prohibition to come to mind is, of course, that on weapons calculated to cause unnecessary suffering. How valuable a standard was this in practice? Sir David had the following to say about this:

> "There are two main difficulties in applying this rule to specific weapons. First, it may be necessary - particularly at short range - to inflict a severe wound to ensure that a man is placed "hors de combat", for a comparatively minor injury may enable him to continue fighting.
>
> Secondly, the requirements of the military task to be performed have to be taken into account. For example, some of the powerful weapons designed for use against armoured fighting vehicles are likely to inflict severe injuries on the crews. But such weapons may be necessary to penetrate the armoured protection on such vehicles and it is a legitimate act of war to put fighting vehicles and their crews out of action. Similarly, a particular level of penetration is required for small arms to defeat body armour or steel helmets, and a weapon which did not do this would not be militarily effective: its effect on an unprotected man, however, would be severe. Ideally, a military commander should have available to him a range of weapons such as to be able to meet exactly the degree of force needed in any particular situation. For obvious reasons, this is impossible: a soldier can carry only one rifle, for example, and the varieties of artillery projectiles are necessarily limited."

His conclusion was that a weapon could not "... be declared unlawful merely because it does on occasion cause severe suffering or injury". As the correct criterion he saw one of proportionality, and "... in this regard a weapon which in practice is found inevitably to cause injury or suffering disproportionate to its military effectiveness would be held to contravene the prohibition". Finally turning to "future generic prohibitions", he considered it "desirable to define a standard of comparison by which it can be determined whether injury is caused unnecessarily". At the same time, he doubted the possibility "to better that which is at present used, namely the degree of injury caused considered in proportion to the military effectiveness of the weapon in question". Yet this standard was certainly not useless:

> "... a prohibition so framed is of value in forbidding the use of any weapon which, while inflicting severe wounds, has no corresponding military significance. The difficult cases, in which the result of the proportionality equation are in dispute, can only be resolved by the agreement of states to prohibit the use of specific weapons. In so doing, they would necessarily take into account the criteria contained in the generic prohibition."

I have included these lengthy quotations from an unpublished paper because they provide an excellent introduction to the difficulties which the Conference experienced, both in its discussion of legal criteria and in the debate on specific weapons or categories of weapon. To demonstrate these problems I can do no better than quote from a statement by Dr. Hans Blix, still in the same debate on legal criteria. Referring in particular to Sir David's comments on inevitable disproportionality as a ground for prohibition of a weapon, he felt that "inevitable" was too rigid a term; and he was

> "... also troubled by the use of the word "disproportionate", because it seems to imply that if a weapon is very effective from a military point of view, then the degree of suffering that would be acceptable would be proportionally high. However, the military effect that is legitimate is only that of putting a man out of combat, to disable him, and there should be put no premium on weapons which may go further than that. This is not to deny, of course, that the element of military utility will have to be weighed against the humanitarian aspects of the use of a weapon, or rather, the inhumane aspects of use of a weapon. That balancing evidently is a central task in determining whether the rule is applicable in a particular case."

In other words, while he agreed with Sir David that proportionality was the applicable standard here he shrunk back from accepting the consequences of its application in all cases.

The concept of unnecessary suffering

In discussing unnecessary suffering, a first question to arise was what had to be understood by this concept of suffering. On this question, there was an appreciable degree of consensus; "suffering" was generally considered to comprise such factors as mortality rate, the painfulness or severity of wounds, and the incidence of permanent damage or disfigurement. Opinion was more divided, however, when it came to an identification of the elements to be taken into account in assessing what suffering should be considered unnecessary. There were those experts who, like Dr. Blix, while conceding that an element of military necessity was involved here, maintained that this consisted solely in the capacity of a weapon to put an enemy *hors de combat*. Even then, the question would remain how much injury is required to disable an enemy soldier. According to the opposite view, military necessity as an element in the choice of weapons included such other factors as (to quote Mr. Ronald Bettauer from the United States):

> "... the destruction or neutralization of military materiel, restriction of movement, interdiction of lines of communication and effects on morale, command and control, stamina and cohesion of opposing forces, effectiveness against particular targets, availability of alternative weapons, cost, and the security of the troops involved."

The debate on unnecessary suffering yields one further interesting detail. This arose in connection with the view, defended by Dr. Blix and others, that the sole legitimate function of a weapon was to put an enemy *hors de combat*. Dr. Pictet grasped this opportunity to confront the meeting with an idea of a somewhat philosophical order, that, "... if two or more weapons would be available which would offer equal capacity to overcome ... an adversary, the weapon which could be expected to inflict the least injury ought to be employed."(16) The idea had already been forestalled by Sir David in his paper, where he also had pointed out that it could not work in practice. The same objection was of course repeated in the debate. An attempt to do Dr. Pictet's idea maximum justice while at the same time putting it in its proper perspective was undertaken by Mr. Frederick Blakeney, Head of the Australian delegation. While suggesting a formulation which closely followed the idea expressed by Dr. Pictet, he accompanied this with the comment that any such formulation

> "... obviously needs to be looked at in respect of the enemy as an individual, and as a group. There already seems a wide measure of agreement that as few as possible should be killed, no more than necessary should be wounded and those lightly rather than gravely. The total so disabled or overcome should not exceed the number necessary to ensure victory in given exchanges and the war overall."

I have dwelt at some length on this discussion about unnecessary suffering because it obviously was of crucial importance to further discussions on specific categories of weapon.[17] It also provides a clear example of the type of inconclusive debate which was so characteristic of the Lucerne Conference. The debate on legal criteria did not yield any agreed formulations. It also was certainly disappointing to those few experts who, like my compatriot Major Gonsalves of the army legal services, had set their hopes even higher and aimed at identifying legal parameters of such accuracy that they could be applied almost automatically to any given weapon. For those who had entered the debate with more modest expectations, it could at least be said to have provided, in Dr. Blix's words, a measure of "knowledge of each other's philosophy for prohibitions or restrictions".

A few brief words may suffice with respect to the other legal criteria discussed.

Indiscriminateness

As concerns indiscriminateness, the discussion turned around the question whether the category of conventional weapons includes types of weapon which are inherently indiscriminate. The difference of opinion was predictable: while some experts thought that such weapons did indeed exist, other experts denied this. According to these latter experts, any conventional weapon could be used indiscriminately or with discrimination, so that the method of use rather than the weapon's properties would be decisive in determining whether the requirement of discrimination had in effect been met. And a similar difference of opinion became apparent with respect to perfidy, with some experts advocating that this be given a separate place among the legal criteria and others denying that it would deserve such a separate place.

Dictates of public conscience

The last criterion brought up for discussion under the heading of "legal criteria" was the dictates of the public conscience. These are mentioned as one factor besides others in the well-known Martens clause in the preamble to the Hague Convention of 1899 respecting the Laws and Customs of War on Land. It is of course very much a debatable point what legal effect, if any, should be attributable to utterances of public opinion. At Lucerne, there was a general readiness to acknowledge its importance. To some, it even constituted an independent legal criterion against which the legality of use of specific weapons could be tested. In the eyes of others, it represented a political rather than a legal factor: governments would be well advised to take the "dictates of the public conscience" into account in making up their mind about the deployment and use of modern conventional weapons. And indeed, in any not entirely closed society this certainly seems to be a sound piece of advice.

Incendiary weapons

The "dictates of the public conscience" have obviously played an important role in the discussions of recent years about the admissibility of use of incendiary weapons. At Lucerne, these were the first category of weapons to come up for discussion, and although it is not my intention to discuss each and every category of weapon, some remarks about incendiaries may nonetheless be useful.

One key issue in the debate concerned the definition and classification of "incendiary weapons". After all, there are many ways of starting a fire, and at times it may erupt as an involuntary side effect of the use of weapons. This question was taken up by the informal working group which I mentioned earlier, and the group was able to reach a consensus at least on the definition of "incendiary munitions". It read as follows:

> "For the purposes of this Conference, an incendiary munition has been considered to be any munition which is primarily designed to set fire to objects or to cause burn injury to persons through the action of flame and/or heat produced by a chemical reaction of a substance delivered on the target."

The group also recognised that there exist munitions which may have secondary or incidental incendiary effects but which do not fall within the quoted definition, and they gave examples: illuminants, tracers, smoke, signalling systems and fuel-air explosives. This was as far as the consensus went: the group had not been able to reach agreement on the classification of other munitions such as certain armour-piercing and anti-aircraft projectiles, which combine incendiary with other distinctive effects.

In the meantime, the discussion in plenary had yielded a wealth of information about the use of incendiary weapons, their military characteristics and medical effects, and possible substitutes. In the final evaluation, the conflicting nature of much of this information led to radically opposite conclusions with respect to the admissibility of use of incendiary weapons. This division of opinion became apparent as much in the assessment of these weapons against the criteria of unnecessary suffering and indiscriminateness as in the views on their prohibition.

Thus, according to one group of experts, incendiary weapons caused exceptionally grave wounds, were of limited military value and could easily be substituted by other weapons, and they could therefore be said to cause unnecessary suffering. These experts also regarded incendiary weapons as inherently indiscriminate. In contrast, while other experts did admit that burn wounds are probably the worst possible type of wound, these experts were not convinced that the use of incendiary weapons would in all cases result in an exceptionally high incidence of casualties, let alone of gravely wounded. These experts felt moreover that the military value of these weapons was far from negligible, and they feared that their substitution by other weapons might even result in an increased number of casualties and of severely wounded in particular. And as far as indiscriminateness was concerned, they once again expressed the view that this depended entirely on the method of use. One method in particular, however, the massive use of incendiary weapons against civilian population centres, found virtually unanimous condemnation.

Views on the final evaluation of incendiary weapons were equally divided, with one group of experts advocating their outright prohibition and the other group holding that insufficient grounds for such a sweeping conclusion had been shown. One interesting detail in this debate concerned the possibility of attacks on military objectives located within population centres: while an expert from the first group pointed to the risk that incendiary weapons, when used in such attacks, might start fires spreading over a wide area outside the target, an expert from the other group drew attention to the responsibility of the authorities who should ensure that no vital military objectives be found in civilian population centres.

The discussions which followed on other categories of weapon were of a similar nature. There might be differences in technical complication or in the level of emotion involved in the debate, but in each and every instance, once it came to evaluating the category of weapon concerned, the house was irreconcilably divided. This caused quite some frustration, especially among those experts who had come to Lucerne with the firm conviction that a number of conventional weapons deserved to be banned from use, and that their view would be shared by all once everyone got to know the true facts. This sense of frustration was voiced, for instance, by Dr. Blix in his closing statement on small-calibre projectiles. The Swedish experts, he said, had found the discussion "most useful"; but still:

> "We would have been even more appreciative of the debate if more of the statements had aimed at a constructive analysis rather than one that has very preponderantly been directed at throwing doubt at whatever data that have been presented and reaching the somewhat sterile conclusion that nothing is known about anything."

When one looks back at the Conference of Lucerne, a first conclusion is that it constituted an important event in that so many countries, and most of the major ones among them, were represented by qualified experts. The experts, moreover, did not confine themselves to being physically present: they offered a wealth of information about a wide range of conventional weapons. In doing so, they did throw doubt on virtually every assertion which one group of experts and the governments which they represented, had previously regarded as incontrovertible truths, whether with regard to legal criteria or where the properties of weapons and their substitutes were concerned. It is perhaps no exaggeration to say that the greatest value of the Conference lay precisely in this element of "throwing doubt" on the earlier beliefs: anyone who thus far might have entertained the hope that fast results were within reach, had by the end of 1974 probably given up those high expectations.

One further conclusion I drew at the time from the totality of the debate, and which was significantly strengthened in a private conversation with the Australian representative, Mr. Blakeney, was that few results, if any, could be expected in the sphere of protection of combatants, and that efforts had best be concentrated on achieving an improved protection of the civilian population.

3. Subsequent negotiations

The rest of the story is soon told. The experts met in a second session at Lugano, from 28th January to 26th February 1976.[18] The report on that session is about twice as thick as that of the session at Lucerne, in inverse ratio to the importance of the affair. This time, there were besides the Plenary Meetings, a General Working Group and several Working Sub-Groups, both official and informal ones. A number of documents were produced and annexed to the report. But with one exception, it would be an exaggeration to say that anything critically important had been contributed. The one exception concerns the proposal, introduced there for the first time by the experts of Mexico and Switzerland, to forbid the use of "weapons producing fragments which in the human body escape detection by the usual medical methods".[19] This proposal on so called non-detectable fragments immediately received widespread support.

The debate on conventional weapons was at the same time being carried on at the Diplomatic Conference of Geneva, 1974-1977, where the Ad Hoc Commission met at regular intervals, more often than not merely to listen to lengthy statements by Dr. Blix and his colleagues, to which no response came. When the Diplomatic Conference terminated its work, it could do no more than transmit the whole business to the United Nations. It did this by Resolution 22(IV), which recommended the convening of a Conference of Governments no later than 1979, with a view to reaching:[20]

"(a) agreement on prohibitions or restrictions on the use of specific conventional weapons which may be deemed to be excessively injurious or have indiscriminate effects, taking into account humanitarian and military considerations; and

(b) agreement on a mechanism for the review of any such agreements and for the consideration of proposals for further such agreements."

It will be noticed that the qualifying elements of excessive injury and indiscriminateness had crept in again, this time, as was to become apparent later, to stay. Another important element was of course the reference to a review mechanism, an aspect that had been much debated at the Diplomatic Conference and to which great importance was attached, especially by those Governments who had their hopes for early results seen frustrated.

4. The UN Convention on Weapons

After two preparatory sessions, the United Nations Conference on Prohibitions or Restrictions of Use of Certain Conventional Weapons Which may be Deemed to be Excessively Injurious or to have Indiscriminate Effects met at Geneva in two yearly sessions, in 1979 and 1980. The Conference produced a Convention with three annexed Protocols.[21]

To start with the latter, they deal with "non-detectable fragments" (Protocol I), "prohibitions or restrictions on the use of mines, booby traps and other devices" (Protocol II) and "prohibitions or restrictions on the use of incendiary weapons" (Protocol III). Few of their provisions provide any protection to combatants; this is notably the case with the one and only article of Protocol I and with some of the provisions in Article 6 of Protocol II on the use of booby traps. For the rest, Mr. Blakeney's prediction came true that the focus would be on the fate of the civilian population. In that respect, there is of course a certain amount of overlap between the Weapons Protocols and the parts on protection of the civilian population in the Geneva Protocols of 1977; but this is not the whole story: both the Mines Protocol and the Incendiary Weapons Protocol contain specific provisions which provide additional protection.

One of these, the rule laid down in Article 2, paragraph 2, of the Protocol on Incendiary Weapons, held the Conference in suspense till the very last minute. The paragraph provides that:

> "It is prohibited in all circumstances to make any military objective located within a concentration of civilians the object of attack by air-delivered incendiary weapons."

As this was virtually the only significant addition to the protection of the civilian population afforded by the Protocols of 1977, it was crucial to a number of Governments that the provision would be adopted. At the same time, the United States in particular found it extremely difficult to accept this restriction on the freedom of action of their armed forces. As long as the United States delegation could not express its approval of the proposed text, the Soviet Union kept silent too. It was therefore a moment of utter relief when toward the very end of the second session the news arrived that the United States had finally decided to accept the text. Already on the following day, the Soviet delegation could inform the Conference that Moscow had given the green light too - an unusually quick reaction on their part. As in the meantime all the problems attending the setting up of a review mechanism had also been resolved, the Conference could ultimately come to its happy end.

The review mechanism, as contained in Article 8 of the Convention, is a model of complexity, and this necessarily so because it attempts to meet a set of virtually irreconcilable goals. There was, first, the goal of those Governments who had wanted more significant, results to ensure that the good work could continue in future. An additional goal of these Governments was to bring even their reluctant partners along in any such future exercise. And there was the goal of these reluctant Governments, to avoid any obligations to accept future meetings, let alone the outcome of such meetings, against their will. All these interests have to some extent found a place in Article 8. Put differently, not too much should be expected of it; or, in the alternative, need be feared of it.

This brings me to my final conclusion. The results obtained at Geneva in 1980 while perhaps not overly impressive, are certainly not negligible either. At all events, they represent the very limit of what could be reached at the time, and in all probability they will remain so for a considerable amount of time to come.

FOOTNOTES

* This paper was first given at a meeting of the Discussion Group of the Laws of Armed Conflict of the British Institute of International and Comparative Law, 16th March 1985.

1. *Journal of the Royal United Services Institution*, London, Vol. 12, 1879, pp. 15-27.

2. p. 17.

3. p. 27.

4. p. 17.

5. p. 21.

6. pp. 2-27.

7. p. 25.

8. p. 26.

9. p. 27.

10. As for the negotiating history of the 1899 Declaration on dum-dum bullets, reference may be made to the article entitled "The soldier and his golf clubs", which the present author contributed to *Etudes et essais sur le droit international humanitaire et sur les principes de la Croix-Rouge*, published in honour of Jean Pictet, Geneva/The Hague, 1984, pp. 369-385.

11. The text of the Convention is found, *inter alia*, in Roberts & Guelff (eds.), *Documents on the Law of War*, Oxford, 1982, p. 467 ff.

12. Much of what follows is based on this author's "The Conference of Government Experts on the Use of Certain Conventional Weapons, Lucerne, 24th September - 18th October 1974", in *Netherlands Yearbook of International Law*, Vol. VI, 1975, pp. 77-102.

13. International Committee of the Red Cross, *Conference of Government Experts on the Use of Certain Conventional Weapons (Lucerne, 24.9-18.10.1974) - Report*, Geneva, 1975. An abbreviated version of the oral report on the Conference, made by the present author at the outset of the second session of the Ad Hoc Commission, was published in the summary records of that Commission: 8th meeting of 5th February, 1975 (CDDH/IV/SR.8, paras. 8-33), *Official Records of the Diplomatic Conference on the Reaffirmation and Development of International Humanitarian Law Applicable in Armed Conflicts, Geneva (1974-1977), Vol. XVI, pp. 68-73.*

14. Along with other documents distributed at the Conference, Sir David's paper was merely mentioned in the list of such documents, included as Annex 4 to the Report.

15. R.R. Baxter, "Criteria for the Prohibition of Weapons in International Law", in *Festschrift fur Ulrich Scheuner* 1973 p. 51.

16. Report of the Conference, p. 9: para. 25.

17. For a further discussion of the question, the reader may be referred to the paper contributed by the present author to the book in honour of Jean Pictet, *supra* note 10.

18. International Committee of the Red Cross, *Conference of Government Experts on the Use of Certain Conventional Weapons (Second Session Lugano, 28.1-26.2.1987) - Report*, Geneva, 1976.

19. Report of the Conference, p. 188: COLU/212.

20. Official Records, Vol. I, p. 215.

21. Text adopted, 10th October 1980, opened for signature, 10th April 1981; in force, 2nd December 1983, 19 *I.L.M.* 1523, *Cmnd.* 8370.

UNNECESSARY SUFFERING? - A MEDICAL VIEW

R. Scott

1. Introduction

The ICRC convened a conference at Geneva in 1973 to which experts in the diplomatic, military, legal and medical fields were invited to express their views on the prohibition or restriction of specific weapons. The experts from the United Kingdom attended in a personal capacity and expressed their personal opinions. The exchanges at this conference were summarised in an ICRC publication.[1]*

In the same year in Teheran the XXII International Conference of the Red Cross adopted a resolution to invite the International Committee of the Red Cross to convene a conference of government experts to look at "Conventional weapons that might be deemed to cause unnecessary suffering or have indiscriminate effects" and to consider the means by which international agreement could be reached to prohibit their development and use. The legal background has been described by Professor Kalshoven.[2]

In implementation of this resolution governments were invited to send representatives to further conferences in 1974, at Lucerne and in 1976, at Lugano.

The physicians and scientists who contributed to these conferences frequently found difficulty in understanding the legal process and in particular, in grappling with the concept of law that may proceed from philosophical and ethical considerations.

I will make some attempt to relate my observations to the legal issues and I will try to describe the application of the

* For footnotes see p. 279.

scientific process to the relationship between the use of weapons and the suffering that may ensue.

2. Weapon Use

As we are all only too aware these days, some weapons are designed not to be used. As far as I know, this is a new concept which followed the development of nuclear weapons. So called "conventional weapons" are designed to be used, and current design criteria normally specify the circumstances of use and the results to be expected. For example, an anti-personnel mortar-bomb can be described in terms of the area in which 50% of exposed personnel will be incapacitated by injury, caused by the penetration of metal fragments. The specifications for rifles and machine guns prior to World War One included their effects on horses, because cavalry was still considered to be an effective arm. Of course the early battles of World War One showed that cavalry was rendered completely ineffective by machine guns and there is currently no need for the designers of small arms systems to consider their effect on the horse. But if the horse was a legitimate target, could one say that the cavalry-man injured by similar bullets had sustained unnecessary injury?

On the question of use I now wish to explore each of these themes further. If one accepts that nuclear devices are designed not to be used then presumably, it is not necessary to discuss the injuries that could result from their use. It is notable that in the current arms limitation talks matters related to suffering are not included.

There is an international group of physicians which is currently attracting publicity for the view that there is no credible medical response to strategic nuclear attack.(3) They claim that, therefore, there can be no credible nuclear defence policy. I will not comment on either of these two assertions except to say that a policy of non-use does not necessarily inhibit all speculation on injury and suffering.

Simple calculations of the expenditure of ammunition during war related to the number of casualties sustained, show that for every soldier hit by a bullet from a rifle or machine gun, many thousands of rounds of ammunition are expended. "Covering fire", is utilised to prevent the enemy from observing movement, or to get into a position to fire his own weapons and uses up a great deal of ammunition that does not cause injury. The machine gun or rifle bullet may also be designed to penetrate protection. In the early part of this century, this was often defined as so many feet of earth or thicknesses of brick but it could also be defined in terms of personal body armour or the light steel of unarmoured vehicles. Can we then say that injury which results following the penetration of such protection must be considered in bullet design?

Not being intimately acquainted with horses I do not know whether his horse experienced the same exhilaration that Winston Churchill described at the Battle of Omdurman. It is quite likely, however, that it experienced the same state of excitability, in which wounds are unnoticed or disregarded and which required that near-mortal injury was necessary to stop his charge. When the horse was replaced by the tank similar considerations applied. The mobility and the fire-power of the tank are its prime assets and its armour is designed primarily to protect its engine and its ammunition and secondarily to protect its occupants. It was of interest to us to learn some years ago that tank crew are not the most vulnerable parts of this system. However, if anti-tank weapons injure the crew, are there circumstances in which their injuries could be considered unnecessarily severe? Apparently not. At the conference in Lucerne this possibility was considered and rejected.

It would seem then, that if we are to consider unnecessary suffering as a criterion for prohibition, the weapon must be designed to attack personnel. Of course, if the weapon is indiscriminate in its effects there may be an additional ground for prohibition on its development or use. This point was debated at length in the conferences which I attended.

3. Anti-Personnel Weapons

For reasons which I will elaborate later, I will look first of all at an anti-personnel weapon designed for a specific purpose - the baton-round. Of course no one proposes to use the baton-round in war. It was, however, developed for use by the military in Northern Ireland as an alternative to the rifle bullet, when the drawbacks of the use of anti-riot chemicals in built up areas had become obvious. The baton-round was designed to be used as a discriminating weapon with specific effects. It was conceded that it would inflict pain, associated with a degree of injury but that this injury would fall within acceptable limits. The alternative was the use of a weapon which, in the circumstances, was likely to be indiscriminate and to cause an unacceptable degree of injury with a high risk of mortality. After its introduction attention was drawn by surgeons to the seriousness of a few of the injuries caused by this device and to its apparent indiscriminate nature. In an attempt to meet these criticisms the baton-round was redesigned and new guidelines drawn up as to its use.[4] These depended heavily on an analysis of riots as they occurred at that time. In the course of the analysis the possible injuring effects of the baton-round on the target rioter were estimated and the probability of serious injury calculated. Subsequently a number of cases of fatal injury due to this weapon were reported and the government found it necessary to defend the use of the plastic baton-round in one case brought before the European Court of Human Rights.[5]

The government accepts that the doctrine of the use of minimum force should apply in internal security operations in the same way that it is currently applied to police operations. In the case of the baton-round the military aim is to inflict a degree of pain which will cause the rioter to desist.

General experience and the experience of soldiers involved in peace-keeping operations is used as the guide as to how much force is necessary. In the laboratory assessment of the baton-round, only the hazards can be estimated, not the effectiveness. There is no way of assessing the degree of pain inflicted by the baton-round and relating this to the probable action of the rioter. As we have already noted, in the excitement of a game, a military action, or a riot, injury which would normally be expected to be associated with significant pain, may not even be noticed.

The weapon may be designed to cause the opponent to desist. The infliction of pain is not quantifiable and, therefore, cannot be a criterion. Can any other criterion be applied?

4. Penetration

Until early in this century the performance of rifle bullets was determined by their ability to penetrate. It was appreciated that penetrating wounds could cause instant "knock-down" and there were at least two views on how this effect was achieved. One was a scientific view which related knock-down to the amount of energy expended on the target. Before I go on to discuss the other view I would like to explore the consequences of this "scientific" approach.

The amount of physical force was calculated at 70 ft/lbs. As far as I have been able to determine this was worked out by calculating how much power was required to cause the center of gravity of an upright fully loaded German soldier to pass in front of, or behind, the point of support on the balls of his feet! To the weapon developer the implication was that if a kinetic energy projectile transmitted this amount of power to the target it would achieve its object. Thus testing, using any sort of material which would enable the calculation to be made would indicate whether the projectile would achieve its purpose and any transfer of power above this level could be held to be unnecessary. The modern equivalent of this approach is the transfer of energy to gelatine blocks or soap or other inanimate material to determine the likely effect of the projectile under test.

I do not wish to suggest that such an approach is without advantage. When penetration is the criterion it is easy to argue (although it would not always be correct) that inanimate materials can be used to compare the penetratability of one projectile with another. If they are the same in the inanimate target, then presumably they would be the same in the human target. It was shown some 90 years ago that in soft targets, projectiles travelling above the velocity of sound in the target would also create a temporary cavity lasting a few milliseconds and it was suggested that this phenomenon could be associated with injury which extended beyond the wound tract. It is to Zuckerman that we owe the first display of this phenomenon in living tissue and we now accept that the cavitation process is associated with a degree of injury which would not be suspected from the external examination of the victim.[6] By measuring the degree of penetration the volume of cavitation and the amount of energy given up in tissue simulants it is possible to compare the injuring potential of fragments from exploding devices or from bullets. The technique of making such experiments and drawing the appropriate conclusions has been dignified by the term "wound ballistics". The advantages are obvious. The disadvantages from our point of view may not be immediately obvious.

5. Knock-Down

One of the major figures in the debates of the 19th century was Sir Samuel Baker. For any one interested in the history of modern Africa he is a fascinating figure. He was an intrepid explorer and also a hunter of big game. It was he who pointed out that "knock-down" in big game was only achieved with certainty when the animal was mortally wounded. Instant knock-down was only achieved when the animal was shot through the heart or through the brain. An editorial published in the Lancet drew attention to the inadequacies of the Lee-Metford rifle in the Chital Campaign.[7] Baker suggested that if the bullet were constructed so that it stopped in the target a greater degree of injury would result and "knock-down" would be more likely and military observations of the time (1895) led to the development of the uncovered rifle bullet, popularly known as the "dum-dum" bullet. The horror expressed over the effect of the dum-dum bullet was not vented on the "spitzer" bullet developed some ten years later, and designed to achieve a similar effect.

We can now appreciate the problems for the weapon designer. Certain "knock-down" can only be achieved by fatal injury. Although the big-game hunter can aim to hit the target to achieve this effect, the soldier cannot do so. The designer of military anti-personnel weapons must therefore, fall back on some development of the theory which relates "knock-down" or incapacitation to the transfer of energy. He is tempted to assume that the greater the transfer of energy, the greater the probability of achieving incapacitation.

I hope I have shown that there is a fundamental flaw in this approach when it comes to be applied to the control of weapon development. The technique is useful for comparing new designs with old; if - for example - the designer wishes to replace a heavy bullet with a lighter one which will have the same terminal effect. It cannot be used to determine whether this effect is desirable or undesirable in the sense that the effect created is greater than necessary. This approach may, however, demonstrate unwanted and possibly undesirable effects such as break-up of a bullet, which may not be intended in the design.

6. Suffering

During the conference at Lucerne in 1974 a number of physicians met together to discuss the concept of "suffering" and to consider whether it could be defined or quantified in some scientific way. They agreed that it could not whereas "injury" probably could. It was suggested that "injury" should be substituted for "suffering" in the legal discussions that followed. However the legal experts agreed that "suffering" was a valid concept, even if the physicians found it difficult to quantify.[8]

From a military medical point of view the most obvious defect of the concept of "suffering" is that it cannot be numerically or graphically related to wounding. Compare, for example, fever. Fever is more than the high temperature that can be recorded on a hospital chart. We all know what we mean by fever but the physician has a measure which, for the last hundred years or so, has enabled him to define the patient's condition and which also has predictive value. Physicians of a thousand years ago, believed that fever was a specific illness, today we talk of it as a symptom. Suffering is not listed as a symptom in medical texts; it is not measurable but we all, layman and physician alike, are aware that it occurs in physical illness and also in mental illness.

There are many accounts of the lack of pain immediately following severe, and even mortal wounds. In the immediate aftermath of wounding pain is undoubtedly a cause of suffering and in many cases the relief of pain will relieve suffering. Mental suffering is not related to pain and in very severe injuries leading perhaps to the loss of limbs the relief of pain certainly does not relieve the suffering.

The sufferings of the wounded are undoubtedly increased when they cannot be removed from the scene of the battle and when the resources for medical treatment are inadquate. I am quite sure that it was this aspect of the battle of Solferino that made the greatest impression on Henri Dunant and led him to found the Red Cross.

Although suffering is recognised as one component of the mental and physical effect of injury on the battlefield, it is extremely variable; it is not measurable; and it is also related to factors other than the severity of injury.

7. Conclusion

Few people, least of all soldiers, would doubt the contribution that the laws of war, and especially the Geneva Conventions have made to the alleviation of suffering on the battlefield, in the prison camps and in the hospitals. A brief look at the statistics of the major wars in this century shows that for us this has been a mainly military experience. It was not so for others in World War Two and there is every reason for physicians to be concerned about the possible effects of the weapons of future wars on the civilian population. Even if self-interest is the main determining factor there is good reason for potential belligerents to attempt to control the development of military weapons. The success of the Gas Protocol of 1925 is one example which deserves careful study.

When we consider the effects of so-called conventional weapons the demands of common humanity play a greater part in the determination to limit their effects. Significant achievements have been made, especially in the agreements to mark mine-fields and in the banning of plastic grenades. A detailed examination of other fragmentation devices has shown that the claims of humanity and military efficiency are not necessarily incompatible. A vast amount of research by a Swedish medical group has improved our understanding of the effects of small arms[9] and I believe that this will, in turn lead to changes in ammunition design which will give improvements in military efficiency and decrease the severity of wounds.

Finally, an increased understanding of the relationship between weapon use, injury, incapacitation and suffering may be relevant at the national level. No one should be permitted to use potentially lethal weapons unless he has a very clear idea of the intended effect and of the possible consequences of such use.

FOOTNOTES

1. Report "Weapons that may Cause Unnecessary Suffering or Have Indiscriminate Effects" *ICRC*, Geneva 1973.

2. *Supra*, pp. 287-310 and Kalshoven F. (1975) *Netherlands Year Book of International Law*, Vol. VI, 1975.

3. Leading Article, *British Medical Journal 1983*, Vol. 286, p. 826.

4. The Yellow card issued to Security Forces in Northern Ireland specifies range and target area. (*Hansard* 21st January, 1977).

5. *Daily Telegraph*, 11th July, 1984.

6. R. Scott (1983) *Clinics in Laboratory Medicine*, Vol. 3, No. 2, pp. 273-294.

7. Editorial (1899) *Lancet*, Vol. I, p. 1573.

8. "Conference of Government Experts on the Use of Certain Conventional Weapons", p. 140, *ICRC* Geneva, 1976.

9. *ACTA Chirurgica Scandinavica.* Supplementum 508. Stockholm, 1982.

TABLE OF RATIFICATIONS AND ACCESSIONS TO THE GENEVA CONVENTIONS 1949, THE GENEVA PROTOCOLS 1977 AND THE WEAPONS CONVENTION 1981

As at 10th October 1988

Explanatory Note

This Table, in addition to ratifications and accessions, includes declarations of succession and acceptances.

For reasons of space, the names of countries may differ from the official names of States.

The date indicated is the day on which the instrument of ratification or accession, or the official document of like effect, was received by the relevant Depositary. The figures are, in order, the day, the month and the year.

The sign d/r indicates declaration or reservation.

GCI is the Geneva Convention for the Amelioration of the Condition of the Wounded and Sick in Armed Forces in the Field. [75 *UNTS* 31]

GCII is the Geneva Convention for the Amelioration of the Condition of the Wounded, Sick and Shipwrecked Members of Armed Forces at Sea. [75 *UNTS* 85]

GCIII is the Geneva Convention relative to the Treatment of Prisoners of War. [75 *UNTS* 135]

GCIV is the Geneva Convention relative to the Protection of Civilian Persons in Time of War. [75 *UNTS* 287]

The four Geneva Conventions of 1949 were adopted at Geneva on 12th August 1949 and entered into force on 21st October 1950.

The Protocol Additional to the Geneva Conventions of 12th August 1949, and relating to the Protection of Victims of International Armed Conflicts (Protocol I) [1125 *UNTS* 3; 16 *ILM* 1391], and the Protocol Additional to the Geneva Conventions of 12th August 1949 and relating to the Protection of Victims of Non-International Armed Conflicts (Protocol II) [1125 *UNTS* 609; 16 *ILM* 1442], were both adopted at Geneva on 8th June 1977 and entered into force on 7th December 1978.

The Convention on Prohibitions or Restrictions on the Use of Certain Conventional Weapons Which May be Deemed to be Excessively Injurious or to Have Indiscriminate Effects (Weapons Convention) [19 *ILM* 1523 Cmnd. 8370], was adopted at Geneva on 10th October 1980, opened for signature in New York on 10th April 1981 and entered into force on 2nd December 1983.

As at 12th January 1989 the total number of States parties to these treaties were as follows:

Geneva Conventions 1949	-	166
Protocol I 1977	-	79
Protocol II 1977	-	70
Weapons Convention 1981	-	29

TABLE OF RATIFICATIONS AND ACCESSIONS

	Geneva Conventions 1949	Protocol I 1977	Protocol II 1977	Weapons Convention 1981
Afghanistan	26.9.56	-	-	-
Albania	27.5.57 d/r	-	-	-
Algeria	20.6.60	-	-	-
Angola	20.9.84 d/r	20.9.84 d/r	-	-
Antigua and Barbuda	6.10.86	6.10.86	6.10.86	-
Argentina	18.9.56	26.11.86 d/r	26.11.86 d/r	-
Australia	14.10.58	-	-	29.9.83
Austria	27.8.53	13.8.82 d/r	13.8.82 d/r	14.3.83
Bahamas	11.7.75	10.4.80	10.4.80	-
Bahrain	30.11.71	30.10.86	30.10.86	-
Bangladesh	4.4.72	8.9.80	8.9.80	-
Barbados	10.9.68	-	-	-
Belgium	3.9.52	20.5.86 d/r	20.5.86	-
Belize	29.6.84	29.6.84	29.6.84	-
Benin	14.12.61	28.5.86	28.5.86	-
Bhutan	-	-	-	-
Bolivia	10.12.76	8.12.83	8.12.83	-
Botswana	29.3.68	23.5.79	23.5.79	-
Brazil	29.6.57	-	-	-
Brunei Darussalam	-	-	-	-
Bulgaria	22.7.54 d/r	-	-	15.10.82
Burkina Faso	7.11.61	20.10.87	20.10.87	-
Burma	-	-	-	-
Burundi	27.12.71	-	-	-
Byelorussian Soviet Socialist Republic	3.8.54 d/r	-	-	23.6.82
Cameroon	16.9.63	16.3.84	16.3.84	-
Canada	14.5.65	-	-	-
Cape Verde	11.5.84	-	-	-
Central African Republic	1.8.66	17.7.84	17.7.84	-

	Geneva Conven-tions 1949	Protocol I 1977	Protocol II 1977	Weapons Conven-tion 1981
Chad	5.8.70	-	-	-
Chile	12.10.50	-	-	-
China	28.12.56 d/r	14.9.83 d/r	14.9.83	7.4.82
Colombia	8.11.61	-	-	-
Comoros	21.11.85	21.11.85	21.11.85	-
Congo	30.1.67	10.11.83	10.11.83	-
Costa Rica	15.10.69	15.12.83	15.12.83	-
Cuba	15.4.54	25.11.82	-	2.3.87
Cyprus	23.5.62	1.6.79	-	-
Czechoslovakia	19.12.50 d/r	-	-	31.8.82
Denmark	27.6.51	17.6.82 d/r	17.6.82	7.7.82
Djibouti	6.1.78 (GCI) 6.3.78 (GCII-IV)	-	-	-
Dominica	28.9.81	-	-	-
Dominican Republic	22.1.58	-	-	-
Ecuador	11.8.54	10.4.79	10.4.79	4.5.82
Egypt	10.11.52	-	-	-
El Salvador	17.6.53	23.11.78	23.11.78	-
Equatorial Guinea	24.7.86	24.7.86	24.7.86	-
Ethiopia	2.10.69	-	-	-
Fiji	9.8.71	-	-	-
Finland	22.2.55	7.8.80 d/r	7/8/80 d/r	8.5.82
France	28.6.51	-	24.2.84 d/r	4.3.88
Gabon	20.2.65	8.4.80	8.4.80	-
Gambia	20.10.66	12.1.89	12.1.89	-
German Democratic Republic	30.11.56 d/r	-	-	20.7.82
Germany, Federal Republic of	3.9.54	-	-	-
Ghana	2.8.58	28.2.78	28.2.78	-

	Geneva Conventions 1949	Protocol I 1977	Protocol II 1977	Weapons Convention 1981
Greece	5.6.66	-	-	-
Grenada	13.4.81	-	-	-
Guatemala	14.5.52	19.10.87	19.10.87	21.7.83
Guinea	11.7.84	11.7.84	11.7.84	-
Guinea-Bissau	21.2.74 d/r	21.10.86	21.10.86	-
Guyana	22.7.68	18.1.88	18.1.88	-
Haiti	11.4.57	-	-	-
Holy See	22.2.51	21.11.85 d/r	21.11.85 d/r	-
Honduras	31.12.65	-	-	-
Hungary	3.8.54 d/r	-	-	14.6.82
Iceland	10.8.65	10.4.87 d/r	10.4.87	-
India	9.11.50	-	-	1.3.84
Indonesia	30.9.58	-	-	-
Iran, Islamic Republic of	20.2.57	-	-	-
Iraq	14.2.56	-	-	-
Ireland	27.9.62	-	-	-
Israel	6.7.51 d/r	-	-	-
Italy	17.12.51	27.2.86 d/r	27.2.86	-
Ivory Coast	28.12.61	-	-	-
Jamaica	17.7.64	29.7.86	29.7.86	-
Japan	21.4.53	-	-	9.6.82
Jordan	29.5.51	1.5.79	1.5.79	-
Kampuchea, Democratic Republic of	8.12.58	-	-	-
Kenya	20.9.66	-	-	-
Kiribati	5.1.89	-	-	-
Korea, Democratic People's Republic of	27.8.57 d/r	9.3.88	-	-
Korea, Republic of	16.8.66 d/r	15.1.82 d/r	15.1.82	-
Kuwait	2.9.67	17.1.85	17.1.85	-

	Geneva Conventions 1949	Protocol I 1977	Protocol II 1977	Weapons Convention 1981
Lao People's Democratic Republic	29.10.56	18.11.80	18.11.80	3.1.83
Lebanon	10.4.51	-	-	-
Lesotho	20.5.68	-	-	-
Liberia	29.3.54	30.6.88	30.6.88	-
Libyan Arab Jamahiriya	22.5.56	7.6.78	7.6.78	-
Liechtenstein	21.9.50	-	-	-
Luxembourg	1.7.53	-	-	-
Madagascar	13.7.63	-	-	-
Malawi	5.1.68	-	-	-
Malaysia	24.8.62	-	-	-
Maldives	-	-	-	-
Mali	24.5.65	-	-	-
Malta	22.8.68	-	-	-
Mauritania	27.10.62	14.3.80	14.3.80	-
Mauritius	18.8.70	22.3.82	22.3.82	-
Mexico	29.10.52	10.3.83	-	11.2.82
Monaco	5.7.50	-	-	-
Mongolia	20.12.58	-	-	8.6.82
Morocco	26.7.56	-	-	-
Mozambique	14.3.83	14.3.83	-	-
Namibia	18.10.83	18.10.83	18.10.83	-
Nauru	-	-	-	-
Nepal	7.2.64	-	-	-
Netherlands	3.8.54	26.6.87 d/r	26.6.87	18.6.87
New Zealand	2.5.59	8.2.88 d/r	8.2.88	-
Nicaragua	17.12.53	-	-	-
Niger	16.4.64	8.6.79	8.6.79	-
Nigeria	9.6.61	10.10.88	10.10.88	-
Norway	3.8.51	14.12.81 d/r	14.12.81	7.6.83
Oman	31.1.74	29.3.84 d/r	29.3.84	-
Pakistan	12.6.51 d/r	-	-	1.4.85
Panama	10.2.56	-	-	-

	Geneva Conventions 1949	Protocol I 1977	Protocol II 1977	Weapons Convention 1981
Papua New Guinea	26.5.76	-	-	-
Paraguay	23.10.61	-	-	-
Peru	15.2.56	-	-	-
Philippines	7.3.51 (GCI) 6.10.52 (GCII-IV)	-	11.2.86	-
Poland	26.11.54 d/r	-	-	2.6.83
Portugal	14.3.61 d/r	-	-	-
Qatar	15.10.75	5.4.88 d/r	-	-
Romania	1.6.54	-	-	-
Rwanda	21.3.64	19.11.84	19.11.84	-
Saint Christopher and Nevis	14.2.86	14.2.86	14.2.86	-
Saint Lucia	18.9.81	7.10.82	7.10.82	-
Saint Vincent and the Grenadines	1.4.81	8.4.83	8.4.83	-
Samoa	23.8.84	23.8.84	23.8.84	-
San Marino	29.8.53	-	-	-
San Tome and Principe	21.5.76	-	-	-
Saudi Arabia	18.5.63	21.8.87 d/r	-	-
Senegal	23.4.63	7.5.85	7.5.85	-
Seychelles	8.11.84	8.11.84	8.11.84	-
Sierra Leone	31.5.65	21.10.86	21.10.86	-
Singapore	27.4.73	-	-	-
Solomon Islands	6.7.81	19.9.88	19.8.88	-
Somalia	12.7.62	-	-	-
South Africa	31.3.52	-	-	-
Spain	4.8.52	-	-	-
Sri Lanka	23.2.59 (GCIV) 28.2.59 (GCI-III)	-	-	-

	Geneva Conventions 1949	Protocol I 1977	Protocol II 1977	Weapons Convention 1981
Sudan	23.9.57	-	-	-
Surinam	13.10.76 d/r	16.12.85	16.12.85	-
Swaziland	28.6.73	-	-	-
Sweden	28.12.53	31.8.79 d/r	31.8.79	7.7.82
Switzerland	31.3.50	17.2.82 d/r	17.2.82	20.8.82
Syrian Arab Republic	2.11.53	14.11.83 d/r	-	-
Tanzania, United Republic of	12.12.62	15.2.83	15.2.83	-
Thailand	29.12.54	-	-	-
Togo	6.1.62	21.6.84	21.6.84	-
Tonga	13.4.78	-	-	-
Trinidad and Tobago	17.5.63 (GCI) 24.9.63 (GCII-IV)	-	-	-
Tunisia	4.5.57	9.8.79	9.8.79	15.5.87
Turkey	10.2.54	-	-	-
Tuvalu	19.2.81	-	-	-
Uganda	18.5.64	-	-	-
Ukranian Soviet Socialist Republic	3.8.54 d/r	-	-	23.6.82
Union of Soviet Socialist Republics	10.5.54 d/r	-	-	10.6.82
United Arab Emirates	10.5.72	9.3.83 d/r	9.3.83 d/r	-
United Kingdom	23.9.57 d/r	-	-	-
United States of America	2.8.55 d/r	-	-	-
Uruguay	5.3.69 d/r	13.12.85	13.12.85	-
Vanuatu	27.10.82	27.2.85	27.2.85	-
Venezeula	13.2.56	-	-	-
Vietnam	28.6.57 d/r	19.10.81	-	-

	Geneva Conventions 1949	Protocol I 1977	Protocol II 1977	Weapons Convention 1981
Yemen, Arab Republic of	16.7.70	-	-	-
Yemen, People's Democratic Republic of	25.5.77	-	-	-
Yugoslavia	21.4.50 d/r	11.6.79 d/r	11.6.79	24.5.83
Zaire	20.2.61	3.6.82	-	-
Zambia	19.10.66	-	-	-
Zimbabwe	7.3.83	-	-	-

INDEX